always
BECOMING

Kim,
you are a beautiful
representation
of His fragrance
& the Love that
remains from
your daughter-role!
Keep proclaiming
Him in your
be coming
journey.
Tamra

sex,
shame
&
Love

always
BECOMING

TAMRA ANDRESS

get connected deeper

Tune in for a quick hello video from the author!

Praise Reports

"Tamra Andress is a world-changing leader who's mission is to uplift and activate women. She shares what matters most to lean into your purpose and bring joy into your life. Her story will inspire and empower you to embrace your blessed life."

- Patricia Wooster, Founder of WoosterMedia Books

This book is a testimony to all of those who find themselves stuck in a "what has been done to me" mindset. Tamra's tears, confessed moments of shame, and ultimate breakthrough presents such a beautiful path to restoring the identity you were created with. Stealing lyrics straight out of 80's hip-hop, this book is "about to ruin the image and the style that ya used to".

- Pastor Anthony Hart, The Pioneer Pastor

This book has changed my life. Watching Tamra's testimony unfold made me realize I am not alone. That shame doesn't have to have it's grip on me and the power of Jesus's love can break any chain. Read this NOW.

- Pastor Morgan Hart, Creative Designer

Tamra has a radiant presence and joy that combined with her process for helping you identify and activate your purpose, leads to deep life transformation. I love seeing the shifts she makes!

- *Mike Zeller, Mindset & Business Mentor*

Tamra inspires me to be my best "me." No more thinking I have to be like anyone else, because God made me with my own purpose and mission. It was freeing to realize I am enough and she reinforces that with every phone call, social media post, and contact.

- *Janis Rodgers, Podcast Producer*

I've known Tamra for several years now and have had the privilege of watching her transform her story of shame and brokenness into one of life-giving vulnerability that shows you what it looks like to have healing in Christ. Walk through her journey by reading her story and you'll find that she points you to the true hope only found in Jesus.

- *Dr. Jessica McCleese, Licensed Clinical Psychologist*

Chains of bondage being broken and hearts set free, because God gave Tamra courage to be vulnerable. Lives will be redeemed!

- *Liz Andersen, Prodigal to Princess Ministries*

Tamra unabashedly follows God, allowing Him to transform past scars into a beautiful unfolding of grace, love, and power. She reaches to the depth of your heart, ushering you into your calling, and cheerleading you into God's sunshine. Tamra clearly walks within her own calling, leading generations of ministers.

- *Elisah McGee, CEO Freedom Farm and Freedom Defense Group, minister to be*

Tamra's life is a vibrant example of abundant living. Her authenticity about her past and her determination toward her future are mutually inspiring. I'm always encouraged in her presence and am grateful the Lord allowed our paths to cross.

  - *Dana Che Williams, Pastor and Relationship Coach*

The more I think about the continued amount of grace I need , the more I truly appreciate the Trail Blazers who have so bravely shared their testimony. Tamra, your story, your honesty, your journey in this ever evolving life truly gives hope to those who need to hear these words. YOU ARE WORTHY. YOU ARE LOVED. Keep letting your light shine for HIS glory and may all your passions sing praises to HIS name.

  - *Lauren Sinclair, RDH Coastal Cosmetic + Implant Dentistry*

Tamra is one of those amazingly unique individuals who has the ability to speak joy into every crevice of your life. As a trusted friend and spiritual sister, Tamra has inspired and encouraged me to grow deeper in relationship with the Lord.

  - *Dr. Michelle Marie Lappin, Minister and Wealth Coach*

The first time I met Tamra I knew she was filled with the Holy Spirit as she just radiated light. Her authenticity is what I admire most and her ability to call out the gold in people. She is fully alive and runs hard after everything God calls her to. She exudes the fruits of the spirit and is the type of person that leaves you better than how she found you.

  - *Kari Tavella, Creative Woman of God*

Always Becoming

Published by F.I.T. in Faith Press

Acknowledgements

I stand in awe of our Father in heaven at this moment. And while I am currently sitting in a local coffee shop, my spirit is erect and humbled. For years my tears have fallen on these very floors, comfy couches, and tables of this bustling roastery. Little do they know their space has been a dream factory, a classroom, a therapy space, a think tank, a business sanctuary, and a becoming mother's haven. And while they don't get my priority appreciation, they will forever be remembered.

To Christ alone be the praise. The fact that I am breathing today, in lieu of the grave I once lived in and ideated to put myself in, is a true miracle and testament to His steadfast love and power. Secondly, to my incredible husband, Gary, who has supported my becoming from day one (counting the day we met when I knew or the day I said I do or the day I laid shaking in your arms scared of the morning or the day we dipped together in the ocean or yesterday when I kissed you good morning). You inspire me to be a better human every day. And I count you as my greatest gift, truest soulmate, and forever love of my life.

To my dear children, Cooper and Waverly. May you always know that your lives were the saving grace to mine. Your very breath brings me purpose every single day and I love you to the ends of eternity. May you always prioritize your wholeness by pursuing God first and foremost and last and not least and everywhere in between.

To my beautiful mama, for prioritizing me even above your own well being. Your big dreams have been implanted into me and will be realized in His timing. I am certain of it.

To my big-hearted dad, I honor you and the legacy you've left in my life towards my health, well-being, and whistling sing-song spirit. I am believing that your own becoming story will be the unlock to the same joys I have experienced on this side of heaven.

To Morgan, Anthony, Liz, and Paul. You are the "framily" God knew I needed in seasons I could hardly breathe, in seasons I was yearning for depth, and now for seasons where we get to pass His breath of life within us to others. Thank you for your simple and yet deeply rooted relationships. I am forever grateful.

To Lauren, Amy, Ashley, Kari and Janis. You've loved me through my becoming and propelled me into greatness even without knowing every detail. Thank you for never leaving my side.

To my editor, Sharon. You never let me give up on the hope of what this should become. Thank you for enduring my limiting beliefs and reminding me of the greater purpose He has for this message.

To my supportive family and friends. You are a massive part of my why. Even when it is uncomfortable, I will step out of the boat for you.

To my incredible community of dreamers, go-getters, and God-fearing becomers; this book is for you, to prove His ability to transform your life, no matter your past, so that His plans for you and the Kingdom will be realized. It has been written. And His will be done.

Contents

Foreword

*L*ife. It really is a box of chocolates: you never know what you're going to get (Thanks Forest Gump). I don't think anyone of us ever grows up to expect or hope that our future will be filled with trauma, pain, divorce, abuse, betrayal, depression, and the list goes on and on. However, I don't think there's one person reading this right now who would say that their life has been all rainbows and butterflies and that heartache has never been a part of their story. That's why it is so important for us to be willing to tell our story, so that we can touch the pain in someone else's heart and hopefully give them hope that there are better days ahead. You know the old saying "what doesn't kill you makes you stronger"? Well, it's actually true. I know that personally because I have had my share of pain and trauma. I was raised in a very traumatic household with physical and verbal abuse. I was raped when I was fifteen (15) years old and never spoke a word of it until I was in my twenties (20's) then I married a preacher and just thought that we were going to run off into the world and storm hell with a water pistol like Superman and superwoman! With the pressures of ministry on top of all of the buried pain that I carried into my adulthood, it all eventually caved in on me. I had an emotional breakdown at 35 that led to nine years of living a double life, while trying to lead a worldwide ministry (that, my friends, mixes like oil and water). I had spent the last 10 years earnestly rebuilding my life, my character, my circle and I am proud to say that today I'm living my very best life, authentically free.

I said all that to say that when I met Tamra, I felt like I met my wonder twin and the wonder twin powers are activating! Not only did I identify with her pain in her story but more importantly, I identified with her fighting spirit. Tamra Andress has been to hell and back, as you will read in this book, but the most important aspect of her story is that she was determined to press her way out of every debilitating season of her life. Like I said in the first few sentences above, troubles and trials are going to hit all of our lives but it's what we do with them that counts. Grit, hard work, dedication, a fighting spirit, discipline, seeing the cup half full, is what you will read about in this book. I am over here in your corner Tamra doing my best backflip and high kick, saluting you for your fierce courage to scratch and claw out of your pain to become the amazing woman that you are today. Truthfully, I don't think you've seen anything yet. Why? Because you, me, and all the other determined-to-be-all-we-can-be people out there are *Always Becoming*, when we choose to dig our heels in and fight. Because if we don't fight, then we don't win! You are the bomb. com, the air in our balloons, the bom-diggity-dog, the voice in our heads cheering all of us on to *Always Becoming*!

Pastor Hope Carpenter,
Redemption Ministries

Introduction

Standing in front of her, young and frail, I felt nauseous and naked, though entirely healthy and fully clothed. Dissecting my body with the quickest mean girl glance and words that pierced my fragile ego, she never hesitated to say what first came to mind. "Looks like you've put on a few pounds," she said with her lips curled into an innocent smile. I felt my stomach churn as she reinforced what I saw in the mirror and what had circled my mind one thousand times since I quit competitive gymnastics a few months prior. Moments after walking in from my first few days of high school, the metal faced braces already a point of concern, I now heard the faint persistent voice inside my head come alive through the voice of my own grandmother.

She meant no harm. She wasn't wrong. She always called the shots as they were, and in fact I love her for that now. Clearly, however, she had no couth or awareness of…well, any of the inner struggles affecting the teenage girl before her. But at the time, my thin skin took every word to heart. The little girl inside me sat at the kitchen table swinging her dangling legs that didn't yet touch the floor and silently riddling, "Sticks and stones may break my bones, but words can never hurt me." Meanwhile, staring back at the reflection in the window across from my nightly seat at the dinner table, I was present in body, absent in spirit, and my racing, adolescent mind sat questioning, "Maybe she's right?"

Eventually, my self-deprecating opinions didn't matter as much. They were quieted by the adolescent boys voicing contrary beliefs about my blossoming body. As a girl craving affirmation in all the wrong ways, I let their votes determine the outcome of my own personal poll.

Meanwhile, God himself was voting for me. He'd cast a ballot that would outweigh any opinion just long enough to bring me back into the light, and then the dark would creep back in to unanimously veto. I was stuck in between lies and Truth, confused and afraid.

I never understood my value. For years I had been playing the game of comparison, and images of the "perfect" woman flashed through my mind long before I could even comprehend what the female anatomy was purposed for. Pornography, unintentionally accessible, empowered a skewed connection I had to a distressing experience as a toddler. Working in tandem, these snares left me constantly striving for affirmation.

For years, I continued to let the opposite sex cast their votes, one by one, until my reflection was not cultivated or kept for myself but instead became a resource to be used in finding my value and worth through the eyes of men. I discredited the gift of my body by treating it like a tool instead of a vessel. I used it for what I thought would bring me joy. I took care of it solely so it could be admired. My mind wrapped and raced around fictitious scenarios, yet through the lens of society, I was a "happy, smart, healthy" young girl.

Eventually, I lost my appetite for health. Food brought me comfort and filled the emptiness I felt inside. I'd binge with full intent to work out endlessly until the calories consumed didn't affect my body frame or pants size. "I am still more ideal than her," my mind would whisper. I bared too much skin. I competed with every female with an internal comparison compass. I chose to be a guy's girl, so I didn't have to be stuck in a mental battle with myself around girl friends. I went on to study the body through personal training and nutrition, thinking this emphasis would propel me into the frame even my grandmother would approve of. And she did.

I taught other women how to love themselves. I taught them how to eat and sleep and carry themselves. They mimicked my wardrobe, and I uplifted their confidence with motivational and encouraging boosts. I masked internal struggles with "a wine me" mentality or other antics, such as retail therapy, that suppressed emotion and enhanced my self-esteem. I loaned my expertise in a healthy way, or so it appeared, but my struggle at the polls still existed.

Eventually, a ballot was cast that I could not ignore. My husband won, and I viewed it that way too. I saw myself as his prize. We were called Barbie and Ken, and the votes continued to be counted. And yet, even as God sanctified what I had lost physically, I was still being exposed and warped mentally and emotionally as our relationship, in its picturesque form, developed and matured.

Y'all, I don't even vote beyond casting presidential ballots...so this analogy has me slightly cringing and also thinking about my politically conscious father. (Oh, what a journey this will be for him to read.) Ultimately, however, the final ballot is not my father's or theirs or yours or mine or even my husband's to cast... Jesus gets the ultimate say. And when I inevitably hit rock bottom, standing in the mirror staring at the reflection of the broken and lost young girl from decades before, He persisted to cast His final vote. He pierced through my downcast soul and said to me, "I see you. You are mine." And I had a choice to make. Would I step confidently into acceptance or stay buried in rejection and shame. The latter had me wanting to take my own life. But with two tiny humans now calling me mother, my choice, though incredibly hard, had legacy attached to it.

You do not have to be what others have called you. You do not have to accept the fate of those who have wrapped you in your own metaphorical death cloth. You are not what they say. Your mirror moments do not have to keep you trapped. You are not meant for the grave. You are worthy and called, and even through your tragedies, there exist triumphs in the midst, and your sorrows will be used to serve. Just as Jesus called Lazarus from the grave, this message will speak that same life and activation over you. And before long, any places that might feel stale, buried, or impossible to resurrect, will be the very death cloths I hope to have the honor to help remove.

At this point, let me guess…you are wondering about #allthethings. I just dropped my life's testimony at your feet, and your brain is circling to connect the dots. Maybe you are thinking, "Do I even like her enough in this moment to keep reading? She's not politically active. Is she even American? She kind of sounds like an awful person. She seems self-indulgent and far from the kind of friend I'd want to take self-development insight from. She doesn't even like women. And now, all of a sudden, she knows Jesus?"

Hold up. Let me stop you right there. I've played this mind game before – the one where we speak for the other person before they even have a chance to process their emotions or open their mouth – the one where we create the storyline of the other person's life before they've even shared the punch line. This book won't just provide one punch line; it's going to provide all the punch lines of my life. I'm not writing it to glorify my works or revelations but instead to shed light on the miraculous works that have been done in spite of my past and hand you the framework that may assist another (maybe even you) in the exchange of fictitious happiness for abundant joy with lasting mind, body, and soul alignment.

But I'd ask you to be patient with me as I walk the process out, just like I'd train you in a physical workout or teach you to build a business. I surely wouldn't throw you on a sprinting treadmill or schedule you to appear on Shark Tank right out of the gate. Though, I have been told by several folks that working with me is a bit like being thrown out of an airplane. I believe my most important work is in the equipping process and gradual growth before I push them out into the vast sky. There's a reason that a treadmill has an option for setting the speed and incline, right? I've surely fallen flat on my face in the gym during an all-out treadmill sprint…so I do know better. The speed comes with endurance and the elevation comes with awareness of your ability, practice, and purpose. Slow and steady wins the race.

I can imagine the tension rising up in your gut right now. The combination of self-help and spiritual development is probably not the most glamorous way you'd like to spend your excess time, but what if I could save you decades of your life?

Trust me. I get it. I'm fully aware that this is a huge ask, especially from a stranger. But I believe we could all use a little more grace these days, so instead of asking you to do the hard work out of the gate, I'm openly throwing my white flag and hoping you'll be the Good Samaritan who stops all along the way. But don't worry. My wounds have been healed and my strength has been renewed. So, I'll be the one to take the time to sit with you, as I know your "Good Samaritan" role can get tiresome and you, too, need some pouring into. This book is the becoming process of my life, the reveal of the ballot moment that changed everything, and how I became fit in faith. I open up the details from my resurrected life with the ultimate goal of showing you how to claim the same banner for yourself. This isn't one of those one-hour cardio sweat fests that will have your heart racing from start to finish and feeling like you're going to die. Slow and steady, remember? This book contains the highs and the lows. It's the warm-up all the way to the cool down and includes all of the necessary components built in for an aligned, whole-body, mind, and soul approach to your wellbeing. It's the freedom factor that will ultimately give you the strength to hold the arms of your friends up to the heavens on their weakest day because you first let someone hold yours. This is your oxygen mask, my friend. Breathe it in. I'm casting a ballot for you.

Faith has been the key to unlocking my strength, my endurance, my ability, my cleansing, and my focus. It is responsible for creating the alignment point of my life, the equilibrium of my being. And while this book was a way to house my story of perseverance, it has more importantly given me the opportunity to illuminate your own ability to achieve what you were made to do and become wholly who you were made to be. It will also allow God, and God alone, to have the final say in your health, your wealth, your inner voice, the voices of others, and the message you tell yourself in the mirror. I've already criticized myself enough and shattered my own mirror, so no matter what you may be thinking about me at this point or by the end of this book...what matters most to me is your process of self-reflection through this process of becoming.

I'm not here to inspire you; I'm here to activate you into a perpetual momentum of becoming. My hope is that you find Hope and never stop seeking it. My hope is that you hear through this message, "Child, Come Out!" And, that by taking the step to say yes in uncovering the state of your own mental, physical, and spiritual well-being, you will walk away from this read with a new motivation to take ownership of your body, mind, and soul with fresh perspective and ignited passion. I also pray that you simultaneously come to the realization that while you are gifted this human vessel for only a short time, your soul is enveloped in eternity. As a result, it is imperative that you place a priority on every facet of who you are. Hold tight to the Truth and release all other opinions in the universe including those of your friends, your family, and even your own mental naysayer. The final say, the final ballot, the final vote is Jesus. I can see Him now...carefully filing out the bubbles on His ballot next to your name.

Hebrews 12:1-3: *"Therefore, since we are surrounded by such a great cloud of witnesses, let us throw off everything that hinders and the sin that so easily entangles. And let us run with perseverance the race marked out for us, [2] fixing our eyes on Jesus, the pioneer and perfecter of faith. For the joy set before him he endured the cross, scorning its shame, and sat down at the right hand of the throne of God. [3] Consider him who endured such opposition from sinners, so that you will not grow weary and lose heart."*

Born Identity

The fitness world has been shaping me ever since my chubby little feet took their first steps. My parents were original gym rats on the West Coast long before the East Coast adopted gyms like Gold's or conceptualized the YMCA or Rec Centers. My dad has stories of drinking raw eggs for immediate protein before pre-made, powdery protein drinks ever existed. And while they were never competitive in bodybuilding or other stage shows, my dad has been known for his hulk-like biceps since high school; just ask his four sisters' grade-school boyfriends.

And so, nature versus nurture, one of the oldest psychological debates, comes into play. But with my proverbial coin, it didn't matter which way it landed; I was literally born to be fit. Honestly, we all are, but I'll hold off on that rant until later.

At two and a half years old, I was tossed into the sport of gymnastics. Maybe this had something to do with having been nicknamed "Bamm-Bamm" from *The Flintstones*. You see, my chubby baby rolls had inhibited my efforts to sit up or walk at the typical monthly milestones, but once I figured it out, I went from rolling into everything right into tumbling. I was a gymnast from then until 17 years of age. I played other sports with my siblings and enjoyed cheerleading and dancing as well, but I am always thankful for my experience in the world of flexibility and flips. Due to those years, my muscle memory is top notch, even though I may have some chiropractic needs that I wouldn't mind living without. Plus, my one season soccer stint didn't serve me well beyond a handful of dandelions that caught my heart's attention.

Now I need to paint a clearer picture here because I realize it is common for kids to participate in sports, but did most kids have a drill sergeant for a dad? Did their punishment for acting out consist of running laps around the perimeter of the backyard, no matter the weather or time of day or night? Or did their parents make time-out a game of "don't touch the wall" (face the corner standing, hands straight above your head, no slack in your arms, and of course no touching the wall)? We also did squats or good ole jumping in place until we could muster up an apology and get back on track. It was also commonplace to have push-up and pull-up challenges post family dinners – but these were just for fun. And to top it off, as a right of passage for prospective boyfriends and instead of the usual meet and greet and "get-to-know-you" conversation, there was always arm-wrestling involved. My dad and younger brother didn't sit around cleanin' metal guns; theirs were the more figurative bicep kind. Can you visualize that country music video? Rodney Atkins should try this one out too.

I'm sure some crunchy moms (I'm crunchy too, so don't take offense) are thinking this was borderline child abuse, but please, spare the CPS concerns. We were a happy and obviously healthy family. Our house was full of laughter, even though we may have been pushed harder than most kids. And although our pantry never had "the good stuff" when my friends came over for sleepovers, I was still allowed my own personal Skittle stash in my room, and Dad would let me get a Hershey Bar on the way to gymnastics at least three times a week. So, it wasn't all boot camp intensity – plus Dad deployed with the Navy often and mom's biceps were, thankfully, not as intimidating.

Although we didn't have a pantry with all "the good stuff," every meal was an event. I can still remember us sitting on the tile floor, all in a row, anxiously awaiting our post nap snack. Like a brood of freshly hatched chicks, snack time in my household always looked a bit like feeding time in the nest. We weren't starving; we had just had lunch a couple hours before. But unlike the neighboring nests, a quick grab-and-go sweet treat or boxed concoction wasn't often on the menu. Instead, bowls of cottage cheese and pineapple became a fan favorite.

The row of children wasn't comprised of just my siblings. My mom ran a daycare in our home, which eventually evolved into a full preschool with twelve little Tweety birds. They, too, learned to eat things their parents couldn't even force feed. It was just the expectation, and mama bird never wavered from the rule: greens first, then the meat, and then the treat (which was fruit by the way, not a bagged mini muffin). The occasional cookie was a delight. Parents were always perplexed as the chicks were sent back to their home nests claiming amnesia to the healthy food choices they consumed during the day. They would have nothing to do with similar items presented by their own parents. It was strictly at Mrs. Brenda's house.

As I got older my adolescent appetite ran wild. Sleepovers with other equally active gymnasts inevitably led to evening pantry raids. Friends often left underwhelmed from my house, while I would be in Kellogg and Hostess heaven in their homes. It became a running joke that my friends would hoard snacks in their overnight bags so we could binge upstairs. Surprisingly, I'm now the parent without the treats…even more so because we try to run a pantry free home to the best of our ability. "If it's in the fridge, you can have it."

Today I'm so grateful for the healthy nest my parents created. And although my teenage self would not agree, it was worth their investment. Without their focus on fitness and health, I'm not sure how I would have turned out. Our environment certainly has an immense effect on our approach, understanding, ability, and desire towards wellness.

Now there are some components of wellness and fitness that I didn't inherit from my parents. I am not a marathoner. I won't say never, though. I've learned that lesson before. Saying never inevitably speaks truth that it WILL happen eventually – God has quite the sense of humor! You see, in gymnastics, running means you have an 82-foot sprint to the vault apparatus. Our endurance conditioning involved running tumbling passes on the floor, not lacing up running shoes to get a good jog on. For all of you runners out there, I have a different interpretation and understanding of a "runner's high" than most. Runner's high to me used to be, "They must be high to run that far." Though, after further study (or hear say), I learned that you are more likely to be lethargic or ravenous when you are high as opposed to going for a run. So now I think it's just a state of temporary insanity. But I'm still uber-impressed with runners and will come out to cheer for you on the sidelines, likely even cry knowing the endurance and pain required to achieve that 13.1 or 24.2 bumper sticker on your car.

I recently ran a 5k. It was my longest run since childhood and just a squirrely idea to get into the sport alongside my family. Y'all, I passed the finish line while peeing... My husband and kiddos came to hug me, and I had to crouch on the ground to let it all go. Mind you, I was less than 50 yards from the porta-potty line up. Imagine my 4-year-old realizing what was going on! Her face flushed, and her jaw dropped. Luckily she's the strong silent type, so my husband brushed them to the side for my privacy. She secretly asked later about the shocking experience. How in the world are women running long distances after having babies (well, unless they're wearing a diaper)? Either way...we've all got our strengths and niches, and running surely isn't mine.

With that being said, your realm of influence has determining factors. Maybe it's your driving force to be healthy because you don't want to deal with the sometimes-debilitating results of being unhealthy, e.g., heart attacks, diabetes, and hypertension. Or perhaps you feel stuck in the lack of movement and activity your family participated in and motivation seems impossible to muster up. Whichever way the pendulum swings in your nature vs. nurture, there are a couple of absolutes. Our generational input into our genetic make-up exists; our DNA is a non-negotiable. In addition, our environments and other contributing factors DO weigh-in to our emotional output, positive or negative. I'm sure you've heard it said, "We are a product of our environment." Both nature and nurture are responsible for the person I am today – physical health being a dominant portion of that.

But the key component, the biggest absolute that is often overlooked in today's society or lineage study, is that we are daughters and sons of a perfectly fit Father. No matter your childhood experiences or pantry shelves, no matter your choice of sport or snack, no matter your heart rate or waistband measurement, you are loved to the root of your being. You are innately good because you are innately well. You are designed in His perfect image. Despite any situation you find yourself in and no matter what your scale, health records, or BMI says; our heavenly Father knit us together in our mothers' wombs. And since our birth, He looks upon us daily with a magnitude of love and adoration that we can't fully understand. This is truth. "Do you believe it?" is the question.

Now, I'm not a proponent of the "everyone wins" methodology that's taken over our children's athletic leagues, but I do believe that children and adults deserve encouragement and recognition for their efforts. Unfortunately, the unintended consequences of these good intentions include the devaluation of achievement, motivation, and opportunities to learn from failure. So, as we mature, we may feel less significant when there aren't accolades, plaques, and prizes being given at every event. Prizes, however, are mislabeled and misunderstood. We must recognize and teach our children that significance is not measured by tangible trophies or awards. Instead, significance is found in character development and obedience as suggested by Paul. For treasures being stored in heaven aren't always tangible here on earth. Does that mean we aren't accomplished? Paul, in 1 Corinthians 9:24-27, talks about the runner's race, the process of endurance and obedience in training, as well as the prize and how it is won. This parallel allows us to visualize the supernatural crowning that occurs when we put in the fight, die to self in the process, don't seek the glory award, and instead seek the eternal crown.

> *1 Corinthians 12:24-27:* *[24] Do you not know that in a race all the runners run, but only one gets the prize? Run in such a way as to get the prize. [25] Everyone who competes in the games goes into strict training. They do it to get a crown that will not last, but we do it to get a crown that will last forever. [26] Therefore I do not run like someone running aimlessly; I do not fight like a boxer beating the air. [27] No, I strike a blow to my body and make it my slave so that after I have preached to others, I myself will not be disqualified for the prize.*

I've "run a lot of races," and whether I peed in private or stood on the podium to accept Gold, I've put in the work. But the treasures that are being stored behind closed doors weren't recorded in a logged manual, weren't completed with a gym membership or race entry, and the price I paid wasn't with money at all. In fact, it was the price our Father in Heaven paid that led me to this very conversation – the conversation beyond the physical and into the mental.

Mental health comes into play in a large way with nature vs. nurture. Did you grow up in an environment of encouragement, love, empathy, and positive affirmations? Did you grow up in negativity, brokenness, shame, and striving for positive feedback? These are drastic variations for sure, and the reality is that we can often experience a little of both during our childhood. It's not specifically because of how we personally are changing and growing but how our adults and caretakers change as well. Just because one of their titles is Mom or Dad or Nana, this does not negate the many other names that make them who they are. They still have to function in their other roles, which can surely change the way they act out each of their identities. We end up being the offspring that represents every piece of their being, even the components that were never intended to be taught, known, or absorbed. Our first title is always child. And this is where we begin to grow.

Each of us has a mental health rap sheet that would intrigue psychologists. Our human composition, brain development, emotional practice, relational involvements, and life experiences are all worthy of a book. We each have a story and mostly all experience some sort of trauma in our lives. The key element of demise versus triumph is becoming the victor instead of the victim. It is the way we get healthy and learn to stay healthy.

My belief is that a fully functioning, healthy person experiences a process of establishing wholeness. They first identify their roots and then discover the strengths and weaknesses of their individual design. (This includes personality composition. Where are all my 3 enneagrams or ENFJ Myers Briggs companions?) Next, they become self-aware in the oneness of how they were created, raised, and are currently living. They then unearth their purpose for existence. This revelation allows them to find joy and peace, which in turn will aid them in building a future where they can walk out their wholeness as a physical, mental, and emotional being. Through this process they learn to establish necessary healthy practices that they then teach their own offspring and thus positively influence their immediate relational contacts – hence the circle of life.

How can we accomplish something so huge and seemingly complex? Like any development of expertise, skill, or physical practice; like any weight loss journey; it's a step at a time. It's a meal at a time. It's a day at a time. And the roadmap we need for this vast process of transformation doesn't exist in a health textbook or trending diet and exercise plan, but instead, it can be found in the number one selling book in the world. With over five billion copies sold and over 700 translations made, the Bible holds the blueprint to everything we need.

So let's take an example from its invaluable teachings to help us understand and witness this process firsthand outside of a gym membership, kitchen, track, or field. In the book of Exodus, the Israelites had lost their identity and were letting their mirrors, the Egyptians, pass judgment and cast lies as truth about who they were. For generations, in fact 430 years, they were called slaves, and therefore they took that name as their own. No medallions, no works could gain them the recognition or authority they were in fact promised. Their individuality had been stripped and their names were taken.

When Moses and Aaron finally came forth in their giftedness, even despite worry and fears of judgment, they helped break the Israelites free from their bondage. In the momentum of their release and escape from slavery, they still struggled in the knowing of who they were as chosen children of God. They even began to find comfort in those false identities and several times wanted to turn back to what was "comfortable". It took 40 years in the desert for the old belief systems to pass from their thought patterns so that they could step boldly into the Promised Land. Their strengths and their weaknesses combined to fortify their faith in God and help them press on toward the promise of a land flowing with milk and honey (Exodus 3:17). When they finally started believing His promises, their authority began to shift the atmosphere. In fact, they were even gifted land that they themselves had not toiled over, cities they did not build, and vineyards and olive groves they did not plant (Joshua 24:13). How good is our God that He helps not only restore our identity but gives us more than we could ask for or imagine. This goodness helps us create a new sense of wholeness in place of what was once breakage and bondage. This new wholeness then allows us to build a new, solid foundation on which our children can stand.

So the questions for this first critical step are many:

1. In what physical, emotional, mental, or spiritual prisons have you been locked?
2. Who do you feel is holding the key to that cell?
3. What lie are you standing beneath when you look in the mirror?
4. Are you willing to release the cycle that has caused you to be enslaved in your own mind, body, or soul?
5. What generational ties do you need to let go of in order to stand within your purposed identity as a daughter or son of the King?

Let me give you fair warning. This part of the process – the first step – encompasses so much more than just the action point. It is saying, "Yes." It's the commitment to yourself. It's the knowing of your why. It's the realization of the ultimate love that has your absolute best interest at heart, a love that has purposed you to expand your ability and placement here on earth, not solely or selfishly, but for God's Kingdom evolution. This is the hardest step and requires that you dive deep enough to accept and reestablish. I think the history books and family trees are useful tools, but on a much deeper level, you have to actually journey back in order to fully understand who you are and how to love that person standing in the mirror today. You must love enough to not be complacent with the current image, enough to want change for them, enough to want to nurture them, enough to want to fly out of the comfortable, safe confines of the nest you currently live in to bring back the essential ingredients that will keep you alive and well. You must love enough so as to insure that the generations that follow you have access to, and will proudly cultivate, the milk and honey you are promised.

So how did I do it? It wasn't just a conversation in the mirror. It wasn't just a miraculous eye contact exchange with Jesus either. It was action based on an "aha" of identity. Ultimately, regardless of my nature vs. nurture journey, it was my turn as a full-grown adult with children of my own to revert back and become the caretaker of the littlest memory of me. Barely past toddler phase, I found myself needing rescue. And even with extremely present and loving parents who were giving life their best foot forward and making a full attempt to provide above the means they were given as children – I still had greater needs. We all do. I had holes I couldn't fill, no matter how many bowls of cottage cheese and pineapples I ate, no matter how many flips and twists I did at gymnastics, no matter how many abs or muscle line definitions were produced, no matter how many affirmations, no matter how many accomplishments… The world could never fill my bucket. Enter our Heavenly Father…

So, I travelled back to visit that little girl and walk with her through her life's voyage, step by step, day by day, and help nurture her needs in a new kind of way. This would be done, not by my own might, but by His. It required recognizing and reminding her that light existed in every single situation, even when it felt like a blackout. I was never alone and neither were you. And honestly, even generationally, neither were they.

Without this first step, even if a little wobbly, you can never fully move through the other steps. The deep roots of who we are and where we came from help us to identify the "whys" that we often question without real cognitive awareness. Exposing the roots is not an easy process. It doesn't take place with a quick payment and click of an ancestry link. It takes time and often extracts some brokenness. It's a discovery process that begins generations before your birth, moves forward to the family dynamics of your home as a child, and even continues into your interactions with them today. And if you've already become a parent yourself, you learn that those lessons, or lack thereof, are also prevalent currently in your own home and practices. This step is a mouthful to say the least. However, it's never too late to take the first step. I encourage you; don't become paralyzed by a lifetime of dissection...start today. The jail cell is open my friend. Don't sit in fear of what awaits you outside.

But first, before you can proceed with your life's work, you must recognize the most imperative piece to unleash the understanding of our creation and purpose of existence (aka faith). And you don't walk into a therapist's office and leave having checked this box, even if all you've ever known is Christianity. Spirituality is a lifelong process, and the vast unknown of His existence is what makes this adventure epic. Sanctification, or the setting apart for a special use or purpose, isn't a one rinse of the feet kind of scenario. Though we are made new in Him, washed white and cleansed, our imperfections leave us in a constant state of becoming. He calls us to be more like Him by renewing our mind daily, submitting ourselves, and pursuing the wonders of His existence.

And, if you know Jesus at all, you know His ways are beyond our comprehension. His DNA existed and still exists in every being and life form that has surrounded you since your conception. Every detail matters, but we must accept the fact that we will not fully know the "why" behind every detail while here on earth.

This understanding is where trust and faith are established. It is the deep knowledge that the maker of the universe has your best interests at heart, even on your worst day. It is the promise given that insures the path this little girl wandered was not in vain, but was instead, incredibly purposed and beautifully paved. Jeremiah 29:11 says, "For I know the plans I have for you," declares the Lord, "plans to prosper you and not harm you, plans to give you hope and a future."

Without searching, you will never find, and you will never fill the void that you unknowingly tried to fill without Him. This step, your first step, is where our perfectionism and brokenness mend. You may be the most physically fit person you know, but even the healthiest bodies only last so long. Your hearse doesn't make a stop in Heaven, so it is necessary to nurture a relationship between your mind, body, and soul. Mentally, physically, and soulfully, we cannot be truly healthy without this step of faith progression.

I can't teach or tell you the who, where, when, and whys of how this process will take place in your own life. No one storyline unfolds the same way. But I can assure you that you will find your intended identity, develop stronger roots, begin a new nest, and crave the awareness of your Heavenly Father in every moment of your journey moving forward. I can also assure you that if you avoid it, your cell will begin to close in around you. The crash and burn will become a part of your story line as it was for some of the Israelites. Although their physical chains were broken, their mental and spiritual chains remained. Similarly, in my storyline, I physically knew strength, but mentally, emotionally and spiritually, I had no resilience, no strength, and no ability to press on towards any prize.

As you become, ask your heart:

Do you know your roots?

_____

_____

_____

_____

Have you taken the time to comprehend your own
established nature vs. nurture story line?

_____

_____

_____

_____

How did you get where you are today?

_____

_____

_____

_____

Can you identify Jesus in your journey?

_____

_____

_____

_____

The Warm-Up

*S*tanding at the end of the apparatus, far enough out of sight not to distract the judges but close enough to smell the chalk and hear the springboard as she mounted the beam, I would stand, eyes closed and fingers delicately yet purposefully posed in my natural gymnast stance. Move by move I would point my toes and wave my arms subtly as my mind spun to precision and each piece of my body nailed every element solid, sharp, yet graceful. As I mentally dismounted, I would step back into the reality of the moment, nerves lessened, focus intense, and my body ready to compete with what I had practiced for months on end.

My physical warm-up would have happened long before the showcased event, but the mental zone, with focused muscle memory exercises, was where I believe the gold was won. Even after decades of this technique, I totally forget about it when I think about a warm-up. My mind instead goes to the movie *Flashdance*. Give me some leg warmers and a fast-paced song so I can jog in circles to raise my heartbeat. This may be because I'm a product of the 80's or just because I love a good dance session in lieu of cardio day, but either way, most of us know warming up is essential to avoiding injury. It helps increase the heart rate at a gradual pace and gets the blood flowing. It helps loosen the muscles and joints. But how often do we miss this step in the process and jump right into the work out?

People don't often prefer process; they like results. They want the finished product. They don't want to know how many testing series were performed to get the completed outcome – they just want it to be good. Let's be honest, I often used to skip the warm-up. I wanted to meet the goal time or the muscle group objective and be done with it.

One of the most common and overlooked components of warm-up, and I'd argue one of the most important components, is the mental preparedness process. In gymnastics we used to practice the simple tricks first to get our headspace set and ready for the actual physical performing of the more difficult moves. If I weren't mentally prepared, I would usually fall. If it takes all of that to warm-up your body and your mind, imagine what it takes to warm up your soul, especially when it's been cold for a long time…but we'll tackle that a bit later.

I'm a coffee lover, but I wouldn't call myself an addict. Although I can give it up at any point, it's a morning practice that I've grown to love. I recall coffee dates and coffee drinkers in the wee hours of my procrastinating library days in college. But during that time, I drank hot chocolate. It sounds juvenile thinking back on it. I sound like a child, and in the grand scheme of things, I surely was. I even worked as a barista for a semester, learning all of the styles, names, and tricks for pouring the espressos and lattes for the sleep deprived college students. But, my coffee acquisition came at the right time in my life. It became my daily warm up after restless nights of nursing my babies. Without it I felt tense. I needed to loosen up, and I'm sure my husband was thankful for a fellow coffee-drinking buddy and a less grumpy morning zombie. I know many people who you just don't speak to until they have had their cup of Joe. It's like their tongue is frozen, and until they can get in that "warm-up," they physically can't communicate.

Starbucks on average makes eight million cups of coffee a day! That's proof alone that our society as a whole goes through a daily thawing period. So many are addicted to the caffeine kick that ignites their mental and physical states, yet so often we avoid the process in other significant areas of our lives. Just like those who bypass the warm-up in a workout and expect themselves to perform at ample levels without getting hurt, I've experienced the coffee-bypass in my daily routine. It often leads to a slow start, slight grumpiness, and usually a headache by noon. I understand that's the sugar and chemical caffeine void, but it makes for a beautiful correlation, don't you think? And for now, with my kiddos, I'm convinced I'm a better mom when I have a cup of coffee. So, I'm not judging you! It's the one thing that is all mine. They drink my water. They eat my snacks and meals. I can't even go to the bathroom or shower alone. But they think my coffee is gross, so every last drop is all mine, and I'm thankful!

As I write this book, social media posts are filled with reflections about the previous year, preps for New Year's resolutions, and highlighted key words to use as personal, annual anthems. I was actually pleasantly shocked by the amount of prep and thought that went into people's goals for the year. Though I wondered how much of it was done just to gain followers versus actually taking the time-out to assess and reflect on their "health."

Reflection is a wonderful heart-level warm-up. If more people would do it instead of passing it off as a silly tradition or useless tool, it could be so beneficial for the collective society. The problem is, most traditional goals generally aren't applied to one's moral barometer or belief system. Most concentrate on finances, fitness, family, and fun, while neglecting the faith component.

I have surely been there. My list of desired achievements year after year were focused on the acquisition of stuff. I wanted more money. I wanted more gadgets. I wanted more of the things "The

Joneses" had, and I equated those things to happiness. I didn't often have fitness goals, as I was satisfied with my frame and my weight, but we know skinny girls can be sick and unhealthy too. The more my warm-up in goal setting reflected materialism, the less happy I became. I was satisfied momentarily, however. The traveling was fun. The shopping and purchasing and showing off were enjoyable at face value, but the root joys were ignored. Even my family goals with my kiddos and hubby were less about the kind of mother and wife I wanted to evolve into and more about performance driven expectations and checkpoints.

Please don't get me wrong; I by no means think setting goals around finances and dreams of things you want to buy is all bad. It's all about the depth at which the other areas are elaborated and the priority placement of those desires. Happiness is established best when the warm-up is rooted in heart matters – in soul matters with a solid spiritual foundation. At the end of the year, if we are fuller in faith than we are in finances, I'd place big bets that we are more than happy; we are filled with unspeakable joy. If, however, we are full in finances but lacking family and friends to share it with, I'd have to argue that we are missing the happiness factor.

So, to go against the grain, I started practicing something new to move past the annual hoopla of New Year's Resolutions and stay more connected with who God was calling me to be in that next season of life. I began by adjusting the emphasis to my birth year. Using a trending insta-shop bracelet concept of clarifying one-word mantras, I began unpacking words that would lead to a centering of happiness for me. Only later would I find out it was actually introduced in a book called *One Word That Will Change Your Life*. Recently, I had the pleasure of connecting with the author, Dan Britton, to share my own take on this experience and practice. In the 20+ years he has been writing and sharing this book and message, he had never heard of my particular methodology. I was, of course, pleased with myself, but more so grateful that others could take it for their own experience too. Essentially, I had this novel idea that this would be the ultimate warm-up. I'd step into the next birth year refreshed in this new pursuit of concept, and I'd spend time seeking God through this lens.

Ironically, the year I put this into practice, I was turning 30. It was a year I now refer to as my quarter-life crisis. I say ironically, because Jesus's ministry really kicked into high gear during his 30th year. In addition, I've also connected with so many incredible humans who, like me, have had catastrophic events coincide with monumental experiences during just such a personal decade change. Regardless, I started that year with the word "expectant." But, what I didn't expect, due to my lack of maturity (which became the word for my 34th year), was for God to show up unexpectedly to surprise me in unexpected ways. During that year, my happiness, or fickle idea of it, was rocked time and time again. I'll come back to that later…but I had to cue this up.

In the Japanese culture there is a term called *ikigai* that has been explored for decades, in part due to this island nation having the world's highest life expectancy. Everyone wanted and still wants to know, how and "what is the secret?" This word is their truth. It's defined as "a reason for being." It's the understanding of their greatest purpose in life. And I believe, based on countless smiling photos of their sometimes-toothless, deeply creased faces, they do truly get it. Happiness and purpose are connected. And nothing about these two critical elements results from material gain but rather from acquisitions of the heart.

Happiness is explained biblically as being "blessed." The Hebrew phraseology from the Old Testament is *ashrê*, which means "flourishing" or "happiness" or "well-being." It's often used when describing those who live in accordance with God's will. Later in the New Testament, this word is translated into Greek as *makarios*, which takes on the same understanding. It is also correlated to concepts in which happiness exists, not just in gifts and blessings, but in conjunction with following the law and abiding in His very nature.

> Psalm 1:1 says "Blessed is the one who does not walk in step with the wicked or stand in the way that sinners take or sit in the company of mockers, but whose delight is in the law of the Lord and who meditates on his law day and night. The person is like a tree planted by streams of water which yields its fruit in season and whose leaf does not wither — whatever they do prospers."

So while the world tells us happiness is defined by exterior items or found in simple heart-filled joys, it is equally as relevant and critical for us to align ourselves with the not so fun Fruits of the Spirit. Galatians 5:22 also mentions forbearance and self-control. I know that doesn't sound glamorous, but even the most awarded "happy" and "successful" humans, like the rich and the famous, have a testimony to their endurance and self-discipline. The variable in question is, are they really happy? Have they experienced true joy? Quite possibly.

So we've talked future, fitness, coffee, and even happiness. Even how coffee may make us happy. And, we've also seen how expectancy towards our happiness can have some unexpected turns as well. But let's go deeper. Let's reconnect with the concept and importance of the warm-up. I think as a society we are so fast-paced and caught up in this microwave movement of "right now" that we completely miss the element of the warm-up. People jump out of bed to an alarm clock without even taking a breath to embrace the fact that they even woke up in the first place. It's taken for granted. It's expected. But the warm-up is critical to this journey we are on, and the most powerful way to warm-up your soul is to pray.

Even as Christians, we can find ourselves cold. You may have been set on autopilot with ministry work or perhaps the prayers are always prayed by you for others or over you, yet you forget to pray for yourself. So, let's be purposeful and begin each day with a warm-up for our soul! Set the time between the alarm and your feet on the floor to pray. Pray in thanksgiving for the opportunity to live this day, in this body, with this breath, in this mind. Or maybe you are one of those aforementioned zombie coffee fiends – it's ok, you can pray in the shower or the car or anytime. He's always listening. I had an enjoyable revelation while stretching in the wee hours of my early morning routine. The next time you go to pray upon rising, I hope this triggers a little smile. The cartoon, the sitcom, the plays, they all do this the same. The person sits up in bed, they yawn, they put their arms in a back stretch position, eyes closed, and then they stretch their arms far and wide to the heavens. Coincidence? I don't believe in those. God wink. Definitely. Try it now. Own the strength of this given day and praise those arms right on up to Heaven. Rejuvenating right?

However, I'm aware, friend. Perhaps the prayer of thanksgiving isn't relevant to you right now. Perhaps "this body" and "this mind" aren't something you are thankful for at this time. If this is your reality, then let's pray for the renewing of those things. Let's get your blood flowing. Let's get your muscles moving in a warm-up for what you are getting ready to do that day. Visualize where and how you want your mustard seed of faith to be planted and grown. Just as Mark 4:31 shares of the resilience of the mustard seed, the smallest of its kind, which bears a massive tree, strong, resilient, and rooted; I, too, desire this magnificent growth for you. So don't be like the man who plants his seed in not-fertile soil, where the birds pluck it before it roots or the water washes it before it is grounded. Focus into good soil and you will reap the harvest of happiness – blessing – ikigai: your eternal joy.

It's your prayer, planning, and reflection – it's your warm-up – that waters your mustard seed and keeps you rooted for what's ahead. You can also use my annual word rooting methodology to keep attuned to your annual vision. Without this practice, your daily apparatus, whatever it is (gym, work, mom-hat, wife-hat, hobbies), will be but a loose thoughtless mustard-seed experience that is lacking precision and good soil.

So girl, grab a coffee, seek His blessings, pray and de-thaw; it's vital.

As you become, ask your heart:

What's your morning routine?

What warm-up are you ignoring that you may desperately need in order to align yourself?

What is one thing you can do today to better your mind, body, or soul (perhaps all 3)?

Read Matthew 13: Where and how are you currently planting your seed?

How can you readjust from self-realization to a God-reflection?

Trainers Need Trainers

and found its way between our toes, in our hair, beneath our sports bra line, and well...obviously everywhere else. It stuck to glistening sweat as we chased the shade cast by the hotels in the afternoon sunset. Each morning, with a jerry-rigged beach buggy attached to my gearless bike, loaded with medicine balls, stretchy bands, cones, and water, I'd race miles to set up the exercises before the women arrived for their morning beach workouts. For an entire summer, my mother and I ran what we called Beauty and The Beach. I lived closer and didn't have a yacht high bridge to cross, so I often got the beach buggy responsibility. Regardless, my twenty-something bikini bod provided ample inspiration to the women who came to get their butts kicked and egos checked. I don't care who you are or how "in shape" you think you are, get on the soft sand and give me ten jumping jacks and tell me you're not winded. This boot-camp style experience, next to the vast ocean that has always been my resting place, was a memory I'll never forget. The women we trained that season aren't still active in our lives, but we have a bond because of what we gained and what we left on that beach. Even sand in all the wrong places was evidence of the hard work we put in. Blood, sweat, and tears; burn marks and sanded wind blasts; we shared life. And though I reveled in that experience, I have come to realize that because I was the one doing the training, my needs weren't ever fully met.

I think often we see these health nuts, either lean or muscular, and we forget about the people who poured into them to get them where they are today. No successful or healthy person exists without the influence, love, and encouragement of others. Their abs, even in their own diligence and mental preparedness, have a story connected to someone who motivated and pushed them.

Trainers usually aren't our favorite people at the beginning of our workout experience. We are angry at their pep and enthusiasm and envious as they hover over us with their blow-dried, bouncy hair while we are forced into painful positions and countless reps. We want quick results. I know because I've been on both ends of the training experience. I've prepped my own goals and assisted others in setting and meeting theirs, however, not usually with the bouncy hair. But we know, just like the warm-up, it's a process. We're trained to train you to reach those physical goals, just like teachers, therapists, and life coaches know what it takes to have mental and emotional wins.

Our culture has negated the importance of the role of a teacher post college. Law mandates at youth that we all must go to school; we all have to have a teacher. But when it comes to adulthood, we're released. We're kicked out of the nest to fly on our own, yet the conditions we are headed for are uncharted territory for every single one of us. We don't know what lies ahead, what mountains we will face, or what barriers will block us. We just set off into the sunset with the hopes of clear skies and fair winds.

I truly think that there needs to be an additional term between childhood, adolescence, and adulthood. The Lord knows I wasn't an adult in my 20s, and I believe many others can relate. Perhaps we can increase the maximum age of adolescence from 19 to 29. Shoot, it's scientifically proven that our prefrontal cortex doesn't even close until we're 25. That's the part of the brain responsible for sound decisions and an awareness of consequences.

Thankfully, I believe that the millennial generation has changed many components of the accepted patterns of aging and life milestones. And while I do not believe it was a carefully considered decision made by my generation, but instead a gradual shift throughout a few decades, it now seems to rest on our shoulders. Though we have been commercialized as irresponsible, selfish, perhaps egotistical, and entitled; I'm standing on the confidence that our generation will constitute the shifters of the Kingdom revival. From a worldly view, we don't get married and have kids in our late teens and early twenties. It's no longer an expectation to have your life's career choice decided and definite at 18, though college foundations still try to narrow our focus. We aren't locking ourselves into one role or one hat or one passion. We don't answer to the man, and we don't long for the same white picket fence that our parents did. So, moving forward, I'll refer to this teetering, adventurous time period as the wandering years.

These wandering years were the years I needed a trainer most; a trainer outside of my beach boot camp role; a trainer who would harness my mind, heart, and body. And thus entered the new age "wandering years" teacher, or more commonly referred to and accepted as, a counselor. Yet unfortunately, there was a horrible stigma associated with someone who visited one of these necessary people. The coined term "shrink" that was established by an author in the 60's, was one of many words used to create the idea that these professionals were only needed by those with psychiatric issues. But, if we are honest with ourselves, don't we all have psychiatric issues? We all have a brain. We all have feelings. We all have social, religious, generational (just to name a few) pressures and opposing opinions being thrown our way daily. Oftentimes, they all struggle against each other and leave us questioning, deliberating, and wrestling with ourselves as we try to make sound life decisions.

In the same breath that the "healthy" American culture discredits the need for a therapist, it celebrates the role of a trainer. In all fields, a trainer has a positive cognitive connotation. Their job's purpose is to prepare and instill confidence in the trainee. A dog trainer, a physical fitness trainer, and a corporate job trainer are all celebrated for their efforts, yet aren't they doing the same job as the shrink? They train the subject (people and animals alike) mentally and physically to do and be their best self.

Call them what you may, I needed, and still need, a teacher. I need a counselor. I need a therapist. I need a trainer. I need a shrink. I believe we all do. Luckily, there is a term that has gained traction since the 80's. This term allows us to not feel like a "crazy-person" when we loosely use it in conversation; enter the Life Coach.

So, if you are a human – get one – a life coach that is. This isn't some new age practice, by the way. The need for teachers and others to guide us through life's struggles is not new and was in fact a common occurrence throughout the Old Testament. Disagreements broke out regularly in different people groups and caused havoc within communities and regions. Religious discrepancies existed between false idols and sound doctrine. Governmental corruption and generational bondage existed and spread throughout entire nations causing destruction to the family unit. Sadly, it doesn't sound much different than society today, does it? And even then, until Jesus, there were few teachers speaking total Truth.

I've had my fair share of trainers. I've experienced athletic trainers and coaches as a child and adolescent on up to fitness trainers and business coaches as an adult. And, as I'm sure you know, I even became a personal trainer and business coach myself. But I didn't experience my first counselor or life-coach (whatever name you choose to use) until I was in my late 20s. Nearing the end of my wandering years, I had literally stumbled off course and felt completely lost.

I, too, had a misconception about their purpose and need. I was "normal." There was nothing wrong with me. I was just living life like the next person...trying, sometimes succeeding, sometimes failing. I was not self-aware in my true identity. But am I entirely to blame for that? They don't offer a high school or college course on that one; though in retrospect, it would be a stellar core curriculum class. However, I would love to see an up-rise of school counselors who begin to teach and share what they know to the younger generations. This guidance might help prevent the crash and burn scenarios that we often hear about in this chaotic society.

The entire counseling experience was so foreign to me. Sitting across the room on a couch, while sharing your deepest thoughts, your history, and your heart with someone shouldn't be so bizarre, but I've never felt so exposed. I didn't even feel that exposed when I was naked with my husband for the first time. That is proof that even our closest relationships, though seemingly intimate, are still only surface deep. The only person you are truly in total union with (other than the Holy Spirit) is your own conscience, and even in that headspace, you can be deceived. I was.

So, near the end of my second decade, I found myself right in the middle of what I referred to earlier as my quarter-life crisis. I woke up frantically searching the Internet to find a place where I could get the help I so desperately needed. After enduring a night of full body shakes, internal anxiety that even the tightest embrace from my husband wouldn't calm, and fear gripping my insides; I knew I needed a trainer. But what do you search for when you're broken, fearful, depressed, lonely, lost, confused, anxious, and full of shame? Which coping mechanism did I need the most help with? What treatment would I ask for?

What I found that day was a massive void in available care. Even the places that made a bit of sense were tens of thousands of dollars, too far away from my babies and family, and required too long of a time frame. I panicked. At this point, I already felt that I had checked out of life. The walls were already crashing around me. In a matter of one week, I was no longer the CEO of two companies; I was no longer the wife and mother I dreamed I'd one day be, and I was a stranger to the reflection in the mirror.

After no luck and continued panic, we called a trusted source in desperation for her sound wisdom. We knew she loved Jesus; we knew she had 11 children that she cared for into their adulthood, and we knew she had read and studied more psychological books and been to more conferences than anyone we knew on the subject. She's one of those people who you can simply melt into their shoulder and know that everything will be OK. She came in the midst of a storm, one outside by weather forecast and one within our home and hearts.

This dear woman is my spiritual mama, also known as my fairy God-mama. Speaking of sound doctrine...holy cow is she a gem of a human being. She was also the brave soul that weathered the first storm with us on our wedding day. She was the officiant that helped us tie the knot – technically twice in one evening – with the outside and inside nuptials. Her prayers on that day, even outside of my true knowing of Jesus, still penetrated my soul. This amazing woman was there for us again on the fateful day of my unraveling.

As we laid the puzzle pieces before her, I was amazed by how many tears could flow from my being. But what I didn't know was that my husband had already been in communication with her for weeks. He had spotted this downward spiral before I would admit to its existence. He utilized her training skills in hopes of breathing life into a dying situation. He had tried to connect with me through the stale expressions, lifeless conversations, and avoidance patterns; but I retreated further.

Have you ever had someone pursue you, someone who saw the best in you when you didn't see the best in yourself? Have you ever had someone love you...fully love you? Well on that fateful day, even with my faithful husband by my side, I would have said no to that question. But, by the time our fairy God-mama left three hours later, the sun was shining, the skies were full of sun rays, our home was freshly illuminated, and a rainbow had appeared within my spirit.

I saw the face of Jesus through submission and admittance that day:

Submission to the love – the personal, unconditional, infinite, and unfailing love of my Heavenly Father; Submission to The Truth – the truth that Christ took upon my shame on the cross; and Submission to my true identity and most important title – Daughter of the King.

Admittance of the fallacies in the arguments and lies that compounded to create a false identity; Admittance of the fear that was not from God; and Admittance of my own incapable, imperfect, impossible humanity, and the flesh that I was at war with.

Submission met with admittance, received through repentance, became my admission to eternity. We prayed. We warred. We shared testimonies and secrets. We shared life and love. And I'll never forget the moment Jesus himself took my downcast eyes and grabbed hold of my chin, lifting my gaze from my feet to His radiant face. Rays of sunshine burst forth through the storm, and warmth filled my soul from the inside out. My shoulders sat high, and my energy was renewed. Color came back to my face, and hunger came back to my stomach. And I clasped the hand of the husband who sat with me, desperate to be met by my gaze and adoration once again.

But the fairy God-mama and The Teacher of all teachers shared a bit of insight that forever changed my life, wisdom that I now gratefully and freely pass to everyone I can. "We love, because He first loved us." (1John 4:19). Even though the pain didn't miraculously lift forever, and I still had a long road ahead, I wept, as Jesus wept, for the sins of the world and for the pain of this side of Heaven. But, I also wept for the glorious revelation that I am fully seen, fully known, and still fully loved, even in my imperfection.

The lessons were many, and in fact they never stopped. This is due to the fact that since that moment, I've lived in a desired state of conviction. This is admittedly a hard place to exist for an overachiever, people-pleaser, and recovering perfectionist. But conviction isn't intended to be destructive; it's a process of iron sharpening iron; it's the truth in the journey of becoming.

One of the most critical components that I believe emerged from this season of training was my ability to communicate. Just as our personal angel addressed us that day, she didn't steer away from the hard questions or the hard conversations. She came in with ease, peace, and Truth. I didn't pick up on this quickly, and the first few sessions with my hired counselor felt like rejections all over again. You've heard that adage that old habits die hard? Well, I didn't want to face the hard truths, and I definitely wanted to save face with strangers. What was actually happening? What did I actually need to do to get past these controlling emotions and fears?

Eventually, bit by bit, and night after night, the Holy Spirit chiseled away the stone that was covering the tomb of my heart and soul. Each counseling session made me feel as though I was having an out of body experience. I seemed to hover over the couch watching myself, onion layer by onion layer, removing the outer shell that the world had assisted me in placing. The reality that I was discovering the root of my design didn't hit me all at once. It was instead one aha moment after the other. And I couldn't have done it without The Shrink – The Counselor – The Therapist – The Coach – The Trainer – The Fairy God-Mother – or The Teacher. His name is Jesus.

I remember, at the mere age of six, my gymnastics coach thrusting me into something I wasn't ready for. I sat with the dozens of other girls trying out for our first competitive level. Their bodies were sandwiched to the floor, resting in the middle split like it was how they regularly slept. I was perplexed and embarrassed. My body wasn't that flexible yet. Trying to help, my coach pressed on my back leg, forcing me into tears instead. I ran back to the viewing room where my parents sat, and I heard him tell them, "She's not mature enough. She's just not ready. We'll try again soon."

This is how I felt on the couch. At almost 30 years old, I knew that I was about to be stretched outside of my comfort zone, but I also knew I didn't want to look back in another 20 years and wonder what if. Even outside of my own desire to press on, I understood that this wasn't a comparison game anymore; it was a critical self-awareness moment. No one else's opinions mattered, and I had the perfect trainer ready to help me maneuver myself into the positions that were the most uncomfortable to face.

How can we adequately prepare our bodies for new fitness levels if we are unaware of how our bodies are designed to move? How can we try a movement that is foreign to us without the instruction of someone who has done it before or knows our potential? Trainers are imperative to reaching and mastering congruent, fluid movement. Their role is to bend you, not always in comfortable ways, and this requires that you trust they have your best interests at heart and that they will not break you.

I felt broken. I felt utterly misunderstood. I sat across from her on the couch, sometimes with my husband by my side and other times alone. I was hesitant. I was unpacking a closet within me that I never knew existed. It took months before I could sit on the couch comfortably. It took years before I was ready to face the "middle split" position again. I needed her, not for the extra push, but instead for her guidance as I attempted to stretch deeper and wider. It wasn't the typical, come in and lay down to meditate, situation. She wanted eye contact and effort, and all I wanted to do was get up and run crying to my mommy and daddy. Now, however, I was the mama and this was my time to make the decision on behalf of the little girl inside who desperately needed my comfort.

Trust is no easy feat to accomplish, and it also shouldn't be freely given. It requires a warm-up process through which you get to know a person and develop a relationship. But I believe the key element in trusting others is to first trust yourself. That comes with a dissection of the heart. It is the place where self-awareness becomes an actuality and not a figurative concept of smoke and mirrors. It's getting to the place where we don't doubt every decision and every thought. Don't get me wrong; it is never an autopilot walk, and there is constant need for salt baths, icy-hot massages, and rest days within our mind and body. However, when all of the aha moments come together and your veil of identity is lifted, when you finally get into the difficult middle split position – you will know. You will then be able to firmly hold the position that used to cause you the most pain. Don't give up too easily, friend. This will be the best gold medal you could possibly receive and one that will not end up in a dusty attic bin. Instead, it will be passed generation to generation, gymnast to gymnast, as your children and children's children tumble through the storyline of their own lives.

Ok, so let me guess. You have no desire to do the splits at this age in your life? I get it. But it is feasible. We'll get on the stretching topic later, but I know you're wondering, "How do I get there? How do I cut the fat, lose the weight, and become the outside body that my agile childlike soul desires to reflect?" My advice: find a trainer and lean on the one true Teacher, Jesus. Let go of your self-righteousness and start to peel back the layers. Expose yourself in a leotard that rides up into the most uncomfortable places. Stop comparing yourself. Stop telling yourself lies that you can't, or you won't, or you shouldn't. It's not an overnight feat. It may take years in fact. Day after day and year after year, we put junk in and on our bodies, minds, and souls. This accumulation of junk has kept us from reconnecting with the healthy heart intended for us at birth, and it will take time to get rid of. (And if you were born with a heart defect or weakness, you were born with purpose, beauty, and intention. Our God does not make mistakes.) So, learn to trust your trainer. Learn to trust yourself. And, when you look in the mirror at the end of the day, refuse to see what the world sees, but instead see what He sees. And then in the sweetest gift of all, learn through example to communicate with empathy, vulnerability, truth, and wisdom to help others push past the discomfort of that first "split" experience.

Ultimately, He is the greatest counselor and trainer of all time. His stretching tactics are gentle and kind. He's waiting to present you with your gold medal. But you must rise to accept it. His eyes are already fixed on you, and He's waiting to lift your chin to His glorious face. His passion is to see you break free and stretch and attain new places, spaces, movements, and people that you never thought possible. So today, the lesson in class is to learn to be ok with waving your white flag of broken fragility. It's the most beautiful piece of our humanity. It is the knowing that we are imperfectly perfect and our Father in Heaven orchestrated it this way so we may know Him and live fully within His borders and love. But we must be willing to be OK with getting uncomfortable in order to emerge.

As you become, ask your heart:

Who are the trainers within your own life?

Have you considered therapy or coaching?

Do you trust yourself enough to trust them?

And if not, can you trust them enough to learn to trust yourself?

Have you ever considered God your trainer, coach, or counselor?

Have you practiced submission, admittance, and repentance in order to receive admission into the Kingdom?

Goooaaalll!

I stood on stage in my sunflower jumpsuit and bright red lipstick, peering at a packed cafeteria filled with my peers, parents, and teachers. I had just given my keynote presidential speech, and on cue from the loud speakers, I asked everyone to join in as we danced to the Macarena. To this day I don't remember how that song tied into my campaign, but I had already visualized my victory and was happily celebrating. I still love that dance and have to giggle at my confident, fashionably bold, 4th grade self running for student government president. The practice of repetitive visualization techniques from gymnastics had already begun to spill over into other areas of my life. I never knew their full potential and power, however, until I learned the Biblical purpose of manifestation and meditation.

I'm a firm believer in the power of vision. From a young age, I was actively involved in student government. Before I continue, let me reshape your likely frame of reference. I know that in most school districts running for school council offices would immediately rank you in the "uncool" crowd, but somehow this was not the case. (Or maybe it absolutely was, and I thought too highly of myself.) Cool or not for your school – we were somehow deemed "popular."

This sense of popularity led to school wide support and cohesiveness for student council activities, and annual goal setting became the foundation for the year. After hours of round table political processes (majority vote most often, but not without much debate), we set a theme for the year. Staff and students alike were involved. I loved the process, but I also loved the popularity, mainly from the stance of the teacher's approval. I was an achievement driven child for sure. (I know you're wondering about nature vs. nurture right now.) As I progressed from 2nd grade classroom representative to delivering that elementary school presidential speech and every year following through 12th grade, I was able to design a dream/goal collectively with a team and go after it. I was a goal setter, a planner, a coordinator, and a dreamer. SMART goals were ingrained in me.

Specific – Measurable – Attainable/Achievable – Realistic – Timely

I'm thankful for all the roles I played in student government and also how I learned from others. I believe these opportunities were some of the most transforming experiences of my adolescent life, and they certainly played a significant role in every path I took after graduation. I realize we all didn't have a two-week dedicated goal setting agenda prior to our academic school years beginning, but what if we did?

Unfortunately, I also set many unhealthy goals throughout the years, none of which were aligned to my true design, calling, or purpose. They were selfish ambitions driven by societal pushes and pulls. My goals were not eternal, and though some were generational, as I hoped for a husband and children, I still was not looking at the grand scheme of community or global impacts. It was all about me. And you may think, "You were only a child," but this type of thinking was still the norm during that whole quarter life crisis stint – so decades in y'all. Although I'm ashamed to admit it, my center was me. Even in the midst of student government and later as CEO of multiple companies and even the CEO of my home, I still focused inward, not outward or upward.

My mental focus was no further outside of me than my physical presence. Even my visualization practices weren't community minded. We definitely live in a me-driven world. Thankfully, Christianity pulls your mind from you to Him and from Him to them. "I" is just a miniscule part of the whole. And it wasn't until this season of unpacking that I started to piece together the ME that I was protecting for so long.

I previously published a co-authored book about one of the many revelations that occurred during this time of deconstruction and reconstruction. *She Writes For Him: Stories of Resilient Faith* was the first opportunity I had to divulge a shadow in my closet. It was a hard thing to release – telling the world about a little girl who had been sexually assaulted on multiple occasions by an older, larger child with a mental handicap. I carried the weight. It was my fault for not saying something the first time or the second time…or any time after. It was then my fault when I repeatedly chose to hide in the closet with nudie-magazines, which led to self-exploration, which later led to cyber sex and further sexual cycles of shame. The reason I share this again isn't for redundancy or rehashing but instead to further illuminate the genesis of self-protection that occurs when we are not being protected when it mattered most.

This is but one example of the many catastrophic scenarios that friends, strangers, and even the many beautiful co-authors of that book had to endure. Wall by wall, plank by plank, through the spirit of offense, shame, guilt, and fear, we create our own hedge of protection. This hedge ultimately ends up trapping us in our own personal prisons, unable to break free. I choose to take ownership of my choices and recognize the free will that was gifted to us. I also choose to not cast blame on others, regardless of what story could be told from that angle. Instead, through goal setting, through vision casting, and through truth telling, little by little and step by step, I escaped.

As a Christian, it may seem strange to parallel my spiritual breakthrough to a goal, but I feel like it's more relatable than a miracle (though I consider my freedom just that). However, it wasn't one of those scenarios where the woman touches the cloak of Jesus and is miraculously healed *(Matthew 9:21-22)*. No, my situation felt more like the 40 years spent by the Israelites in the desert that I discussed earlier. But honestly, knowing the actual time it took compared to the Biblical 40-year stint – my life is pretty miraculous, and only by the grace of God is that true. But even so, for three years, each day felt like an eternity as I faced the fears, admitted truths, and revisited the dark places of my childhood and my current life.

Triggers existed everywhere. A trigger, in case you don't know, is when a memory, often in imagery or by way of reminder through one of your senses, brings you back into a place of trauma. It is similar to a flashback, but your adrenaline can race, and you can go back into a state of anxiety caused by the exact emotions that occurred during the actual event. This would happen at all hours of the day, even while enjoying sweet moments with my children. I'd have to snap myself back into the reality that I was safe, loved, and made new in Christ. They haven't fully diminished, but by goal setting and meditation, I've been able to slowly release the nightmares by night and the triggers by day. These were the moments that kept me isolated, the assaults that left me shamed, the choices that left me scarred, the people that I had to forgive, and the most important piece – the me that I had to forgive.

So, how do you set a goal to forgive yourself? How do you set a goal to break free?

I believe it's already been exemplified by The Teacher, by the ultimate goal setter. But if you like more practicality, let's chat.

The concept of SMART goals was developed in 1980. Since then SMART goals have evolved into SMARTER goals and then into SMARTEST goals in 2010. SMART goals are realistic in nature. SMARTER goals add E (excitable, ethical) and R (Re-ward, reassess). The E and the R provide the element of energy, thrill, and success. We all desire the WOW factor, and when we allow the dream to be bigger than our human potential, that's where God can do His miracle work. It's been said before, in relation to ministry messages, that there is no new content. But, God is the master of goal setting; He's the ultimate visionary, and therefore, I reject that statement. Even if there is no new content to Him, He surely reveals new things to me on a daily basis and in a language that's uniquely mine.

Isn't a prophecy a dream? Couldn't it be considered a God-sized goal and plan? They were spoken at creation. They were written in the Old Testament. God was held accountable, and He checked each of them off His list one by one...the greatest check being the birth of His son and His three-and-a-half-year ministry here on Earth. But, to top it off, every one of His goals had a head-turning, life-changing WOW factor. So, shouldn't we take notes from the true visionary? He is the SMARTEST (E = evaluate, S = share, T = tailor). The 'est' is the key. So you must prepare ahead by setting your intention on the outcome and stepping beyond your SMART goal to evaluate and share. Then you will truly be standing in your gifted confidence from God, and He will direct your tailoring through His lens, just as the potter does. This tailoring makes way for you to lean into your authority as truly SMART and SAVED.

So, as we develop ourselves in mental, physical, and soulful ways; we put ourselves in concordance with what He has already spoken over us. Make your goals the smartest by allowing Him to be a part of the dream, the vision, the checklist, and the goal.

You can think them up. You can dream them into existence. You can write them down. You can post them. And it is likely, you can even complete and accomplish them. But, you can only exceed them with His help. Be the smartest in the room because you are partnered with the SMARTEST.

Now I can't possibly move on without helping you process how meditation can align to your goals and how manifestation, through partnering with Jesus in His promises and His will, can help develop a framework of pursuit. Fast-forward five years from these pivotal growth moments between self-reflection and God development. I'm sitting with two feet planted on the floor in my office, learning from a new trainer and amazing business coach, Mike Zeller, who had immersed me in a practiced group mediation. He invited me into a space, a room, where I stood in the doorframe peering in at an old version of myself. The room was white, as was my body. My old self, a smaller white blob of a being, sat at a lone table. He directed me to approach that old sense of self. But quickly, before my mind could let me, Jesus came into the frame. I was initially worried. I sensed the temple scenario where He was going to flip the tables because of what was transpiring inside the house of God. But instead, He calmly approached the table and placed a bag of coins on its smooth surface. The little person looked innocently in his direction, but He walked away without speaking. Moments later, Mike had me name that figure. I called him "Lonely." I was then instructed to take him outside and put him on a waiting bus. He walked toward the back seats, the place where the "cool" kids used to bully me.

Yes, I know I mentioned my popularity before, but these kids didn't care about that. Again, perspective is everything. I was the goody two-shoes, cheerleader, class secretary, and thus their target at the time. So I watched little Lonely meander to the back as I took the driver's seat with authority. I drove the big vehicle down the road and stopped. Looking back over my shoulder, I kindly asked

Lonely to get off and never come back. The people-pleaser in me felt terrible. "What would he think about me?" I wondered. Mike didn't allow me to ponder much longer. Before I knew it, I was back in the room that was no longer occupied by that past version of myself. But it wasn't exactly the same as before. The colors were a bit more vibrant, and the room was packed with people. Mike instructed me to go from one side of the room, where the money bag Jesus had given me was still sitting, to the other side. Like a party host or birthday girl, everyone tapped my shoulders and hoorayed me as I dipped and ducked through the crowd. At the opposite side of room, I stood on a table and proceeded to do the floss. Everyone in the room happily joined in. I remember smiling ear to ear thinking back to the Macarena from my childhood.

Now there were surely parallels with events in my current life, as I was in the middle of planning a virtual flash mob for Glenn Lundy's #riseandgrindshow. But the lessons that persisted throughout the remainder of the meditation had me in awe of the power of presence and in the ability to communicate with the spirit and His ultimate desire to help us connect the dots of our goals, our past, our dreams, our realities, and our futures. Today, I know that bag of coins was a part of a promise He has whispered to my heart. I also know that lonely isn't something I'll ever have to face again, as the next portion of the meditation had me linking arms with men and women of all shapes, sizes, colors, and smiles. I felt assured that they were going with me in an unbreakable chain rather than a solo Red Rover run. And, I'm also fairly confident, it won't be the last time I'm on a table dancing. So stay tuned.

As you become, ask your heart:

What are your goals mentally, emotionally, physically, and spiritually?

_____

_____

Have you considered the larger view: turning your goals from me to we?

_____

_____

How can you parallel meditation and manifestation to your prayer life?

_____

_____

Meditation – Psalm 1:2 – but whose delight is in the law of the Lord, and who meditates on his law day and night

Manifestation – 1 Corinthians 12:7 – To each is given the manifestation of the Spirit for the common good.

54

Set Your Intention

I've been a beach girl since birth. My parents would bring the playpen out to the sand, with a strapped umbrella for safety and shade, as they fished on the shoreline for dinner. I guess technically, I've had sand in all the wrong places since day one. Thank goodness for the baby powder trick that I learned later in life (hint: it's a magic sand remover). Hopefully my mother utilized it for my Bamm-Bamm rolls on those beach excursions. Truly though, the ocean was my lullaby and sound machine. It's no wonder it's my safe haven today.

Let's fast forward to a time when the safety of my little beachside playpen was long gone, a time when I couldn't find my shoreline, and I didn't know which direction was north, south, east, or west. The waves tossed me to and fro and unexpected crashes had me gasping for air between untimely wave sets. I wasn't aware of the depth or danger because I didn't have the energy or bravery to seek the distance. There was no consistency, no pattern, and no visibility. I was in a washing machine with no timer.

Thankfully, I had a buoy. I was prepared for this fearful adventure rather than helpless and abandoned. My flight hadn't crashed, my boat hadn't sunk, my surfboard hadn't broken, and I wasn't being attacked by any sort of sea creature. I was in training.

Ultimately the whistle blew, and the sound brought instant clarity and immediate relief. My directional sense returned, and the physical pattern and know-how of a strong freestyle stroke kicked in. The adrenaline for survival turned into the desire for land and rest. Safely ashore, I sought out and counted all of my red-wearing, lifeguard companions to ensure everyone was accounted for. They had been only feet away from me in the ocean, but the unrelenting waves did not allow for visibility, and my laser focus on keeping my own head above water drowned out the hoots, hollers, and camaraderie that were taking place around me.

I'll never forget that hurricane exercise experience, the strength of the ocean, the lack of self-awareness, and the fear of "what if." It's ironic that the shadows and vast depths can comfort us when we're on the shore, but when we are in the midst, both in our external and internal environments, the fear and panic set in.

I'd heard identical whistles since the days of 5 a.m. summer swim team practices in elementary school (yes on top of 20 hours in gymnastics weekly), but that was unlike any swim test I'd ever taken. That whistle blow brought feelings of thankfulness and completion rather than the anxiousness caused by those signaling the beginning of a competitive swimmer's heat. And though breathing in both scenarios was equally important, my focus in that drill was on survival and endurance, not breathwork or winning.

Focus, in my opinion, is synonymous with vision. Without focus we falter. You have to have knowledge and understanding of what it is you want to accomplish and then keep your eye on the prize. It sounds fairly simple, but if that were the case we would have many more successful visionaries on our hands. I think many of them do exist, but they are stifled by the lack of control in their environments. You hear of dreams and intentions all the time, but it's the follow-through that makes the story. It's the action after the goal is set. It's the details and not the destination that matter.

Unfortunately, it can be difficult to concentrate in today's society. There is noise everywhere. These constant interruptions and distractions silence our inner thoughts that are so critical in directing the way and keeping us centered. Crashing waves and whistles pull our attention in so many directions that we often don't know which way to go. Instead, we frequently choose to follow the crowds. If they are going this way, then we must too. And just like Jesus's mother and father, who unwittingly left him in Jerusalem, we can so easily be distracted and assume all is well. Thankfully, his parents recognized his absence a day into the journey home and found him unharmed teaching in the Temple *(Luke 2:41-52)*. I can easily relate with this mother, who I'm certain was in a panic for the three days before she found him. Her mind was surely filled with thoughts of the horrific things that could have happened to him in her absence.

We, much like Mary, think because the masses are here, all must be well. But what is your spirit saying? Do you have a moral compass that you rely on, a moral barometer that steers you right every single time? If you can't find a way to drown out the noise of the masses, then the sounds of social media, sexualized marketing, vulgar music, discrimination, negative press, and polarized mass media can consume your waking hours. I have learned how to close my eyes in a noisy environment. Simple actions, such as singing an uplifting tune to fixate my mind or putting on invisible headphones, allow me to drown out the noise. But I wasn't always capable of that practice. I used to tune in to what they were listening to, to what they were saying, to how they were acting, to what they were watching and reading, and to where they were going – rather than taking inventory of my own belongings and barometers.

Undoubtedly, all five of our senses are inundated with different kinds of noise from the moment we wake up until the moment we go to sleep. And while it is easy to whistle blow on what is happening around us, the biggest area of noise and distraction isn't fully the fault of others; it's our own mind, our own battlefield, our own washing machine storm. We can easily get stuck inside that place. And when it hasn't been calibrated to the right tune, it will sound wretched. You will go to sleep, and you still can't turn it off. I've been there. I've lain awake with my eyes closed, desperately needing sleep after an already long, emotional day, only to find that I am unable to silence the noise, the fears, the what-ifs, the to-dos, the horrific things that could happen to me.

No matter if you've been saved since you were young, or you just got saved yesterday, or maybe you're still teetering on the edge of that place of rescue – this is often a struggle that connects us all. We run ourselves ragged. In the midst of my internal fight, and likely long before, I lost sight of me, and I lost focus on what was important and true. I was holding onto other people's perceptions, using their crutches to get by, and following the direction of their mis-marked maps. To be totally honest, I was a walking zombie (despite the coffee), treading water out of habit, growing weary, and convincing myself even still that I was strong enough.

It was just like treading water in that training drill in the midst of a hurricane. I was lost and searching for the shoreline while not sure what was below me or how much longer I could last. As a 17-year-old lifeguard, it was an easy whistleblowing situation to get out of – the training was complete. I dried off and the fear was gone. As a 29-year-old woman, the "getting out of the storm" phase took a lot more effort. And while no one technically blew a whistle, many figurative whistles were blown in my direction. Even with my fairy God-mama rescue and "meeting Jesus miraculous moment," it still took daily practice. The life-altering difference, however, was that hope was restored in that moment, providing me with guidance and security. And instead of treading, I found rest. And here I am, years later, finally landside and dry, just as my dad promised I would be on that stormy wedding day. But the critical component of this rest, this peace, is that confusion, chaos, and fear have also subsided. I'm with a new crowd, a new team, and we rely on trusted whistles to get us back on track.

The effort involved in getting out and drying off included the help I previously mentioned with community, church, counseling, and the Great Counselor. I couldn't do it alone like I had for so long. It included insight. It included deep communication (which I had grown really good at avoiding). It included a time-out to just "float" and feel my true feelings. It was almost like a detox, minus some of the more drastic side effects. And I say some, because sleepless nights, nightmares, sweats, and nerves still occurred in the process.

Coming out of a place of perplexity and stress into a place of unknown calm was scary. Imagine the Israelites as they walked into the parted Red Sea split by Moses (by way of God). It was an unknown; there was confusion. I had panic attacks and questioned if it was worth it, as I'm sure they did too. I can hear the masses now, "Are you sure this is a good idea? Moses, are you crazy?" But I can tell you today, and I hope it gives someone a bit of courage out there, the effort is worth it, and the shoreline is near. But you must be tuned into the Spirit for your mind, body, and soul to take rest and trust again.

So how did I do it? I surely wasn't surrounded by people keeping me in check every minute of every day. I had choices to make, just like you. I set my intention daily in clearing out my chaos and noise, while setting strong boundaries around what I would receive and what I would reject. These ideas can feel abstract when we hear about them in church, but I've discovered the beautiful symmetry that takes place in the natural when the supernatural is at work. Just like the lifeguard training experience…He is always teaching in parables. And through those lessons, I started to release control and let go.

But this intentional clearing out or releasing or de-cluttering is so much more than a trip to the Salvation Army store. Between the counseling, church, deep communication practices with my husband, and hours immersed in the Bible and worship, I recall the sense of loss as I submitted daily. I felt unrecognizable. And re-constructing my identity, as Jesus did with the woman at the well, didn't feel so instantaneous, even as I grasped hold of His truth and blessing.

I was wrestling with the loss of titles, the loss of relationships, the loss of direction, the loss of intention, the loss of contentment, the loss of peace, and it all left me exhausted. But a message in church upon the birth of a new year gave me hope towards this new life and a clearer perspective on what I had left behind. "I am still standing," said my pastor. And that was the only way I was able to keep pressing forward each day. When you keep waking up, when you keep moving forward, the loss begins to leave, the waves begin to subside, and you have the energy to press on toward the new goal. But you have to set your intention.

At the beginning of a yoga class the instructor will talk you through a series of movements and breaths, and she will ask you to "set your intention" for the hour journey you are about to take. It's the same concept as fixing your focus, as I mentioned before. I believe that phrase is what makes the practice of meditation and yoga so soulful. It's about your body, yes, but unlike the typical fitness trainer, they are asking you to align your mind and soul at the very same time. It goes deeper than "do 20 toe raises holding this weight." Not to discredit a traditional exercise program, because I love that style of workout, too, but you catch my drift.

Other yoga instructors use the coined term "dedication": to dedicate your practice to something or someone. The purpose of both intention setting and dedication are meant to bring your physical process beyond the mat and into your life practice as well. To live an intentional life is part of my new life's mantra. It is crucial that I know why I'm doing what I'm doing, why I'm saying what I'm saying, and why I'm going where I'm going. And just as crucial is that I am doing all of those things in honesty and openness with my husband, my God, and myself. My moral barometer has been intentionally reset. Intentionality is not rigid; it's fluid and leaves openness to creativity and evaluation.

But before I could move forward fully intentional, I had to look back on some of the things I had previously dealt with (some unintentionally) in order to move past them and know how to approach them if they arose again in the future. You see, we live our life in cycles. There are so many studies on this concept from time and calendar cycles, to life cycles, to seasonal cycles, to menstrual cycles, to what can feel like day-to-day mundane cycles, and more. But we also have emotional cycles that can lead to mental, physical, and spiritual patterns that leave us dizzy, completely out of sorts, and far from where we are intended to be firmly planted. So by studying the details, even though the final destination is the Hallelujah prayer and the celebration once you get there, it's healthy to know how you can stay steadfast in that place of health and wholeness.

Just like the weight loss journey, shedding "pounds" becomes a part of the process. And although it's never easy, it's worth it. I had a lot to lose, but I also had a ton to gain. The giving up, the releasing, the downsizing, and the diminishing scale will give way to abundance and growth in a way you can't quite process while letting go.

One by one, I shed the figurative pounds that also resulted in literal pounds, and I'm confident you can too. Loss can feel stifling, but if we set the intention in the practice, knowing we are letting go of burdening weights, and even if we have become comfortably strong in treading with them, at the end of the day we get to be free and light. My hope in sharing my own losses is that you too will gain perspective in the areas you need to let go of.

I handled lost titles by identifying what those titles really meant to my life and my identity, and I redressed myself in the titles intended for me to carry with dignity and grace. Though the "SAHM" (stay at home mom) title took some real adjusting to – it was less about the name and more about the constant expectations of that role and the comparison game of where I had come from and where I truly wanted to be. As new opportunities arose and new hats were placed, I have chosen titles that are representative of the entirety of my calling versus just a character trait of position. I'm not the CEO of my company, though on paper it may appear that way. Instead, I'm the creator and the visionary. I'm the facilitator and the passion behind its mission. I'm not just a mom. Instead, I'm a teacher for them and a student to them. I'm not just a wife. I'm iron sharpening iron. I'm a supporter and a friend. I am a bride.

I handled lost relationships by finding rest in my relationship with self, growing new connections, and replenishing old friendships. And when the time was right, I reassessed the loss and prepared myself for rekindling or total separation. I poured into the people that existed in my nuclear entity, my home, instead of giving them my leftovers. Boundaries were reluctantly set, but the outcome gave me the opportunity to replace what was causing harm with what would restore. Safe people came in while destructive people were pushed out. (I highly recommend *Safe People*, by Dr. Henry Cloud and Dr. John Townsend as a resource.) This even included those who I knew deeply loved me but weren't currently capable of calling out in me what God had purposed.

I handled loss of direction by slowing my pace and establishing a new God-highlighted path. Previously, I was moving so fast that I didn't really know where I was headed or why. I didn't have a clear end game other than monetary satisfaction, and we know that can't go with us to Heaven. Jesus teaches us in Matthew 6:19-20 that earned or stored incorrectly here on earth, moth and rust may destroy our treasures and thieves may break in and steal. So clearly, in order to store my riches in Heaven, I needed a new road map. Luckily, the Bible was created as just that.

I handled loss of intention by stripping down what I knew as truth, reestablishing The Truth, and clarifying how to be deliberate each day, with each decision and with each emotion. I learned to practice this simple yoga concept in my daily life through mind, body, soul, and spirit development. True intentionality curbs the "busy" I was so used to living beneath. It gave me purpose in being present and not existing in past shame or future glory... right now is our promise.

I handled loss of contentment by taking the time to find what true happiness meant to me and establishing the places, spaces, and people that help create that joy and peace in my life. I explored my Ikigai and found that by taking the time to practice gratitude each day, I was able to actually breathe again without the weight of the world on my shoulders or in the forefront of my mind. I believe we all want to be happy, and although there can be many limiting factors standing in our way, thankfulness can bring clarity beyond the limitations. It brings you out of the surface situation and into the heart – from exterior items to interior gifts.

I handled the loss of peace by simplifying and minimizing my tangibles, my mind, and my heart. I rid myself of clutter that kept me heavy, distracted, and unhappy. I discovered that less is more – which has much more depth of meaning than just tangible "stuff." Worship became my warfare. I began leaning upward and inward to grasp on to the calm buoy of life, rather than outward toward the masses of other treading humans.

None of these things were easy. It took some kicking and screaming and a heck of a lot of tears. Psalm 56:8 reassures me that every tear has been caught and recorded on His scrolls. None of these losses were reconstructed by me alone. None of them are fully complete either – I'm not sure they will ever be on this side of Heaven. I still wave my white flag, and I still have whistles blowing, but now I am assured in my safety on the shoreline. And I am confident that I have placed other guards on duty, surrounding me in prayer and strength and assurance, so that at the end I will still be standing! Your fellow guards, your inner circle, are critical to stand watch. But you must invite them only when you know their assured Truth is in sync with yours and then grant them access into your life through vulnerability and sharpening.

So are you ready to let go? Are you ready to declutter and reorganize your life by way of stewarding your life? My continued desire, even as I regularly have to clean my closets (both literally and figuratively), is that my outside and inside body are both nutritionally, physically, mentally, and spiritually displaying the freedom and wellness that I feel on an emotional, heart level. And when I need to reset my intention, I have the Word as my wisdom.

So, I set my goals. I fix my focus, and I prepare my mind, body, and soul by settling into the Holy Spirit. That is where true, whole, clear health comes into play. The alignment of those four components will get you faithfully fit for life. And don't be discouraged when you have to readjust. The process of becoming never ends and the destination is never fully reached on this side of Heaven. Clarity exists in the action, not in the comfort or confines of the boat. He says, "come" (*Matthew 14:29*). He doesn't say sit. He doesn't say stay. He commands movement. And just like the ever-changing tides of the ocean, movement requires a steady force. The gift of freedom and life and "the walking on water" come from our routinely setting intention to keep our eyes fixed on Jesus.

Each season of life, each trial, each tribulation requires different calibrations. The storm may cause unexpected disorder, but no matter the environmental truths, He remains constant. His Truth reigns supreme and provides the buoy (his outreached hand - *Matthew 14:31)* during your sinking moments and storms.

As you become, ask your heart:

In what area of life do you feel like you are treading water?

_____

_____

_____

Have you been ignoring the whistle blows happening around you?

_____

_____

_____

How can you be more intentional about who is surrounding you in the waves?

_____

_____

_____

What are you willing to lose in life so that you can gain a full life?

_____

_____

_____

Hydration

*I*made my bridesmaids wear bathing suits on my wedding day. I also gave them about a 3-hour warning instead of a 1-year training plan. This was not intended to be a sick joke, however. They had their dresses purchased, tailored, and planned. My little girl fairytale fantasies never included half naked bodies at the altar. My $2000 dress was hanging in a room as I walked the aisle in a white bikini to greet my barefoot, bow-tied, board short wearing, soon-to-be husband. 300 other people hooted and hollered, halfway out of thrill and perhaps mostly out of fear as lightning and thunder surrounded us on the sandy shores of Virginia Beach.

I wanted a wedding that exuded the rainbow. The girls' dresses and all of the décor popped every color instead of a simplistic two-tone experience. This was pre-Pinterest, so I hadn't had the opportunity to make many comparisons at that point. I just ran with what I loved. As I walked over the staircase dune, the rainbow was exactly what I saw against the dark ocean skyline. Umbrellas of every color had popped up to protect the guests from the rain they were now standing in.

This was not the plan. But the one plan that was being stuck to was "toes in the sand." It was the plan that had been sealed with a good night kiss less than 24 hours before. We were both beach babies. We fell in love on the sandy shores of our hometown. That was where we were planted, and that was where we promised to be.

In that moment, nothing else mattered. The ceremony was quick, the winds were high, and my girlfriends (especially the 9 months pregnant one, the 3 week post-partum one, and even my mom) rocked their suits! Although they have never let me live it down, it surely was an adrenaline full adventure and one which we've been living ever since. Oh, and the icing on the cake, I can't forget the fun detail that the building entrance, less than 200 yards away, was struck by lightning during the "I dos." I see it as a blessing, however, since we had 300 people with umbrella lightning rods on the beach with us, and no one got hurt. We also enjoyed an epic fire truck greeting as we signed the official ceremonial certificate with the city officiate, once safely inside the building.

Although we didn't get the traditional professional photos or videography due to the weather, my altar experience was unlike anything I've ever witnessed since then. Safely preserved in my mind is the picture of me standing beneath our white umbrella, staring at my husband's grin, and knowing that even in the storm, he was my safe place and my calm. Thankfully, we were able to share our written vows later in the safe haven of the building, but I could never have guessed that our special day would unfold that way. The dress didn't matter, though I surely ran to put it on for the reception. And the girls in the bathroom with blow dryers and straighteners may have been distraught, but it wasn't their day or lifetime moment...though I've been told it was quite unforgettable for them too. Shoot, they basically risked their lives to witness the ceremony!

The months and years to come weren't entirely out of line with the scenery and adrenaline of that day. Emotions soared high to low as the pendulum swung left to right from season to season. And we had choices to make along the way. Would we press on from the sealed kiss moment of I do, or step back into the comfortable expected plan of society. We've experienced a lot of rain, but we've also seen a thousand rainbows.

Water is a critical element and a fundamental resource that brings new life and restores that which is dying. I knew my love for it from an external perspective, but I never had a clue of the importance of its internal workings. Without full intent of the outcome or purpose, a few years into our marriage adventure I started to pursue water instead of it pursuing me. The rain clouds, though still abundant, served the same cleansing role as before. But now, I was doing the work prior to the storm rolling in rather than after with an unplanned clean up scenario.

It started about a year after my baby girl was born. I was struggling with a continuous pain in my legs caused from varicose veins that had developed during both of my pregnancies. They were bad enough that I was wearing compression stockings in the heat of the summer. And for this sundress-swinging, bikini-wearing, beach-lover that was simply unacceptable. I was also struggling with back pains that had literally been occurring since my middle school gymnastics days. I don't know if it was the continued twisting and flipping or the many neck tweaks and injuries, but I had kept my chiropractor in business for almost 20 years at that point.

Although I had been doing monthly maintenance for years, I had never gone after the root causes of these painful issues. Please do yourself a favor, don't mask a problem with a quick adjustment and one or two weeks of comfort only to find yourself in the exact same place time after time. The daytime compression socks, feet raised evenings, and random leg massages weren't doing the trick. I had a bulging vein in my crotch, you guys! This was real. And while I didn't like the aesthetics of the veins, that was the least of my concerns when the pain kicked in. I had an infant and a waddler (a baby who waddles around but isn't yet a 2-year-old toddler). And, of course they wanted me holding them, and I wanted to, but that added weight to the problem. It hurt.

And just like the physical pain that would not go away, the emotional brokenness and pain in my heart that I kept suppressing, masking, and avoiding was always present. I wasn't even sure from where it originated; I just knew there was isolation and dehydration. The happiness I was exuding as a façade to the world was not mirrored internally. I knew I was "blessed," as they say, and continued to say. However, the juxtaposing reality was exhausting, and so I just kept pressing on in continual pain. The physical pain I was comfortable to share; the emotional pain I kept hidden.

How often do we live our lives in this state of sparring, pressing on past what we know will present itself as a roadblock eventually. Even knowing no quick fix is going to do the long-term job, we push it down; we keep going, and the breaking persists.

I believe my breaking point wasn't unlike the instant pop of a bone. And although I've never broken a bone, I have sat amidst my broken soul, feeling every piece of myself fragmented, and I believe that pain is immeasurably worse. I needed deep fixing – fixing that no doctor or psychiatrist was capable of.

We called ten churches. No one had a midweek service anymore. But the 11th call proved to be different. That call was made off of a faint memory about a HVAC client who my husband had worked with two years earlier. He recalled them mentioning that they were pastors, and with his computer-like brain he was able to store it away to be referenced at a later time. It was truly a seed planted in good soil. The poor couple experienced a wave of anxiety when they found out we were coming. They shared that their third-string team would be "playing" that night. Their first-string was at a conference, the second-string had other obligations, and the third-string needed some playing time. Privately, they even considered cancelling, but thankfully they pressed on. And later, we were the fruit of their good seed. Harvested from broken souls and eager to be watered by the living water.

I hadn't stepped foot in a church since my first-born was an infant, and I had surely never driven 30 minutes out of my way to attend one. Based on my past experiences, all I knew was that they would be well dressed, smiling white people (no offense) who greeted their flock with the same superficial hello and propped door, week after week. The worship show would be nice. The lights and smoke would be cool. The skits would be funny. The pastor would reference the Bible throughout his canned analogies. And, in my opinion, there wouldn't be anything wrong with it. It would meet me where I was, which I later discovered was empty.

This time, however, the smiling faces didn't greet us. Instead, we swung open doors to a fairly empty hallway. The brick building wasn't pretty or new or splashed with pops of color or marketed materials. Emotionally drained from facing conversations and realities I never imagined would happen, I couldn't even make eye contact with the people who tried. When we stood, hand in hand, for the worship segment, I joined my hands with those around me only because I was in need of strength to stand. I had never been so tired.

Unlike the showy, practiced performance of the big box church I had attended, this was raw and unrehearsed. They talked about a spirit. They held their hands up towards the sky. I cried at the words, but I had cried on the car ride there, so that part was no surprise to me. What did surprise me, however, were the public displays of desire, adoration, and community. What were they doing? Why were they so desperate? Minute after minute, as the songs played, my perfectly curated walls came tumbling down. I wanted what they eagerly sought. I needed it because nothing else was working. I knew of Jesus. We were friends. But He was never my beloved. I didn't really know Him, and I had never let

Him in. Even though He pressed, I pushed. And the storms never stopped. I just held umbrellas in hopes that I wouldn't get struck.

The service ended, and I wished it hadn't. The smiling faces I had anticipated at the welcome, bid us farewell. With tear stained cheeks, I nodded my head and left, knowing I'd be back for more. It was Wednesday, and I knew I needed something between then and Sunday. So, we began calling again. Wherever we could find a service, we were there. This time it was right up the road in the same church I first had memory of attending with my parents. You know, those holiday churchgoers all dressed up to check the box. How ironic. How purposed. But the seed had been planted… it was breaking surface.

It was Friday night and a pop-up church was utilizing the space. The pews I remembered from my childhood had been removed, and lights and screens had been added to enhance the experience for my eclectic, technical generation. This time we came in desiring to not be greeted by anyone. We sat in the back row hoping God would meet us like He did two nights before.

The pastor was an older white gentleman, like I was used to, and I tried not to write him off as unable to meet my needs. I listened and I watched the screen light up with the picture of a field of dry bones. I felt like I was in that very scene within my own life. I was broken and fragmented, even with two beautiful babies sleeping in their cribs and bringing laughter and light into my home. I felt lifeless.

It wasn't just postpartum. It was burnout. It was perfectionism. It was a lifetime of hiding and lies. It was a broken heart. It was childhood trauma. It was new age commercialism. It was the American Dream. It was marriage. It was motherhood. It was corporate pressure. It was achievement mindset. It was loneliness.

It was confusion. It was a battle, and I had lost the fight. My bones were all that were left, and they were scattered.

The pastor, Steve Lentz (father of megachurch pastor, Carl Lentz), introduced me to the breath giving experience of Jesus. He gave hope. He restored the imagery of life. And bone by bone, piece by piece, He began to put flesh and tendon back on a lifeless being (a must read - dry bones Biblical reference – *Ezekiel 37*).

I couldn't have planned what would happen next. I didn't even know that authenticity to this magnitude could be possible. I had no idea that people could be so real, that we weren't just a bunch of bones walking around aimlessly doing the next thing that felt good, the next thing in pursuit of "happiness." Pastor Lentz' message was amazing and will stick with me for the rest of my life. It was a change agent to my compliance with living a dry life. I discovered that church is more than a message and a building; it's a home, a place where family resides. It's a brotherhood and community. And I hadn't really known family like this before. Now don't get me wrong. I have a huge, vibrant, boisterous, fun-loving family that has helped sculpt the person I am today in so many beautiful ways. But this was new and different and intriguingly not shiny. I was tired of shimmer and shine. I wanted someone to meet me in my murky mess, in my field of dry bones. I wanted someone who would not just help me out but understand how I got there in the first place. I didn't want to be dressed and adorned for a Sunday meal. I wanted day-by-day nourishment. My dry bones needed sustenance. I was starving and parched...

Months passed, and my casted heart was mending. And though recovery has components of pain, it is also beautifully light. The quote that kept circling my brain, that is now a staple in my home, was the very message my dad spoke to me as we stood in the rain before he walked me down the aisle. He said, "You've never been wet, where you didn't dry off." And boy, was he right. The promise of the rainbow that God made to Noah after the storm was the same promise God had for me *(Genesis 9:13-17)*.

I was smiling brighter than I had ever before in my life. I was living and loving even the mundane moments to a new caliber. I felt like a new person, alive for the first time since my first recollection of memories. And all I could think about was my desire to stay in that place of fulfillment and life.

I invited myself to a church leaders' conference all the way in Greenville, SC at Pastor Ron Carpenter's Redemption Church. I had barely even found footing in my pile of dry bones at that point, but when God knocks, you answer. Or at least I highly suggest it. I drove seven hours with my legs feeling heavy and full, reminding me of my epidural elephant feet at delivery. But this time the feeling pulsated instead of numbly lingering. Sitting was no better than standing, but I found myself dealing with the pain and standing among strangers as the man on the stage spoke about an altar. He shared about the weight-bearing experience of Jesus's ascent to his crucifixion hill. Feeling like I had been carrying a cross as well overwhelmed my soul. Physically, from my painful veins, I struggled. Mentally, from the constant battle between my desired sense of self and my past self, I struggled. Spiritually, as I pressed into the unknown of this Jesus I had been presented with over and over again throughout my life, I struggled. And although I had already experienced many altar moments at the new church we were attending (basically every Sunday I was on my knees), this wasn't a great exchange experience. I wasn't handing anything over to God.

But, unbeknownst to me, He had planned a renewal of my veins as the living water flowed through a well-known Christian pastor and teacher, Tony Miller. He told me to build an altar with my life. To be the altar for everyone who needed a place to rest and experience their own transformational moments with God. The vision overtook me. I saw myself walking through a stone castle towards a coffin-like table. As I lay on the table, like Sleeping Beauty, all of my surroundings turned into a monochromatic grayscale. Rock. (My own version of Frozen) Dead. I stared at the scenery waiting for a message and trying to decipher what this meant for me. Was I going to die? Yes... I would die to my sense of self. Suddenly, the flower in my cold, gray hand started to blossom. In hindsight, as I reflect on this experience, I may have watched too many Disney movies. But this was the Beauty and the Beast part. Instead of a single rose, the vibrancy of rainbows flooded back into my life. Flowers cascaded down my body and up the stone-cold walls of the room. My body stayed gray, but the beauty of the room, the scent, the silence, the energy, and the aura can bring me back to center whenever I lay on that altar.

Just as Abraham took his son Isaac, Tony ushered me to that altar not knowing what God's actual plan was for my life. Unfortunately, I never had the chance to tell him this story, as he passed unexpectedly a couple years later. But I have a comforting peace knowing He's at the right hand of the Father, and like Abraham, took claim on that mountaintop. I took claim of that altar as well, calling it by the name given by Abraham: The Lord will provide *(Genesis 19:1-22).*

This was my second altar moment. No Chippendale replica (like my hubby) awaited me here. No hooting and hollering. No storm. Instead, the rainbow awaited me. It was solely my turn to say I do to the King of Kings, to the Lord of Lords. In my own castle, He awaited my "yes." I never left that altar. I never turned back into a colorful princess to go about her merry way. I'm still on that stone table. And while you may see my pinked cheeks and blonde hair, colorful wardrobe and bright smile; when I look in the mirror, I happily welcome the gray version of myself. You see the color is not from me. It's from Him.

In reflection of that altar moment, I sought further insight into its meaning. A prophetic friend shared in a message from Heaven that the vision of the flowers that grew in my castle (representations of the vibrancy of my life in Christ) was actually the calling to give the flowers away, stem by stem, so as to share what it was that had been gifted to me. This book is my flower to you. I hope it brings color to the gray skies that may surround you.

What a gift that vision will always be to me and now hopefully to you. But, regardless, I left with mind blowing, mind numbing questions. How do you step back into your worldly body, throbbing legs, and dehydrated soul? How do you act out what was just presented as your life's purpose and destiny? How do you share that moment with other people? And, how do you reveal this transformation to the spouse who has only known you as a pile of dry bones?

I turned the page. I stepped forward. And from that moment on, I reached for the water as often as I could. If you see me today, I'm usually attached to a 50 or 60oz canteen or bottle of some sort. So much so that my nieces inquired, "Why are you always carrying that?" But, flowers on this side of Heaven wilt and die eventually, so my water bottle is my minute-by-minute reminder of the altar that defines my life.

Hence, I drink alkaline water and share with others the physical transformation of my life since actively pursuing 100 oz. a day. And yes, with my pea-sized bladder I feel as though I take a thousand trips to the bathroom, and I'm usually floating by the end of the day. But guess how beautiful the representation is and how joyful I feel when I get to share the gospel in this unique, simple, tangible way.

Alkaline water heals, neutralizes, penetrates, provides, oxygenizes, eliminates, detoxifies, cleanses, energizes, reduces, filtrates, and removes. Are you reading this?! He calls Himself the living water! He is the fundamental element.

> *John 4:14 "but whoever drinks of the water that I will give him shall never thirst; but the water that I will give him will become in him a well of water springing up to eternal life."*
>
> *John 7:37:39 [37] On the last and greatest day of the festival, Jesus stood and said in a loud voice, "Let anyone who is thirsty come to me and drink. [38] Whoever believes in me, as Scripture has said, rivers of living water will flow from within them."[a] [39] By this he meant the Spirit, whom those who believed in him were later to receive. Up to that time the Spirit had not been given, since Jesus had not yet been glorified.*

There is a beautiful consistency between the sound machine of my playpen beach days, the alkaline ocean I stood next to on my wedding day, and the 100 ounces of alkaline water I now carry around daily. He has always been with me. But now, instead of just choosing when I visit the ocean, He goes with me and before me and flows through me, and I get to bring life wherever I go for the Holy Spirit is within me. And it is that same Spirit that can dwell within you *(1 Corinthians 6:19)*.

As I headed home from the conference, I was on an energized high. I felt like I had just received an IV full of Jesus. Even taking a 4-hour detour due to driving two hours in the wrong direction, didn't get me agitated at all. I was mindfully sharing all that had occurred with my spiritual mama while mindlessly driving home through Greenville, NC and back to Greenville, SC after my pee-break. I didn't let the detour steal my overflow. Instead I used it to my advantage. I was rehydrated to my core. And it was during that same drive when I called my dear friends and pastors, Anthony & Morgan Hart and asked, "When are we opening a church?" Little did I know the Holy Spirit had already deposited the same pull and revelation within them. You'll learn the evolution of that story later.

That conference was timed perfectly, and today it still feels like it was orchestrated for me alone. It was the catapulting point that led to my vein surgery (yes, I had to get those suckers taken care of medically). It also led me on a voyage of addressing root problems and reestablishing alkalinity in every area of life.

If you haven't realized by now, there is a kinetic theme to my full-speed-ahead life. I don't do most things slowly or in a calculating manner, though I'm learning the importance of that too. Down shifting isn't nearly as fun as the upshift, in my opinion, but we know that doesn't always mean it's the safest.

My bones had new breath and were mending by way of the Holy Spirit. I flushed my veins and then proceeded to restore my eyesight with Lasik. I could be cheesy here and give you the restoration-of-sight story from the Bible, but I'll spare you the explanation. I have no doubt you are seeing the parallels by now. Next, I started approaching fitness through my spirituality instead of outside of it. My body was becoming a vessel for Him *(Philippians 3:21)*.

As old mindsets began shifting day by day, I kept drinking water, increasing my intake from 50 oz. to 100 oz., and began finding a new stride and a new way of life. But He called me deeper still... Standing on the edge of the ocean, less than a mile from the exact site where we said our vows, we once again found ourselves wearing our bathing suits and watching the storm clouds gather, the rain pour down, and the waves toss to and fro. I couldn't help but recall that I had prepared for this moment since my teenage life guarding experience. Who knew it would all connect? He did. He planned it. And I stood there, hand in hand with my husband, without an ounce of fear, and we took the plunge...this time together.

It wasn't our first time being baptized. Actually, it had been less than a year since our first experience. But as the scripture states in Psalm 103:12, "as far as the east is from the west, so are our transgressions removed," this was our east coast cleansing. No, I'm not suggesting you need to get baptized in every ocean or multiple times. This was a needed part of our journey, our first time being baptized together, the representation of our martial rebirth. We weren't saying I do to each other; we were saying, "we do" to Him.

I couldn't have known the storms we'd face. But after nine years into marriage, thirteen years into "love," I'd still stand in a storm with him any day, confident in the full security of the maker of the storm. Our mission now is to show up in the rain for other people. Our altar, the gray-scaled version of ourselves, represents our vulnerability and authenticity. It means giving people water when they've shriveled up into the colorless, lifeless, fleshless versions of themselves. Dry bones – we speak life to you.

In our wedding vows to each other, I wrote something not knowing it would surface years later as a message from the heart of our Father. "I will strive to give you the feeling of sand between your toes." Our altar looks different than yours. I know people who hate sand and wear tennis shoes to the beach. Heaven help them. But I need you to hear me…God doesn't need a huge illustration of faith. He doesn't need you to take the plunge into a churning, tossing ocean. He doesn't ask you to carry around a 50-ounce water bottle. But He does desire all of you…even your veins.

I believe our physical beings are aligned to our spiritual man. Your soul is yours, but your spirit belongs to God. Think of it like a radio. Without being tuned in, you cannot hear or enjoy or exist within the frequency, but upon contact, spirit to spirit, we can connect with God. The moment we accept Jesus as our Lord and Savior, our dry bones, our body, our soul, and our spirit welcome the Holy Spirit. Addressing the issues that impact your body is critical because they impact the strength of your soul. Without full submission and acceptance, we are simply stagnant in the pain. Don't sit with pain. Confront it. Address it. Treat it. And let God restore, mend, and heal it. Bring your minds to the altar. Bring your bodies to the altar. Bring your soul to the altar. Allow His spirit to impart into you the same promise of eternity, the same rainbow. Each part of you is connected to part of Him.

Friend, wherever your ailing, dehydrated self is hurting today, may you know the importance of pushing into the pain instead of past it. May you know the representation of God in your storm. He is not the thunder and lightning crashing down on the buildings around you. He is not the gale threatening harm to your windblown, upside-down umbrella. Just like Jesus calmed the wind and the waves that tossed the boat where the disciples cowered in fear, He can speak one word to calm and silence the chaos *(Mark 4:34-41)*. Ultimately his heart is in the promise of the rainbow.

If you're reading this and you're standing in a valley of dry bones, within a storm, in pain, or perhaps you just feel like your glass is empty, may you allow His alkaline spirit to fill you up and His breath to breathe new life into the dried-up places of your mind, body, soul, and spirit.

As you become, ask your heart:

Take an inventory of your current position – Mind, Body, Soul (mind, will & emotions), and Spirit.

_____

_____

Rate yourself (whole=10 to depleted =0)

_____

_____

What is something you feel is lacking or dry in each area?

_____

_____

What areas in your becoming (sanctification) journey could be brought to life in order to obtain further purpose of God's glory?

_____

_____

How can you start seeking God in that area?

_____

_____

Mind Over Matter

*I*was standing in front of the mirror, freshly showered, naked, and broken. A time where my mind ran wild with a frenzied rush of self-inflicted barbs and hurt. I was brushing my teeth and staring at myself as tears streamed from my eyes. I heard, "You are disgusting. You are ugly. You don't deserve your life." And the sad part was, each time I stood there, I believed it more and more. At night I would shake in convulsions without the ability to stop. I can only describe it as paralyzing fear. I thought it would be easier to live with the lies in my head than it would be to face the truth of who I was and was not. I had worn a mask for so long, I no longer knew what I actually looked like.

Instead of taking my life, instead of giving up all of the good and letting the bad win, I brushed my teeth for over a month in another room where there was no mirror. I put post-it notes in places reminding me Whose I am and who He sees me as. These affirmations from scripture included:

- I am pure.
- I am flawless.
- I have purpose.
- I have peace.
- I am free from chains of guilt, shame, and condemnation.
- I am a woman after God's heart.
- I don't have to be perfect to receive God's perfect love.
- I love myself.

- I delight in honesty and Truth.
- God is my strength.
- I am blessed.
- I am grateful.
- I am beautiful.
- I am alive.

Day by day my identity emerged. It took years. It's still emerging. I am ever becoming. In the beginning of this process, tooth brushing was a task I couldn't do in the mirror, I think in part because of the fragility of my early morning reflection, tired eyes, and empty spirit. I still freshened up and did my hair, but those things required concentration that diverted my attention and allowed me to finish and walk away. For some reason, I find tooth brushing to be much more of a thoughtless process. Shh, don't tell my dentist. It's two minutes of silence with myself. That was my battlefield. Silence was my enemy.

We are beings designed with a mind, a body, and a soul. Our souls are comprised of our will and emotions. By definition our spirit and self-identity exist within our soul, but if our mind, will, and emotions are misaligned from our intended design of wholeness, we come into conflict with ourselves. We end up living our lives battling for one area to be known, seen, or developed while others are left starving and fragmented.

The phrase "mind over matter" is defined as the use of willpower to overcome physical problems. As a gymnast, as a business student in college, as a fitness enthusiast, as a business owner, and as a laboring mother this phrase has spoken to me throughout my life. Putting my mind to work by focusing on the task at hand, hard and painful as it may be, I will succeed. If I can control my focus, I can get through it. But it is important to restate again, if we are limiting our focus or our battle to one arena, we are missing the entirety of the picture.

I lived a majority of my life in an unrealized war with myself. How do you fight a battle you don't know you're standing in? How do you lose or win when society has deemed your demons as normal and some even as constructive? Sadly, it took an unarmored, weaponless combat to render my entire being lost and bloodied on the field. I didn't even have enough strength to wave my own white flag. My mind was warped. My body was broken. And my soul was vacant. Dry bones, remember?

My life, up until that point, had seemingly been picture perfect. I had managed to create a picturesque version of what I wanted others to see while ignoring anything sub-surface. I had a family, a GQ-model husband, and two beautiful children. I was a wife and a mother; two titles that I thought would finally deem my life's resume as whole. But, I used them as a Band-Aid when what I needed was a full body cast, possibly even a straitjacket if I want to be really honest. Ironically, I was spending time artistically casting pregnant bellies by profession and yet avoiding my own need for a casted healing process to occur.

In order for my healing process to begin, I had to first intentionally break down my mind, my sense of self-identity and self-worth, and who I told myself I was. I had to remove the mask... In order to draw a more complete picture of this process, I'll ask you first to put yourself in the shoes of Joseph, the most loved son of His father. He was even adorned with a robe of many colors to prove it. I'm sure his mirror moments felt fulfilling. He had big dreams; he was gifted from God. But his brothers, and even his Father, rebuked him for these dreams. Eventually the brothers couldn't handle the jealousy and rage they felt towards him. They ripped the robe from his body and threw him into an empty cistern in hopes of getting rid of him. Later they would conspire to sell him to some passing Ishmaelites, who in turn sold him to an Egyptian. His identity was stripped. His family was gone, and he existed in an unknown territory as a slave. Lies were continually spread about Joseph. This placed him in question by many and even resulted in him being thrown in jail. However, Joseph was secure in his identity, and God continued to use him and bless him with favor in the eyes of the King through the very dreams that had caused his family to reject him in the beginning *(Genesis 38-50)*.

Self-identity is a process, and doing something to this magnitude is exhausting. It's not reading one book or listening to one self-help podcast. It's surely not listening to the naysayers or even to those who may be closest to you. Instead, I had to find the gumption to attack my thought processes and perspectives. As 2 Corinthians 10:4-6 says, "The weapons we fight with are not the weapons of the world. On the contrary, they have divine power to demolish strongholds. We demolish arguments and every pretension that sets itself up against the knowledge of God, and we take captive every thought to make it obedient to Christ." Like Joseph, I had to rely on the affirmations rather than the commentary of the world. I needed a reason and a purpose to be fulfilled, instead of feigning sanity. I needed dreams instead of nightmares.

In a fitness-oriented realm, putting our minds to work connects two components at once: mind and body. Although I believe true wellness and health come when combining all three realms, this is surely a step in the right direction. Mental sickness can inhibit every other area of health, especially our spiritual man. It becomes an inhibitor and a blockage to growth. Woven intricately within this battle of the mind is another battle. Through jealousy, hatred, wrath, confusion, control, greed, and so much more the enemy has staked his claim. We are at war with our brothers, and our family units have been broken. In the resulting isolation, the seeds of doubt and destruction begin to emerge, and Satan himself enters in to steal, kill, and destroy what is rightfully God's.

Of all places we stand, the battle within ourselves – our mind – is among the most dangerous of places. Our society today has left us unhealthy, and its approach to fixing the issues warps the mental focus even more.

- Achieve Greatness
- Work Hard, Play Hard
- Hustle
- Dream Big
- Just Keep Going
- Failure is Not an Option

How can we constantly live in a state of performance? We can motivate ourselves to work harder for the end goal. Perhaps it's your dream house or car. Perhaps it's your dream vacation. Perhaps it's to gain a position in the company or the salary you've always wanted. Perhaps it's to retire early or hit the 401k mark that you set. Perhaps it's the ideal weight or measurement of your waist or breast line. But Philippians 4:4-9 provides the true practice of mind over matter that will enable us to stand as examples to the final storyline of Joseph. Instead of discrediting or dishonoring our brothers, who at first condemned us, we now have the sound mind and spirit, along with the critically important emerging fruits, that will allow us to feed them nourishment, in kindness, grace, and humility.

⁴ Rejoice in the Lord always. I will say it again: Rejoice! ⁵ Let your gentleness be evident to all. The Lord is near. ⁶ Do not be anxious about anything, but in every situation, by prayer and petition, with thanksgiving, present your requests to God. ⁷ And the peace of God, which transcends all understanding, will guard your hearts and your minds in Christ Jesus. ⁸ Finally, brothers and sisters, whatever is true, whatever is noble, whatever is right, whatever is pure, whatever is lovely, whatever is admirable—if anything is excellent or praiseworthy—think about such things. ⁹ Whatever you have learned or received or heard from me, or seen in me—put it into practice. And the God of peace will be with you.

Whatever your goal is, uncover whom it is benefitting and how you will get there. But once you've achieved it, what is next? Is your life passing you by in the meantime while you hustle your way into this next phase of life? Are you seeking something that is void of emotion, longevity, and ultimately something that you can't bring to Heaven? Are you wearing a robe and flaunting its colors, or are you willing to become a servant in order to give back to the very ones who first scorned you?

My hope is that I have been preaching to the choir, and you have already gained that mental compass and moral barometer which sets your motivation on an aligned intrinsic and extrinsic scale. You are motivated not by worldly pleasure or the satisfaction of how others perceive you but instead by bringing positive growth to humanity and the world and by finding a sense of self-worth and happiness that brings you inner peace and ultimate joy. This is only fully discovered and experienced in a relationship with God.

> John 14:27 - "Peace I leave with you; my peace I give you. I do not give to you as the world gives. Do not let your hearts be troubled and do not be afraid."

Conversely, I had simply and without second thought taken popular taglines and let them be my driving force without diving deeper into my purpose. My mind raced with big American dreams. It never stopped. I never rested and rarely reflected. My cistern/pit moments were self-inflicted and eventually, I took as my identity what the world said I was. This was vastly different from the Truth.

So when push came to shove, and my dreams started to be taken over by nightmares, I lacked clarity in who I was and was unable to stand in authority. I had to retrain my brain and realign my heart – listening vertically instead of receiving horizontally. I began motivating my mind to broaden my perspective. I did this by asking questions that framed the purpose of life and looked outside of self to the bigger picture of God's ultimate dream and plan. I know the same truth questioning Joseph had to rely on time and time again.

Questions like:

- Who are you?
- How do you identify yourself?
- What is your purpose?
- What are your passions and gifts?
- How can they help others?
- And most importantly, Whose are you?

These aren't answer-on-a-whim type questions. Perhaps you've never asked yourself who or whose you are? The answer is not an adjective. It is not "I am strong." And it's not as simplistic as "I am an entrepreneur" or "I am a mother." It's an internal dissection of what makes you whole and what defines you as an individual.

Even if you spend your life in ministry or non-profit work, this question still applies to you. You could already be helping the greater good, for Him even, but until you have identified yourself, you could be doing all of those things in the absence of a larger purpose and a positive motivation. We know faith without works is dead *(James 2:20)*.

We have to stop believing the lies of who others say we are. For before we were born, we were set apart *(Jeremiah 1:5)*. And yet upon birth, into sin, we are told who we are. We are sweet girls. We are strong boys. We are smart or artistic. We are silly or shy. These words begin to identify us before we can even develop our own spoken language. We hear them, and so we act them. We become who we are called, instead of being called to Whom we belong.

I have seen this up close more than ever before as a mother to young toddlers. I've used these exact describing words for my son. "You are strong and brave." And while that seems harmless and encouraging and intentional, it can be skewed as vapid and vain and leave him broken in years to come when he experiences loss, weaknesses, or feelings of being scared or nervous. Or, without realizing its effects, I would warn a stranger who tried to approach my daughter, "Oh, she is just a little shy." Soon, she began describing herself as such when she was in the company of someone new, even though shy was not an accurate description of her the other 98% of the time. She grasped hold of how I viewed her, what others said about her, and she walked into it.

Now, as I travel on my becoming journey as a mother, I've started to call out the Truth rather than the perception of the truth. I do, however, realize the difficulty in refraining from explaining or labeling our children. But, because I now know the words and phrases that made me who I am, even as I speak positivity over them, I have a new heightened awareness of what I am saying. Without recognizing or intending to, our words can be detrimental to our own and other people's sense of identity.

They are saying I am this, but I feel that I am that. They are expecting me to be or act this way, so I can't let them down. They have told me I am all of these things, but what if I don't want to be any of them? I didn't always contest the language or titles given to me. I was smart. I was outgoing. I was athletic. I was determined. But it was the expectation that left me broken.

This concept doesn't just apply to parent-child relationships. We place everyone around us into categories, labeling them as this way or that. Even when meeting a stranger, within five minutes we have summed up who they are by their clothing, their speech, their job title, their car, their shoes, their purse, their hair style, their age, their ring, their accent, their color. It's instantaneous and it's not necessarily wrong. It's how an animal would recognize a friend or a foe. But we do so even before we have a chance to find out who they are and without being aware of the harm this pigeonholing can inflict.

The most difficult battle of the mind isn't about who strangers, friends, or loved ones say you are, though that has major effects. The most challenging part is breaking the mindset of who the enemy says you are. Those are the lies that we tend to believe the most. We hear them in our subconscious, and we speak them over ourselves. We shame ourselves into believing that we aren't good enough, that we aren't worthy enough, that we aren't smart or pretty enough. We miss the mark. We doubt our capabilities. We doubt what we truly deserve. We can even doubt our purpose.

Through deep mental diagnosis with my therapist, I found my answers in the one place I could truly trust, and that was outside of my own mind. I found the answer through Him. Jesus Christ, our Lord and Savior, identified us the moment He breathed life into Adam and Eve. He said in Genesis upon our creation that we were created in His own image, and in the image of God He created us, male and female he created us. And He said, after seeing all that He created, it was very good *(Genesis 1:27, 31)*. And yet, we still stand in question. Who does He say that I am? How does He see me? What does He say that my purpose is? Where does He intend my path to lead?

God has already scripted my identity, just like He has scripted yours. He has held it in His hand since before we were born, before He breathed life into our lungs. He knows the crevices of our mind that we need to bring light to, and He knows how to shut the enemy's lies out. It takes great trust. But if your mind has conjured up reasons why you shouldn't trust anyone and it is hard to open up and let the light in, there is good news, my friend. When you do trust, when you do let the light in, it's like airing out your house in the spring. It brings newness and life. It brings freshness and air. You can literally breathe again. The suffocation of the titles and expectations and comments and claims about who you are will be lost in the wind, and you will gain strength to redefine who you are, despite any old cobwebs. Your mirror moment will re-emerge and the beautiful eyes, whether blind or not, will have a deep knowing and utter gratitude. For you were created in the image of the perfect living God with intention and great purpose.

It sounds heavenly, doesn't it, to stand in the full knowing? But this book isn't called *I Became*; it's called *Always Becoming*. You see, the nagging taglines still battle with my emerged internal woman, even when I stand in confidence of His Truth. I cycle backward. Sometimes I hustle. Sometimes I find myself on the rat wheel of achievement looking for the pedestal previously prepared for me. But there is centering and a knowing and affirmation that awaits me and surrounds me. He doesn't allow the enemy to take root in my soul anymore. And like the Martha of the Bible, my energizer bunny self just keeps going. I was an achiever before, but now, as I have uncovered my true self and listened closely to His mind instead of my own, He has reassured my identity as a daughter, a momentum mover, an illuminator, and an activator. My energy source is never ending. I'm simply a conduit for Him.

Mind over matter still carries weight. The difference is where your mind is focused. Don't live life to get from one pain point to the next. Learn to be aware of your mental focus. Put your mind to the test by putting your mind into the Word of Truth.

I remember stepping in front of the mirror again for the first time after my break down. Loved ones had been watching the shift and evolution of my sense of self for a few months. They would tell me I was glowing, like the new pregnancy or new mama-glow. They would tell me I was beautiful. And even though I didn't always believe them, I let God lead the way instead of pushing out the compliment with negativity or shame. Others during this time, combatted the emerging me. I felt like an outcast because I didn't blend in anymore. They didn't recognize me, and therefore they isolated me. But that was OK. I pressed on towards the peace instead of the previous prison. I wasn't strong enough to unshackle anyone else at that point.

I stood in confidence that I would no longer walk in the mental mindset of defeat or brokenness. My chains had been broken. I would no longer believe who everyone said that I was. I am a child of the King, just like you. We are beautiful and strong and brave and artistic and loving and kind and powerful. We are uniquely designed and purposefully created. We are covered and protected by the armor of God, and because He is in us, we are capable of standing on enemy ground and fighting the fight.

I never thought sharing my darkness would bring about more light. But after living most of my life with a negative internal focus, I desire nothing more than to stand up to the fight in confidence and clarity. I am finally dressed in an impenetrable suit of protection, and while I am far from perfect, and the enemy still finds ways to deceive me, I am bound and determined to not leave another soldier stranded alone in the same cistern of despair. I'm going back for the people that didn't embrace me, but I'm not going back to the enemy lines. I have planted myself near the hydrating river, and like Joseph, who was able to feed the very brothers that threw him out, they will come, and I will be prepared with ripe fruit, a place to rest from their travels, and forgiveness… because He first forgave me *(Ephesians 4:32)*.

But it's important that I acknowledge that those mirror-less, tooth brushing moments and nighttime convulsions and fears have since occurred again. A couple years later, post baptisms and pastoral studies, post new births and new friendships, post sanctified homes and restored mental-health practices, I found myself blanketed in fear again. I need you to know this expedition of wellness is not leading to a final pinnacle. Each mountaintop of clarity and beauty always leads to a valley that requires another ascent. I'm not getting into the details of the why's or how's of that experience in this book, however. You'll have to stay tuned for the next, as that is still a part of my current healing journey. But I couldn't let it go unsaid, as that is the truth of this side of Heaven. Brokenness still exists. Even in our glory days we still reside in a fallen world.

Despite these difficult truths, I want to help by way of word, by way of love, by way of light to remind you that when your mind is fixed on the One thing that matters, the One thing becomes your reflection; the One thing reestablishes your well-being – you become wholly you. By His might, you have the ability to stand in front of the mirror soundly and safely, secure in your confidence because you emulate His reflection through your very existence. You were created in His image, on purpose, for a purpose. Mind over matter, friend. Press on toward the goal.

As you become, ask your heart:

What do you say to yourself when you are brushing your teeth in the mirror?

_____

_____

Do you love the person you're looking at?

_____

_____

Do you see Him in your reflection?

_____

_____

Have you been tossed out and rejected?

_____

_____

What is it that you are believing because of that experience?

_____

_____

Detox

*E*ach part of our being is like a sponge. From the moment of birth, we are immediately consuming what's provided, from our mother's milk to the invisible toxins within the air. And like we just unpacked, even the words being poured out over us are being taken in and stored. Without comprehension of the process, we become living, breathing machines fueled by exterior inputs. And as common science shows, our output is only as good as our input.

> *Luke 6:45* - A good man brings good things out of the good stored up in his heart, and an evil man brings evil things out of the evil stored up in his heart. For the mouth speaks what the heart is full of.

I have a bad habit of mindlessly pumping gas, partially because it's a free moment to myself outside of a vehicle filled with kiddos teasing one another and testing my nerves. Can I get an Amen from all the mamas? Anyhow, I stand pump-side with the assorted gasoline options – diesel vs. regular vs. premium. (I don't even know what guzzles the middle supreme option, but that's not the point.) I've spent my life deciphering these options, and because of my varied car lineage, I often forget my current need.

My first ride was a stick-shift diesel Volkswagen. Yes, my dad ensured I'd never be stranded anywhere. This girl drives stick and can change a tire and her oil – but shhh, don't tell my husband or AAA. After college I was partially gifted a Hyundai Santa Fe. Diesel gas turned to regular, and it felt amazing not having to shift anymore. My next car was a surprise pearly white Ford Explorer. That baby felt like luxury. Then, during what I've previously explained as my one and only quarter-life crisis, somehow my cool Explorer morphed into a minivan. It was tragic. My pride was gone, and I felt certain it was a dirty prank or backlash from my husband. But it was love at first ride when I pushed the button that opened the double slide and what I pretended were the *Back to The Future*, DeLorean doors. I never hate anymore. But I did transition to an Infinity as soon as it was practical.

Let me get us on the same page here. My husband loves cars, and I get to be the beneficiary of his enjoyment. When we first started dating, he'd come pick me up, and I'd never know what to expect him to pull up in. One time he pulled into the center of the neighborhood cul-de-sac with a Mercedes c155. (And yes, I had to ask my husband the name of the car for this chapter. His hobby, not mine.) He has tried to teach me makes and models, but as much as I'm a mindless gas pumper, I am a mindless driver too. He could be at the same traffic intersection and I'd have no idea. My mind is usually in a million places (hence my constant need for meditation and prayer re-centering). That might be why I get lost all the time too. Oh well. You win some; you lose some. Now back to the Mercedes. It wasn't his by the way, just a rental. But like every one of the other 29 cars we've owned or sold collectively in ten years, it was fun while it lasted.

Our friends and neighbors think we're crazy, but it's a side-hustle and a passion. I've had many conversations with girlfriends when I show up somewhere and they see that I'm driving something new. They can't keep track, and I don't attempt to either. They'd mention how that hobby would drive them crazy. But honestly, I've never been one to claim my identity in a car, and it really doesn't much matter to me. Though, as mentioned, the mom van was a bit crushing at first. Regardless, it keeps me humble to know that it's not really mine anyway, and it's just a mode of transportation. Plus he's never brought something home that didn't have a shiny new appeal. They are always used but new to me, so I've always found it a bit exhilarating.

So picture this. I pull up to the gym in the wee hours of the morning to get a good burn in. Afterwards, one of the women walking out with me expressed her love for my shiny Infinity. "OMG, That's my dream car!" she said earnestly while climbing into a silver Suburban. I laughed at the irony of this situation and said "you can have it today." My husband's car salesmanship knack had obviously rubbed off on me by this point, but she shook her head, and pushed it off to "one day when I can afford it." I quickly let her know we traded my old minivan in for it. She couldn't believe it, and when I told her its make and mileage, she was even more dumb-founded.

Ok, there is a point to this whole car analogy, so stick with me. Actually, there are many. First, no matter the shape, size, color, or interior design, each requires the right kind of fuel for its particular engine in order to operate at maximum capacity. Secondly, the make and model will never define you as a person; what matters is if it can safely get you from point A to point B. Thirdly, you always want to have an intended destination (even if you get there much later than planned due to a lack of direction, like me). And lastly, what you see on the surface may not be the full story.

You see that Infinity, like all the others, was used. It was a 2011 with 100k+ miles on it. The body style was the same year after year, so the date wasn't recognizable. The outside was shiny. And, even though the engine was no better than the one in her Suburban, her dream still appeared to be a far too distant realization. She limited herself to what she could easily have, based on a false perception.

As humans, we are no different. There are different makes, models, shapes, sizes, colors, interiors, exteriors, rear views, bumper stickers, etc. I believe it's one of the most beautiful things about humanity. However, we fundamentally need the same things. And just like when a car gets the wrong gas, it doesn't mean it's destroyed forever; it means you need to flush your system and start new. And similarly, what's shiny on the outside may not tell the full story.

That car has been with me a few years now, and its true colors are starting to come out...or should I say, off. It has some torn leather, crusted snack foods in its crevices from my tiny humans, and some chipping, shiny paint that's now exposing its true age. I'm often asked, and teased, why my husband is driving around in a Tesla and I have a chipped paint beater. But like the shedding mind over matter conversation we just had...I've risen above this too.

It's just stuff; it doesn't define me; it just provides me transportation. And quite frankly, even if I end up on the side of the road because I've gotten lost, I've used the wrong gas, or the engine decides it's seen better days (all highly likely), I'll just call an Uber anyway. This was a process though. I drove a brand-new car off the lot when I had my driver's permit at 15. I had a brand new car smell again when the other car was still serving me well. New, shiny things are distractions. They are no different than the crowds. I had to detox. And just like I had to fix my focus and gain mental strength, my body needed some new fuel too. But detoxing, like decluttering, ain't easy.

Detoxing gets a bad rap from those who like food. But come on, who doesn't like food? I mean a good pizza, plus the garlic knots and the hot brownie sundae... YUM! I may be healthy, but I still have taste buds and a YOLO sized sweet tooth. I also love a giant homemade salad. Detoxing is less about giving up the food and more about the replenishment process. Our minds and souls are no different and should be the place we begin. If we stick to the previous mind over matter idea, detox becomes secondary and easy. It's the letting go process needed in order to get where you want to go, in order to enjoy the trip, in order to show up to the destination fully well. And there are many components of the detox process that take place at the rest stops, whether voluntary or not, of our journey.

If we ignore the road signs of our health and wholeness and if we fill ourselves with the wrong gasoline mentally, physically, and spiritually; we end up stuck in the middle of nowhere, on the side of the road, without a cell phone, and no way to call an Uber. I'm also a road food junkie and always pay the price later. Why do we choose these mindless, commercialized concepts over what's valuable, raw, and good? It's habit, likely – enticement, sure – lies, definitely – quick satisfaction, inevitably.

I didn't set out for this book to be a how-to journey, but boy are there a lot of processes to becoming! And I hope you know, I'm not preaching at you; I'm walking with you. I have to empty my own mis-fueled tank often. So, let me get us back to empty so we can refuel correctly.

My detox journey began with titles. It began with letting go of the exterior concern of what car I was driving, or in parallel, what my business card said. And although I had all of those previously mentioned losses ahead of me, the first was surely one of the toughest because it felt like the world was watching that one closely. My status and job titles changed on social media. I had placed my achievement driven, image-conscious nature ahead of my healthcare. This in turn left me completely on E with no destination and no map to get me out of the detour I had self-designed (unintentionally by way of following the crowds).

Being a CEO of anything isn't glamorous. I've seen Facebook profiles of full-time mamas transform from the title of "stay-at-home mom" to CEO, Chief Everything Officer, of the household. Touché, I get it. Been there, done that. My hat goes off to these women in acknowledgment and recognition of this incredibly important position. But that role, too, probably even more so than the business executive, is filled with a lot of...well, shit. Excuse my language but pun fully intended. And yet depending on perspective and experience, there are full tanks and there are empty ones. There are mis-fueled ones and glamorized ones. Titles and jobs aren't always passions. Self-identity isn't discovered through them either. But we're conditioned and fueled to believe otherwise. "What are you going to be when you grow up?" carries more weight than who they are right now as little creative beings.

From my own childhood, through my desire to please others and perform, I had completely hidden my true self from everyone – later even my husband, and sadly even me. I had unconsciously blanketed myself in shame for the "me" I wanted to be and the "me" I was currently being. I was surrounded by people at all times of the day, from sun-up with my kiddos to sun-high in the corporate office to sundown in the happy-hour meetings that turned into nighttime office hours. There was no time for self-reflection and absolutely no time to detox. But eventually, as any good mechanic could guess, I ran out of gas. The titles no longer sufficed. I had not only lost the energy to my battery, but my engine was blown, and my exterior paint was chipping by the chunks.

Insert the forced detox. I know you can relate. You checked into rehab. You were laid off or fired. You were sitting in the hospital hooked up to an IV and God knows what other machines. You got divorced. You had to file for bankruptcy. You had a nervous breakdown or an anxiety attack. You lost someone close to you. You miscarried. You were abandoned. You attempted suicide. Or you were affected by Covid-19. One way or another, we've all been there. We can all share that feeling of emptiness, the feeling of attempting to turn on the engine and nothing happens, the feeling of being broken without the slightest idea of where to go. And having no mechanic on speed dial is terrifying. In that moment, we are alone.

My poor, car-loving husband looked at me like I was his favorite FJ-40 broken into pieces and only partially returned after a promised rebuild. I was fragmented again, mis-fueled, and there was nothing he or anyone could do about it.

After training and dedicated time for self-analysis, I was trying desperately to grasp hold of this new life I was living. But, I still wound up broken down and out of gas. This time, nothing, not even jumper cables, were bringing me back to life. The passengers I knew so well, my family members, were jumping out of the car one by one. And sadly, the battlefield in my mind had me circling around the idea that I was soon to be sent to the junkyard for good. I had already released my job titles, and now the titles of sister and daughter were being stripped from me too. The enemy was coming after my family. One by one, roadblock by roadblock, my identity was being shaken to its core. I resonate with Joseph on so many levels, but unlike his abundance of faith and continued right choices, I felt betrayed and empty no matter what fuel I was putting in.

Finally, amidst a rainstorm, just like in a good Nicholas Sparks' love story, the skies parted, and I saw Him again. At a worship concert dedicated to prophetic sharing, two women laid their hands on my shoulders. As they poured into me, the truths of my past surfaced. They identified, to a T, my current state of loneliness and isolation within my broken family unit. What used to be family road trips and Sunday dinners had turned cold, quiet, and distant in communication and proximity. They also revealed the enemy's tactics at play and professed life over what was to come in the restoration of our family bonds and greater purpose. But before the refuel, detox had to happen.

I crashed to the floor, knocked out cold in that moment. I saw crowds of people. I was teaching on stage. I was sharing the Good News. I looked healthy and restored. I looked vibrant and lively. I wasn't dancing on this stage, but I was peering into the eyes of my family in the front row. I felt within me an engine trying to turn over, but I knew I needed more.

I also knew the pain wasn't over. In fact, I was left broken on the side of the road for years without them. I felt like my own flesh and blood were on enemy lines. How had weekly Sunday dinners turned into distant hellos and ignored drive-bys? How was this possible? Why was my minivan, previously filled with nieces and nephews, void of the laughter and light that had previously sustained me?

This felt more like a forced experience, one I had chosen out of desperation. I detoxed other titles in my life as well, such as the roles I played within my family: the middle child, the therapist, the best friend, the "perfect" one, the poster child, the normal one, the happy one, the reliable one, the successful one, the Daughter, the Sister, the Fun Auntie. Some of these titles I willingly claimed for myself. Some felt like a scarlet letter while others were a privilege. Either way, they were weights I could no longer carry. They were figurative bricks that I had to put down.

I had to release preconceived notions about who I was, where I was going, and who I wanted to be. My vehicle didn't matter. I had to stop the façade of who I pretended to be and claim who I was. I had to release the expectations that others had placed over my life, expectations that I, too, had grasped hold of as my own. I had to understand that I couldn't always be the driver, and I also didn't have to be the passenger. We all have our own vehicles, our own purpose, and our own destinations. I couldn't control the outcome or the vantage point of this journey, so I gripped the wheel, even with chipped paint, and drove on into the rainstorms I knew were brewing ahead of me.

Rain is detoxing - if you let it be. I went from a clogged, discombobulated, self-absorbed, unidentifiable, abandoned vehicle to a T-shirt wearing, white flag waving, ignition starting machine. The rain was a catalyst to my comeback.

But after 30 years, my tank was contaminated. I had been fueled by junk through food, language, music, conversation, media, friendships, family, accolades, expectations, rules and regulations. You see, I was so far from being fit, even though from the exterior I was the shiny new vehicle, the skinny size 6, the athletic type. I was still broken. Even the God I knew seemed fragmented. Even after a year of direct pursuit and counseling, this new scenario left me questioning God and His purpose within this pain. Why, after such critical development in my own home, would someone be fueling my tank with the wrong gasoline to cause destruction?

What I learned, after continued seeking and finding and question by question, was that it wasn't really anyone else's fault. Instead it was each person's journey that had led them into a catastrophic collision at the same intersection. In the midst of this multi car accident, He showed up again in every facet of His being, as He always does, as the medic, as the fire fighter, as the mechanic. And He made sure that during this season of detox, I wouldn't have the energy to drive the vehicle on my own, as I had been so used to doing. He made sure that I would have to release my grip on the wheel, release my control. He made sure that this accident was different. I needed deeper healing and deeper detox than the surface layers or titles or stuff. And finally, my eyes stopped being fixated on the relationships around me and started being fixed on Him alone.

He is the replenishment. He is the only one who can fix and mend and restore something so utterly broken and misused. He doesn't just jump-start. He's the endless gasoline that keeps you running in fullness and health. He's the fresh paint and the new tires. He's the lubricant to the engine and the ignite to the ignition.

It doesn't matter how you got to the detox point. It doesn't matter what the collision looked like or who it involved. What matters is how you restore. I felt like a newborn baby or even my daughter who still enjoys a cup of cow as often as possible. He is the milk, filled with nutrition and goodness and healthy fat. He is the warmth of a nurturing father and mother and the adoring words of affirmation that fuel the first coo and smile. He is the only source of exterior input that revitalizes the interior output.

Remember when the prodigal son came home, cast down and heavyhearted? His father was open armed and ready to feed and clothe him in abundance. The path he had taken for years prior didn't matter. The places he had visited or the way he had perceived himself didn't influence his father's thoughts. His dad saw him as the same child he laid his eyes on so many years before (Luke 15:11-32). He was just as he should be. Surely a little mis-fueled but still purposed. God sees you no different. And He doesn't require a broken down experience; you can turn around and go home right now, today.

Let go of the bad habits and the shame of what you have done or what you haven't yet become. Let go of how others perceive you and what expectations they have set over you. You still have the ability to be transformed from broken and weak to whole and strong. Detox may not sound easy; in fact, it may sound downright scary. The process of withdrawal, the vulnerability of getting honest with yourself, the feeling of loneliness, the concerns of relapse, and even the fear that the car may never come back to life are all valid. But if that proves true, the outcome, the promise, the new vehicle will emerge, and it is always greater than before.

But just as the mechanic must empty the containers that were filled with the wrong fluids before the correct materials can be added, you, too, need to be flushed out and drained. And sometimes even the entire motor may have to be removed. Withdrawal, no differently, will be like fasting. It is the removing of the wrong fuel that was poured in initially. It is a hard, but purposed, process. It is the letting go of what was old and the creating of a healthy habit, a new normal. It is a refuel where you replace self-inflicted pain or man-inflicted pain with purpose and purity. It is the replacing of nicknames, and even previously valued relationships, with newly purposed people.

We often consider the process of detox from alcohol or drugs as the only physical forms of withdrawal. But there are so many other areas where detoxing is just as painful and just as necessary. Some of these include pornography, junk food, dieting, TV, social media, negative or un-safe people, beauty regimens, lies, and even fitness. Anything you do or think or say in excess that prevents you from being fully free and healthy is a hindrance to your completion and alignment.

This is how the world can trick you yet again, and to be honest, this gets me quite heated, especially for the younger generations who don't know any better. When you look at that brief list above, I'm sure you notice components that we are made to believe are healthy. There's nothing wrong with dieting or exercise – those are good for you right? You see the commercial, you buy the thing you don't need, and you assume it will bring you peace or happiness or temporarily solve a problem. This is materialism, consumerism by choice. So what if I want to wear makeup or get my hair done? What's the harm? The harm is not in the simple acts of putting on makeup or getting your hair done. The harm is when these superficial things take root within us in conniving and unintentional ways in order to define us. Without control and recognition of our inner selves and full purpose (thus my concern for the younger generations), anything, good or bad, can become excessive to a point of detriment and therefore require detox. The same goes with people. In a state of fragility, safe-people are a requirement and all others, those who don't support your detox or the changes you are trying to make in your life, must be removed.

Don't wait until the collision happens. If you feel like you've lost control of the vehicle or deep meaning in the why behind your emotions and/or actions, there is no shame in practicing the submission process again and again. There is no shame in saying to yourself or a loved one, "I'm not ok. I need help." I had to. And I can assure you; I'm better and more connected now than I have ever been in my entire life because I let someone in to help.

That someone, the one who knows cars, now has an owner's manual to me too. And while that may cause immediate red flags or fear in some of you because of your inability to commit or let someone in, believe me, I get it. That was me too. Let me be your example. I'm over here with a king-sized white flag for heaven's sake!

But once again, it took depletion before completion. The lessons learned from that multi car collision took us all down our own individual roads to recovery and led to a restored family unit. And just as each car engine needs all the wrong fluids removed and flushed based on its unique systems and design, we each experienced our own unique version of detox.

Perhaps your white flag, like the abandoned car on the side of the road, is an old, ripped, white shirt. It doesn't matter what you use or when you wave it, help is waiting for you. And while God may seem so intangible in your current solitary rainstorm, healthy therapy is a step in the right direction. One act of bravery - throw up a thumb to the next passing car and take a chance on the driver being the one to lead you to your destiny. I don't believe in random acts of kindness. I believe in purposed moments of magic. It's a Mercedes moment of hope. It's a minivan moment of humility. It's an Infinity moment of clarity, a moment where you recognize that you can't keep on this road any longer. And it's our job, as passersby, to pick up those who are broken down in this season of life.

Don't be forced into your detox, especially not by others. Choose yourself. Choose your health. Choose your heart – the engine of your being. Allow the Good Samaritan to show up on your behalf, and let him introduce you to the ultimate mechanic who will help you replenish, refuel, restart, and renew in a right spirit.

Psalm 51:10 - Create in me a clean heart, O God, and renew a right spirit within me.

As you become, ask your heart:

Are you running on E?

_____

_____

_____

What is weighing you down that you need to release?

_____

_____

_____

What do you need to detox in order to be refueled correctly?

_____

_____

_____

Who can you ask for help to keep you accountable in the detox process?

_____

_____

_____

Fuel

O f course, the natural progression post detox is refueling. It is the process of nursing yourself and your system back to health. The key element of staying healthy is how you fuel yourself. I've heard it said that 90% of your body's health and fitness journey happens in the kitchen – it's about what you eat, not how you work out (though I surely don't discredit the importance of that remaining 10%).

Often people who diet aren't successful. They don't make it past the 30-day mark of the fad-fix. Or maybe you are the rare one that commits and doesn't deter from the program, and yet you still don't see the numbers on the scale or measuring tape diminishing. I've tried quite a few fad diets. The get skinny quick thing always works for me, but it has never stuck. And I know it's not the natural process my body deserves anyway. As I've adjusted into womanhood and God's definition of beautiful versus my own perceptions during my early 20s, I have a huge desire to have my body mirror image reflect what my heart and mind feel. And yes, I know I'm skinny and look fit, but all women who work out know the difference between feeling loose and being toned. I want to feel strong, not just look thin. Let me help energize your perspective for your own progress.

Moderation is the necessary well-being state of health and fitness. Our bodies need a rest day from working out, just as our minds need a mental rest and reset day from work. Now my husband, who began a paleo plan cold turkey at the announcement of our first pregnancy (yes, such horribly bad timing, as I wanted nothing more than to consume every carbohydrate in sight), has a different view on moderation than I do. Again, to each their own. And, just as I allow myself grace on family pizza night and with birthday treats, find YOUR healthy balance.

Sometimes, however, there is a time when moderation needs to be cut off at the knees and when suppression mechanisms, whether through food or drink, need to be addressed as well. This is true in every realm of life, be it fitness, body or mental health, work life balance, finances, etc. If you maintain your generalized idea of moderation, you'll never know if your definition is wrong.

A perfect example in the realm of nutrition is with the new trend toward gluten-free. It may seem silly to some. It may seem like a marketing ploy and money making machine for the fat cats in certain industries, but it has relevance and truth all the same. I recently had a friend who constantly experienced headaches, mood swings, blood pressure issues, skin irritations, bloating, and gut and bowel issues. She honestly lived day to day not knowing any different state of normalcy for her body or mind. She came across a mutual friend who had made the transition to gluten-free months prior and offered her some advice on the subject. Her first reaction was probably how most people would have responded...no way, gluten and me go together like bread and butter. I personally love a good carb load. Give me all the pasta, pizza, and breadsticks. But, after further research and taking a quick health checklist test, she realized she might have met her enemy, regardless of her affection for it. She gave up gluten and within days her symptoms lifted. She is never going back to her previous way of eating. Again, moderation comes into play. She loves a good cupcake. Don't we all? But why battle with your body and mental state when you can live more peacefully and comfortably.

Fuel is fundamental to our becoming. Without it you'll never be full or focused, both in the literal and figurative sense. The food we consume is a key element to our overall health, but I would like to adjust the percentage rates of kitchen and gym by adding the necessary factor of the mental game. It shifts the entirety of the equation. So don't get your panties, or should I say gym shorts, in a bunch; hear me out first.

50% mental fuel, 40% food, 10% fitness.

If your head game isn't strong, your food and fitness time will fall by the wayside in one weak moment. As I visited my first mental personal trainer, aka shrink, I simultaneously called on my fairy God-mama to become more of a life coach. While my counselor broke me down, she lifted me up. She was my nutritional planner. She gave me my spiritual diet plan. She fed me when I couldn't feed myself. I don't mean food – I mean FUEL. Food is a hamburger, fuel is The Apple, the Fruit we need to sustain.

It was what I was putting into my body, mind, and soul. It was the places I was going to eat, metaphorically, though I literally changed locations too. I stopped going to happy hours, and I started logging counseling hours. I stopped focusing on the external gains and started learning about the internal needs of my heart. I went back to church, a place that had hurt me previously. Instead of a sanctuary, it had been just another place to wear my mask, just another place to plaster on a smile and act like the world hadn't grown dark and cold. But this time, the more I went, the freer I was to be me and the deeper I went into who me was all along.

It was the repetition. It was the constant fueling that brought me out of the shadows and into the light. If you try to cut out all the carbs and sugars cold turkey, you most likely will fail. There is the mental game of starvation and detox that most are not strong enough to play. You relapse. You give in. You let the normalcy of the dark extinguish the point of light off in the distance because it's easier and because it's comfortable. That's why we have rehab centers. Church was my rehab.

Don't let this concept of "church" deter you from your spiritual opportunity of connection. Church to you may mean being outdoors or a place you go for corporate worship and prayer. We, not a building, are technically The Church by way of spreading, sharing, and declaring the good works (the God works) in our lives. But for this season of replenishment, I needed someone else to feed me and keep my thoughts from self-destruction. And, feeling abandoned by my family, I needed a sense of community. So, I listened. So, I read. So, I sang words I couldn't quite grasp hold of. And eventually, this focus on and repetition of the Word became the fueling source of life.

My life coach gave me snacks, and she even prepared some of my most hearty meals. She gave me Bible verses instead of cultured mantras. She gave me books instead of fantasy reality shows. She gave me worship songs instead of the vulgarity that consumes secular music. She gave me hugs when I wasn't getting them elsewhere. She was my angel on earth. And if you don't believe in angels just yet, then she was "my person." She saw me and still loved me. She was my fairy God-mama. She could see beyond my rags and was able to help me transform into the princess I was always intended to be by teaching me about the Creator who made me that way.

Over the course of time, my incredibly patient husband has shifted into that position (though I don't refer to him as a life coach or fairy God-mama). In the beginning of this process, even he wasn't capable of loving me to the capacity I needed to feel loved. This was not because he wasn't doing everything he could to love me the best he knew how, instead, it was because I had to learn to love myself first before I could allow myself to be loved. Those previous affirmations from earlier chapters, met with habit development, through fuel choices and prayer, led me to be able to overflow into others. As I have gotten more fit as an individual, we have gotten more fit together.

The understanding of fuel far exceeds the process by which we eat or drink. It's how we grow and become nourished. It's how we then operate based on what we intake. We can consume all natural or organic everything, but if we are feeding our head and heart crap, we will never find abundance in health. If you haven't watched the Netflix documentary *Heal*, you should absolutely do that next (not now...next!). It shows powerful examples of how mental health is fundamental to our physical well-being and how our mind can control the inner workings and capabilities of our bodies. Alongside the powerful spiritual component, I believe fully that we are capable of far greater than modern medicine provides. It's a matter of how we set the table to eat. And it is also realizing, just like Sunday Church, we can't just consume a meal once a week; we have to keep nourished and fed.

Part of my personal detox journey (the parallel influence of whole-body health and my continued state of desired conviction) led me here, two years into my sobriety. Again, I wasn't an alcoholic, but it became a crutch. I started thinking about it before my feet hit the ground in the morning. Heavily in my faith practice at this point and years into my ordination and ministers licensing, my one glass of afternoon wine began to cloud my judgment and morning mindset. How you start your day is how you finish your day, and that mentality of "Is it 5 o'clock somewhere?" and "Mommy needs a marg," started to become commonplace, just like gluten had for my friend.

I've been so grateful that God blessed me with children that I not only parent but learn from daily. When my son came over and asked me, "Can I have some?" and I snatched it from his hand, I knew something had to change. I was being a hypocrite. We preached so much about landscape design (I'll explain this more later) and positive healthy fuel for their bodies and minds, and yet something I was putting into my own body was in fact not safe for theirs. That revelation, paired with the spiraling vantage point of alcoholism that surrounded me on many levels, led to a decision to stop, at least for the time being. And what led to a daily choice, led to months and now years of choice. Habits are formed out of action, and we become clearer when we choose healthy habits.

You can view the process of detoxing as fasting. When Jesus went into the desert for 40 days and 40 nights, he fasted while also being replenished through the spiritual and mental practice of prayer and supplication. He is our ultimate meal prep enthusiast. A hearty meal is set before us when we open the Bible, but often our plates are filled instead with convenience and culture.

If you shared your daily meal plan with me (and/or a counselor since they are trained professionals in the matter), I would be able to dissect your output. What you feed yourself will determine your success and the depth of your happiness. Although you may feel happy with a lot of surface level things, it is critical that you feed your mind, body, and soul with the right food, the right information, the right people, the right encouragement, the right sound, and even the right music.

If you look at yourself as a garden, there is no more beautiful imagery of restoration and need for fuel. If you let others plant in your garden as they please, their plants may be like weeds and crowd out or weaken those that are necessary for your nourishment. If you ignore your own garden and focus on others, your intended crop will die, and you'll be left starving. But if you nurture what has been given and designed just for you, fueling yourself with the living water and talking to your leaves with nurturing kindness, your garden will flourish and sustain you. You will never experience fullness, wholeness, and true health without fueling your roots with the substances needed for growth: sunlight and water (the maker of the sun and the true living water). Your garden won't ever be perfect on this side of Heaven, but just like the gorgeous imagery in the movie *The Shack*, if you take a drone image perspective on your life's garden, you will see abundance, even in the places that you ignored and stepped on until they were muddled and in disarray. Restoration comes with rain, even perhaps a storm. Let it be fuel for your soul.

You, my friend, are a garden. How will you tend to yourself today? What will you fuel yourself with? Are you willing to fast in order to find further clarity? Are you cultivating an organic farm or feeding yourself with toxic pesticides...inevitably, by way of free will, the choice is yours.

As you become, ask your heart:

If you were to create a "nutritional" overview of your life on a daily basis, what percent would go to your mind, body, and soul, and what would be wasted inputs?

_____

_____

(Wasted calories if you will)

_____

_____

How can you re-evaluate your fuel inputs to create a better output?

_____

_____

What would God say about the quality of fuel you are providing yourself with?

_____

_____

Beats

Give me a beat. I need it, and if I don't have a speaker, I'll hum and dance to my own tune. Music inspires me. It always has. I love how a song can change your mood, change your thoughts, change your demeanor, and change your direction.

You likely will not walk into any gym and hear silence. No matter the genre, it propels me into movement. I love to dance. There is a component of freedom that I don't think you can experience in any other form of fitness. There are no rules. There are no limitations. It's an expression that aligns all hemispheres of the brain and body. People claim to be uncoordinated, but my belief is that dance is innate and that it's actually mental constraints that keep us from flowing in dance. Rhythm, or lack thereof, may be a valid argument, but studies show there are ways to overcome that too. So, give up your self-conscious inhibitions and take to the music like we are able to take to the language of the song.

Children have such a freedom in their bodies. They let music connect them emotionally, physically, and mentally. I love watching a toddler move with their little squat motions and bouncing diaper butts when they hear a tune. My parents loved musicals and nurtured this love in me. To this day I can still recite every song in *The Sound of Music*. We'd also attend the play, *A Christmas Carol*, each year. The music, mixed with the motions, brought me so much joy. And of course, I got to live out my own form of theater through gymnastics floor routines, flipping to the tunes of *Greased Lightning*. Later, I would dedicate every Friday, for an entire year, to a gifted dance academy at school and then to the high school dance team.

The melodies can move us, but the words have power too. They can be motivating or debilitating. I went through a phase in high school when I became entangled in some melodramatic friendships. "Emo" music brought out a side of me that I hid from the public. And while I don't blame the honesty of the artists, I blame the access I gave it to my heart. But I also give myself grace that I was young and impressionable. I surely wasn't aware of the deposits that resulted from these tunes.

Songs about heartbreak, being out cast, suicide, loss, sex, and love would fill my mind on the very same day light-hearted worship songs would be sung in a group of classmates at Young Life (youth public school ministry). How was I to make sense of these combatting emotions and conversations when there was no arena available to disclose the confusion? No one on either side of the spectrum was willing to discuss the elephant in the room (secular vs. non-secular?). I didn't know why it mattered, but I knew when to shift the radio and what was appropriate where.

In this same season of life, I began to write. But the words that came out were to appease the same person that introduced me to the negative music in the first place. I was conflicted all the time as I lived out the version of who my parents expected me to be, who half of my friends were acting to be, and who the one applauding the manifestation of darkness that gripped me hoped I would be. Back and forth, beat to beat, I'd collide and hide beneath the sounds.

Humanity is surrounded by sound all the time, but sound can also be noise. Anything that was intended for good can be manipulated and perverted to infiltrate us with negativity if we are not mentally sound. (See what I did there!)

Later, the same people I partnered with in worship music left me on a solo emo train to darker days. They had discovered that my actions outside of our youth camps and meetings did not correspond to the songs I was singing of hope, purity, and love. And I wasn't just rejected with the disgusted side-eyes and silence of my fellow students; I was also turned away by the adults who led the ministry, the very people who were supposed to call me out of the dark in the first place. With such rejection, which genre of music do you think took over? And although God can and will find a way to speak to me and to you no matter what type of music we listen to, if we give access to the devil through sound, he will take advantage. And he did.

As my interests and friend groups changed, so did my musical preferences. Most of the time the gym chose my music for me, as I was not one to walk around with earbuds in. (I'm not trying to sound high and mighty; I actually just have small ears and they bother me most of the time.) But my dad to this day has never run or exercised with headphones, even with the many marathons and miles he has tracked, and I've always loved that about him. He prefers nature. And although I can understand that now, for a long period of time silence was something to be avoided. My thoughts were deafening, so I welcomed music as often as I could – Anything to drown the thoughts that constantly circled over my self-worth.

Before getting faithfully fit, I was often being manipulated mentally; it was an internal, unconscious battle that seeped into my reality. I remember how harmless, relaxation music by the pool or during a run would take my mind on a pursuit of the song's theme or meaning. I would question the reality of the existence that the song described and make comparisons with my own. I would belittle my life as it compared to the life they were singing about, a life that seemed like a far-off dream. I would imagine myself in their realities instead of my own. I was lost in the sound of music. I grew up watching MTV videos, which corresponded to the child pornography experience and led to dancing in all the wrong ways. I would often fantasize about how much money I could make as a stripper. But besides my college years, I never left home to live in another city and didn't want to risk my dad or his friends walking into the local club. Thankfully, I kept that fantasy hidden, but it still tainted the sweet intimacy of my marriage bed. We are unfortunately living in a superficial fantasy world, with words and songs we can never live up to and where orgies and sexual sin are romanticized by Playboy bunnies and lingerie.

I worry over other women, over our daughters, and over our sons too. I worry about the way in which a woman's body is presented by the music industry. I worry about the way they describe love and relationships, sex, and heartbreak. I worry about the confusion that sets in from the words that are implanted. There are many styles of music that pervert the truth of our design and God's intent for our lives. The pursuit of money, fame, material gain, and glittering rock star lives distort and corrupt God's beautiful plan created for each of us. And all of this, so grossly flawed in comparison to how we are identified in the eyes of our Father and what this life, here on earth as it is in Heaven, is promised to be. What is reality when every song appears to send the same message and every "old" Bible verse appears to be its antithesis?

After having my children, I felt a natural shift in the way I moved. What used to feel normal and fun, dancing on stages or the sticky nightclub floors, now felt somehow wrong. I felt physically restricted from the motions and disturbed by any thoughts of my children moving or being danced with in that manner. This was simultaneous to the renovation happening within my soul. So, I simply listened and stopped dancing. But the words of the songs still penetrated.

Thankfully, after battling my own identity and existence and coming to know my self-worth and the beauty of how God sees me, those words began to fall on deaf ears. I no longer struggled in the battle of comparison but instead shared the heart of Jesus in my sorrow for the society that had shaped and often mirrored these sad, lost, broken, and hypnotic songs.

After my brokenness became externally apparent, I had to shut out secular sound for some time. It was a musical detox. But because music was so ingrained in our household and my life, I craved it. And so, He replaced it. I stopped worrying about my subconscious thoughts and began to actively pursue my love for music through worship and praise songs. If you grew up in the hymnal church, don't shut me out just yet. There are Christian artists for every genre of music and talk about a powerful movement. These songs won't let you sit still. There is a true freedom in expression when your words are connecting with the sound and speaking into your soul in a positive way.

The Church didn't dull my love for music; it enhanced it. In fact, one of my first Holy Spirit guided experiences led me to pursue a yearlong worship school called Burn 24/7. I was no musical artist. I couldn't play an instrument, and I didn't plan to grab a mic anytime soon. But, I am a worshipper and a dancer. God restored that for me through this program. He taught me about the intimacy of sound and music and the revelations that emerge from the congruency. I learned about the harps and angels in Heaven, the temples filled with musicians releasing heavenly sounds, and the revivals that would break out in the midst of sound and worship and praise. I was renewed in my perspective on what it means to dance, and the words that filled my spirit, home, head, and car were pure and purposeful in nature.

After my mental and emotional state became more secure, I was able to work on my physical state again. For a long time, I couldn't workout. I felt depleted of energy and in need of the repositioning of my spirit to pursue my body again. It took time, but music and dance were a part of that restoration too.

Sadly, the gym didn't care about my musical preference, and I was participating in group personal training, so headphones weren't an option. I remember hearing some of the vulgar songs that used to be a part of my regular playlist and cringing at the sound. "Jesus, Jesus, Jesus" resonated through my brain. I had to block out the sound and focus on the muscles and movements. I escaped the words, listened to the tune, and used it as a driving force to strengthen my physical self. Months later, the words fell on deaf ears and my mind, body, and soul were in alignment no matter what was being pumped through the speakers. But it did sadden me. In unison the songs from my childhood would be recited and sung and laughed over in community uproar. Why had my heart and mind been opened to this idea of destruction? What am I to do with it, I still wonder. But I do know I have a responsibility as a mother to steward what is deposited into my own children's souls.

And don't worry, I still love a good beat, and I can sing aloud to the catchy songs of pop and country music again. I also have a girlfriend who loves to dance. She constantly wants a girl's night to go and groove. I finally gave in when she offered a country line-dancing bar. I thought – OK this will be harmless. No booty shaking. No grinding. No need for sexy. I was hilariously shocked by the truth when we walked into that bar located in a strip mall. I was actually a bit traumatized, but in a comical "this can't be real" way.

I don't believe dance is bad – in fact, I believe as the dancing diaper babies prove – we were born to dance! But, like the consumption of food and the concept of addiction, there are healthy limitations to everything. Now, after inner healing and focus on mental strength, I'll dance my heart out on a dance floor filled with my girlfriends, not needing a single sexual connection, but instead just enjoying the freedom in laughing, moving, and creating with my body. I'll even bust a Fortnite move to show the teenyboppers what's up and give my son a good, mortified laugh. Afterall, I did floss in my Jesus meditation I shared with you earlier! And hello - Flashmob!

What God intended for good, the enemy can use to manipulate as evil. We are not robots for a reason. You are allowed to move and play and DANCE. The purpose and motivation behind your movements and your mental thought patterns are what matter. I want my children to love dance as much as me – my son has my natural ability to move while my daughter moves a bit more like her dada. We've said many thankful prayers over that gift!

Did you know that sound, in and of itself, is a part of what birthed existence in the beginning? If you haven't wrapped your head around that yet, and you are still grasping hold of the creation concept, we can look at this from a strictly human perspective. The power of musical vibration is proven beginning in the womb. The yet unborn can hear our voices, as well as the music and vibrations around us, and respond. We are designed with the ability to respond to sound. And no matter where in the world your birth certificate is filed, music (as is love) is a universal language.

There are over a thousand references to music, sound, song, instruments, etc. in the Bible. These references can be found at celebrations and weddings, in remembrance of miracles, and in moments of rejoicing. How can it not be from God when it can communicate across linguistic, ethnic, cultural, geographic, and generational bridges? I've also found an even deeper access to vision through worship music and praise that reignites my goals and brings me full circle with intention and purpose. So, when I dance, I dance freely knowing it is a God given gift. And when I sing the words of a song after God's own heart, I rejoice in the eternal resonating frequency that hits the heavens and scares the enemy.

And when I am not the one in control of the radio, I remind myself of the importance of words and invisible headphones. We must be ever vigilant to arm ourselves against the enemy's tactics with positive distractions, tuned-in conversations, and prayers sent up for protection. And like the cycles we discussed in earlier chapters, although the enemy isn't too smart, he is conniving and will go after the very thing that tainted you in the past.

As you become, ask your heart:

What are some of the lyrics to your most favorite songs?

What stations do you put on in the background without thought to the words that are infiltrating your spirit?

Do you ever break free from your body and mind confines to just dance before God?

Find time this week to freely explore Christian music and movement.

Frequency

The sounds of high-spirited fun and enjoyment pulled me outside during my little brother's 6th grade birthday party. I would be intruding, and I wasn't sure how he would respond to his "lil big sis" barging in, but my curiosity got the best of me. I knew his new crush, Tameka, was outside, and music mixed with laughter was clearly a scene this soul has always been drawn to; so I risked the rejection. As I walked outside, they were moving their feet in a way I had never seen. I needed a lesson, and fortunately my intrusion was welcomed. Insert, and still one of my favorite moves, the heel toe. I'll never forget her. She had a bright smile and was getting a kick out of teaching this quick learning "white girl." The hooting and hollering continued as we showcased different moves, but eventually my overprotective brother didn't like the attention his buddies were giving me, and I found myself quickly uninvited.

But, I didn't care. Inside to practice I ran, eager to move heel to toe, switch back, heel to toe, slide and shift, hop, heel to toe, bend and twist my hip, heel to toe, over and over again. Frequency is the number of times we repeat something. This can be related to every component of learning, including dancing, but even to larger concepts in life – and like most things, even the negative.

We've heard it 1000 times, "practice makes perfect." But I've diligently practiced countless goals in my lifetime, and I've never hit perfection. My take on "perfection" is that it's unattainable and impractical and honestly just too much of a burden to carry. So I'd like to alter the saying:

Progression leads to positive performance.

Progression doesn't come without practice. And performance, though not always perfect, will be more often on the positive pendulum if you have diligently practiced. Without frequency, progression would be impossible. Frequency produces habit, and habit produces results. Although I'm not really writing to share with you my workout regimen or how practicing a pull-up will eventually lead to a pull-up, it's important to understand that, literally and figuratively, you can't go out and run a marathon without first hitting your 5k milestone. You have to go "running" – Repeatedly and Frequently. My finish line bathroom break story proves that.

Often the idea of frequency makes people uncomfortable. We simply want to reach the finish line without having to experience the "no pain, no gain" part. But just like we have to start our physical training using lightweights and learning the movements and posture, we have to remain consistent. Choosing a consistent rate of frequency goes hand in hand with our previous discussion on choosing our personal level of moderation. If we remain diligent and the chosen levels of moderation and frequency conform to our personal needs, we will achieve the end goal quicker. But that doesn't mean the process is any simpler.

Before we move forward, let me revert back to my brief note on perfection in order to give you some deeper insight. I lived most of my life on a pedestal. I was born there. I was a daddy's girl thru and thru, and he had formed and fashioned that lofty resting place before I was born. As I grew, so did the hopes, dreams, and expectations of those around me. But it wasn't just my parents. They were only doing their parental best, just like we all do. Now, especially, as a mother, I find myself taking a step back from too frequent kudos or praise to my little ones. I simply do not want to risk compounding the myriad of titles and expectations that society as a whole will naturally place on them. We all feed off of the affirmation and encouragement from birth. We look to our parents, before we can even talk, for praise reports and big smiling, hand clapping reactions as we hit growth milestones. It continues with the report cards, teachers, and coaches who embolden and leave notes of congratulations when we do something great. It's not a bad thing. It's important to know good from bad and right from wrong. Instead, it's the frequency at which that applause continues and is internalized. It's the process by which it can eventually progress from a pat on the back to a necessary addiction that rewards us based on performance. I was a performer. I got really good at acting. I did things for the applause and always went after the standing ovation.

You can call it what you want: perspective change, mindset shift, heart change, reality check, or aged wisdom. Regardless, the emotions you experience with each scenario have similar frequencies. You have moments when you feel like you are living outside of your body and are in the audience watching yourself performing on stage. There may be a sense of deja vu as you watch those around you mimic your past self. You know what you used to feel, but the same emotions aren't making their way to the surface. Am I just getting old?

I wonder as I stand watching the old me, "How did I not realize my state of confusion and loss? How did I deal with the daily struggle of me vs. me?" How do you do it? Do you just get into a routine like you do with everything else in your life? Do you make a conscious effort not to listen to the inner conversations of good vs. bad? Do you do things out of the expectation of praise from others? And, because of the applause, do you just keep going?

I hid. I masked. I disregarded. I forgot. I even "prayed," or so I thought. Regardless, I was not wholly me. I was a shell of what others wanted and expected from me. And all the while I was secretly running from that expectation and surely from the heart of God, a God who had called me from a young age to stand out.

Now, as a disclaimer to the loved ones and friends who walked through my adolescence and 20s with me, I was not trying to pull the wool over your eyes, acting fake, or being someone I was not. I was living in a state of unawareness. You knew as much about me as I knew about myself. And the areas of nondisclosure, which I believe we all have, were places I didn't reside in cognitively; I was always running from the non-simplistic.

But escaping life isn't possible because it eventually catches up to you. And there will be a "come to Jesus" moment when He is finally heard through all of the noise, beats, and applause. Where will you be when it happens? Will you have hit rock bottom? I did. And every day since, I've put on the armor of God (*Ephesians 6:14-17*) and climbed out of the pit of despair. This was only possible through the frequency of my fuel – that's how you always get the best results.

We have to align our minds, warped as they may be, with our faith. Even if that faith is the size of a mustard seed (*Matthew 17:20*), God can use it, and He will. Sometimes your rock bottom isn't from your own doing but instead is due to external factors. Perhaps a loved one passed away unexpectedly. Perhaps you were diagnosed with an illness. Perhaps you lost your job or your home or your spouse. Perhaps your child is in anguish and out on the streets without your guidance. Whatever it is – He will help mend, heal, and grow the areas of loss in your life. He will take your broken, weak body and make it fit for performance. He will use all the areas of your life for good. And this time the performance is not for others; it is solely for Him and His perfect redeeming plan.

> *Romans 8:28 - And we know that God causes all things to work together for good to those who love God, to those who are called according to His purpose.*

The world has a way of taking hold of our mind, which then can affect our heart. We aren't intended to be influenced. We are intended to be influencers of the atmosphere and culture; God has equipped us for this. Your mustard seed faith will lead you to that place of positive force if you nurture it well. Don't run from the still small voices. Don't lose sight of the life you've always dreamed of. God gifts dreams and visions with intentionality for you to pursue holistically. Tune in to the frequency of Heaven's sound instead of the blaring beats of a warped society. There is freedom, even if you're currently experiencing darkness. The darkness will teach you how to be brave. Don't stop. Don't give up. Set your eye on the prize, not by striving, but by being. He will not only salvage your soul, He will help you discover your own frequency for salvaging the lives of others. And through this process you will have life, and have it abundantly.

> *Colossians 3:1 - Set your minds on things above, not on earthly things. For you died, and your life is now hidden with Christ in God. When Christ, who is your life, appears, then you also will appear with him in glory.*

God has the power to change your mind if He becomes your frequent fuel. He showed me the light and led me away from all that was dark in the dungeon of concealment and pain and performance. He set me free from the ploys of perfectionism, and he can set you free too.

I thank God for not dealing with just my exterior world, for not just changing my place of being, but instead for changing my internal home. I can attribute growth to counselors and many books and podcasts, but the voices that spoke into my life the most, the church, the worship music, the podcasts that shared about a Truth I only halfway understood...that is where my victory was won.

I encourage you, if you're lost or can't climb out of a state of sadness...seek light, seek peace, seek freedom, and do it frequently and at a higher frequency than you ever have before. It does exist through Him. And while tuning in may seem like only a minimal sense experience, I'd encourage you to experience Him with all five senses.

Matthew 7:7 - "Ask and it will be given to you; seek and you will find; knock and the door will be opened to you. ⁸ For everyone who asks receives; the one who seeks finds; and to the one who knocks, the door will be opened.

You will never know the feeling of true reward and true praise until you practice progression frequently. We aren't perfect. We never will be. But we were made in His likeness, which is perfect. Rest in knowing that as you look in the mirror at your stretch marks, scars, weight, and wrinkles you are beautiful, and He is giving you a standing ovation.

Frequency, while dealing with duration and numbers, also has to do with sound. Are you tuning in to His frequency? Can you hear Him through the chaos that has become our world? Astonishingly, His voice is capable of creating utter silence over the entirety of existence. I can just imagine the great silence as humanity slipped slowly under the floodwaters in Noah's day, the silence that must have enveloped those at the foot of the cross as darkness fell at mid-day and the temple veil was torn, and the silence of the empty tomb at His resurrection. Just as his person cannot be measured or weighed, His frequency has no measure of depth, width, length, or weight. And yet, He has given us a taste of His frequency by providing us with our very own wavelengths.

Resonant frequency is a natural vibration – every object known to man, every living and nonliving particle, has a sound – a frequency of differing magnitudes. And in that variation there is an understanding that each of those things is only a speck of His entirety. God knows each of our frequencies intricately. He knows what will break us and what will make the perfect melody. But each of us can only comprehend His frequency by understanding our own. This is His gift to us, our very own superpower – the power of our physical presence and the power of our voice. But, in order to recognize and utilize the power we have been given, we have to tune in to the frequencies of our existence through Him. In fact, Jesus promised that we would do far greater things than He did when He was here on earth.

> *John 14:12-14 - * [12] *Very truly I tell you, whoever believes in me will do the works I have been doing, and they will do even greater things than these, because I am going to the Father.* [13] *And I will do whatever you ask in my name, so that the Father may be glorified in the Son.* [14] *You may ask me for anything in my name, and I will do it.*

What does that mean? It means in order to hear, we have to find stillness. We have to push through the hard times (the hard workouts), and find His strength made more perfect in our weaknesses. Then we can find quietness and fulfillment through the connecting of our fueled and whole body, our hearts, and our spirits to God. And the more often, the more frequent, we tune in to that mind, body, soul, and spirit aligned design, the more we will hear Him. This is done through hydration, focus and prayer, detox, fasting, fuel, and every layer of release, such as worship and praise that I've spoken to thus far.

1 Timothy 4:7–8 - *Have nothing to do with irreverent, silly myths. Rather train yourself for godliness; for while bodily training is of some value, godliness is of value in every way, as it holds promise for the present life and also for the life to come.*

Don't let frequency become rote memorization or second nature. Hearing the voice of God is a gift, so we want to match the frequency with fragility and ultimately with legacy. Our continual practice of leaning inward and upward will become the example for others to emulate. And remember, people don't want perfect people; they want present people. Be frequently present.

As you become, ask your heart:

In what area of your life can you eliminate the need for perfectionism?

What are you practicing most frequently in your varied forms of self: mentally, physically, and spiritually?

Are those choices serving your legacy in the Kingdom?

How do you tap into the frequency of Heaven?

Actions Speak Loudest

I stood in the grocery line sensing their stares towards my smiling son who looked a bit different than the common waddler. Perhaps it was the story I was telling myself, but I could feel their critical and concerned eyes focused on both of us. They didn't want to make eye contact, but they wanted full scope of this child's predicament.

He was wearing a helmet for 23 hours a day at 12 months old. I was 20 weeks pregnant, exhausted and yet still on the move, suppressing most all emotions in order to maintain a smile and sanity and press on toward the many goals I had in play at the time. Twice a week we would drive 40 minutes one way to a neighboring city in order to receive specialized skull chiropractic care for his diagnosis of plagiocephaly. So when kiddos or adults stared, pointed, and asked questions, I would muster up the energy to share and slap a smile on my face, even when I wanted to cry.

I couldn't press his cheek to mine like I did every night before his first birthday to sing him "Que Sera, Sera," the same lullaby that my adoring father sang to me. I couldn't snuggle or hold him in the same way. I didn't photograph him as much. I looked forward to our 30-minute breakfast routine and 30-minute bath and book time during the evening, which gave him freedom from what felt like captivity. It was purposed. It was a joint decision based on hours of research and professional insight. His flat head was clearly not from lack of love or interaction. We noticed it really early on but chose to wait it out. It was even suggested sooner, but we opted to let time do the healing, trusting that eventually it would become even. Dada had wanted to take action months before, but my mama heart, and concern for opinions, expectations, and outcomes kept me frozen in disbelief. We do that so often in life, don't we? We tell ourselves to wait it out, let time heal and often end up letting the thought patterns of others determine our own choices.

This next piece of the puzzle, I cannot place for you. It requires movement, awareness, mobility, and willingness. You have to act in order to see change. And your choice in action, or lack thereof, determines the positive or negative outcomes in your next situation and season. In close parallel is the need for preparation in your intended choice.

This concept is easily understood through our eating patterns. When our stomach growls, our reaction is to plan our next meal. We either take the short cut, the quick alternative to full preparedness, the generally less healthy option, or the quick route to curb the appetite. Or, we've prepared for this moment and meal prepped, stocked healthy options, and/or planned necessary time for cooking and eating, all which has been thought out and intentionally put into our schedule.

Which action do you think, or know, yields better longevity to your overall wellbeing? Isn't it odd that no matter the chosen example, the choice or action that causes the most friction and takes the longest time is usually the answer to the big, hard questions?

Action without preparation yields poor performance. It is a planned failure. There's no getting around it. And in the same breath, preparation with no action yields stagnant results, which result in less than hoped for circumstances. I must confess that this is completely derived from my husband. He is a natural researcher, detail desirer, and question asker. He's an interviewer, which fits well with my extroverted, interviewee tendencies. I'm known to share based on flamboyant emotion, and we often laugh at my quick responses based on preconceived notions and assumptions. And even when I'm proven wrong and finally able to admit it, he has always applauded my confidence.

Planning is the next natural step to goal setting. But the goals can never reach fruition without implementation. Eventually with practice, like any skill, this becomes second nature. It is not unlike muscle memory. I still recall standing there staring at that number, the number that was the deciding factor, the number that resulted in the decision to place my son in a helmet. The hard truth is that even honest faith filled prayers can't change the course of God's larger plan in our lives. And although it was a difficult pill to swallow, especially because it would affect a sweet, innocent child, it taught me many lessons.

Fears of adjustment can keep us locked in our own cell. And if we let our fears become bigger than our faith, then the enemy has us right where he wants us, just outside the manifestation of His faithfulness and our corrective growth.

My son's head was basically forced into a planned circumference that would instill a growth pattern intended to yield a more balanced, sphered shape. The chiropractic helmet was intended to mold and shift the plates at the suture junctions of his skull. This was possible because his soft spot wasn't developmentally closed yet. Y'all this hurts my head even thinking about it. I can't even wear a headband for more than a couple hours. But this baby boy, lying on exam table after exam table, was cool as a cucumber as they measured, moved, and pressed. He has been resilient since day one, and even in his abundant energy in every other facet of life, he's still the most calm at a doctor's office. Oh the endless, trying lessons in motherhood.

So the goal was set. The plan was good. The implementation, though difficult and uncomfortable and seemingly lasting forever, created a worthwhile result that left us pleased with our emotional and his physical transformation.

Change is hard. But guess what friend? We were made for hard things. We've been built "Ford tough" for decades now; it's time we get with the program, disavow the marketing that is brainwashing us, and face the hard things head on. We have to take action before action takes us. The struggle IS real. I'm not negating the difficulty involved in making change a comfortable norm in your life, but sugar coating and coddling aren't going to help. So I'll be the trainer, coach, teacher, and friend that you haven't yet positioned in your life to tell you the truth and the Truth.

I've watched the process of enabling unfold in my own life. I've encouraged negative patterns and gifted authority to actions that led to devastation and despair. Why do we do this? Are we blinded by the outcome? No, it's because we've seen the patterns cause problems and pain time and time again. We've chosen to allow the hard things, which are the wrong things, to take precedence over the lifelong things, the eternal matters of our souls and our health. I've even been a culprit to my own enabling by making excuses for bad choices that left me disjointed and despondent. Unfortunately, the uncomfortable had evolved into comfort, so I suppressed recognition and feigned "okayness."

As a bystander, it's so much easier to see things clearly. You aren't immersed in the emotional relationships that create cause and effect drama. You have a clearer view of what should or could take place. It's the very reason that the AMA Code of Ethics states that doctors should not treat themselves or members of their family. The waters are too muddied. The lines are too faintly drawn. Yet, out of a desire for consistent, current comfort, we continue to discredit or put off taking action that may result in mental, physical, emotional, or spiritual pain even if that pain leads to healing. Honestly, it's so idiotic. We sound and look like complete dodo birds.

I love that we love big. I just think our understanding of love isn't big enough to allow us to comprehend what the larger plan of the universe entails. So we coddle, and we ignore the warning signs. We put blinders on. We mask the realities. And yet inevitably, without action, we end up in a greater catastrophe, a catastrophe that could have been avoided had we chosen to act sooner.

We can't go back. We can't live our life in regret. The only constant is change. I've learned, by way of destruction and through the development of empathy and humility, that when I tune myself in to the things that break our Father's heart, the emotions and spiritual drive that result can allow me to affect change so much sooner, even if that change is selfishly for my own internal adjustments and wellbeing.

What if we approached each opportunity for growth by asking, "What's the best that can happen?" instead of the fear-based version that inquires about the worst. We can't fear the next step because then we fear learning, and learning is the fundamental building block to wholeness.

We are ever becoming beings, ones that need change even though we are constantly trying to avoid it. The Bible does not avoid this idea of approaching fear. In fact, it's mentioned over 365 times. Yes, once for every day of the year!

Isaiah 41:10 - So do not fear, for I am with you; do not be dismayed, for I am your God. I will strengthen you and help you; I will uphold you with my righteous right hand.

Ironically, we often stand within a sea of people feeling completely alone and wondering why we don't feel God. Why do none of our shifts left or right put us in the ideal position of closeness to Him? I challenge you to consider that He never moved…you did. He's always been right there. He's always been right here. But it is our active steps towards the wrong things that lead us in the opposite direction of our right standing with God.

It's only one treat. It's only one lie. It's only one sip. It's only one try. Indulgence, though seemingly harmless, leads to brokenness when not controlled, when enabled, and when ignored. The shifting current of the world pulls us farther and farther away. Enemy lines creep in from every direction as our very creator and identity are attacked again and again. We are being chipped away. Our freedoms and birthrights are being questioned and condemned. We are being silenced and manipulated.

I believe there are many ways for us to approach our wholeness. We're multifaceted beings, and just because my mind, body, soul, and spirit journey led me one way, it may not be the correct roadmap for you. However, let's be clear. Although our paths are personal, diverse, and unique, there is only one path, one way to Heaven, and we cannot rely on our own logic because the serpent taints our judgment. I am confident that God does not intend for us to slither, crawl, scratch, claw, or cry our way back into goodness. Grace is abundantly free. You simply need to accept it through the person of Jesus Christ. His love is not earned; it is gifted. Ephesians 4:8 says, *"For it is by grace you have been saved through faith – and that is not from yourselves, but a gift from God."*

And while our works are not the way by which the gift is given, we still have to actively receive this gift in order to open, unwrap, use, and explore it to become anything like Jesus.

The way to life is clear – just as the disciples discovered 2000 years ago. They left their comfort zones, their homes, their families, their jobs, their satisfactions and lack thereof, to experience the gift of life and salvation. They left these things to witness miracles and define salvation through the lens of the Messiah Jesus. Matthew, a likely parallel to some of you reading this, was living a life of materialistic comfort. But, his 9 to 5 was void, heavy in fact, and felt shameful. Although he was satisfied with his privileged lifestyle, occupation, and societal clout; as a tax collector, he was hated by his fellow citizens and isolated in his discomfort. Eventually, however, he witnessed miracles and firsthand teachings that resulted in him leaving it all behind to follow Jesus.

He was brave. And I question my own bravery in comparison. Although I have chosen to follow Him, have I fully left it all behind or am I one foot in and one foot out of the boat?

Years after my son's helmet ordeal, I yearned for my own molding and shaping experience. I finally felt like I had worked my way into the light, into the shape He'd intended for me. Instead, He called me into further stillness. I struggled with the popular Christian concept to "be still." I was told that I'm a human being not a human doing and that my works do not define the magnitude of His love for me tomorrow, no matter what I do today. But in my study of Mary and Martha and my eagerness to learn to sit at His feet like Mary, I was shockingly awakened while reading the book of John *(11:17-44)*. I read that Martha ran to Jesus! She was expectant for His miracle working abilities. She knew He could raise the dead, and I immediately aligned with her heart and her desire and her eagerness and her knowing that He was a miracle worker. I believe, as did she, that we can be raised from our own deathbeds, just like Lazarus.

I know this Truth because I was dead. And if dead, the only way to "rise" and "pick up my mat and walk" is by actively moving and actively believing. By researching, I learned that to "be still" is an active pursuit of dying to oneself, letting go, and surrendering. The very next action is to "know" (Psalm 46:10). Knowledge is not stagnant. We must seek and find and knock (Matthew 7:7). We must uncover and reveal. You may figure out how to do this without exertion of your physical self; prayer and meditation come to mind. Action does not mean exhaustion, but it does require energy.

Like physical exercise, mental and spiritual activity isn't easy. You will sweat; you will be sore; you will shift; and you will change, but you will do it all for the betterment of the person you are today and the greater good of the Kingdom. You will do it for knowledge of the one who provides you restoration from the strongholds that have kept you hindered from living in abundance. Your enabling ways will be revealed, and it will spark empathy in your soul towards others who are struggling in the very same way. Your earlier pursuits will fall dormant, and your newly immersed person will develop vocations that speak to your transformation. Like the potter who presses and mends, molds and yields; like the chiropractor who practiced those same skills on my son's tiny head; we are moldable beings. We are capable of shifting and moving. And just as the Word is active, we are in pursuit of its knowledge – His knowledge. So take up your mat and walk (John 5:11).

Hebrews 4:12 - For the word of God is living and active, sharper than any two-edged sword, piercing to the division of soul and of spirit, of joints and of marrow, and discerning the thoughts and intentions of the heart.

If you have no valid example on how to move or when to move, turn to the Bible. Our Heavenly Father knows when to act and when not to act. He knows when to be still without movement and when to be still with rapid pace. Learn to rely on His motives as good and well, though highly outside of our humanistic norm. I had to develop my sense of trust. I had to practice contentment with being still. I had to be more like my sweet baby, who showed me that you don't have to be content with it to be content in it. Just as he knew we were acting in good will towards his wholeness, we need to know that God is doing the same for us.

I had to learn to stop chasing contentment, to stop worrying about what their eyes were doing and where their minds were wandering as they stared in my direction. I had to actively practice inaction in my mind. I had to "crash the chatterbox" as Steven Furtick so eloquently puts it. That concept applied to so many compartments within my head. The action, the workout that was harder than any I had ever done, was learning to exorcise my demons so they would stop exercising me. I eventually learned that most of my demons I had created myself, and if I had built them, I could break them.

So I put on a spiritual helmet of protection *(Ephesians 6:11)* and armed myself with His breastplate. Clothed in His dignity and strength, armed with His sword, I heel-toed my way to the front line as He called me into action alongside His army. So here I am...showing up to fight for you and to pass the helmet on to my fellow warriors. My son's helmet had the *Finding Nemo* scene with the shark on the front. He'd stand up on his changing table, look at himself in the mirror, and roar. A couple years later, I experienced my own mirror moment. Affirmations flowed until I began to roar. This book is intended to help you gain the strength to roar as well.

As you become, ask your heart:

What action have you been avoiding in your life?

_____

_____

What area do you need molding in?

_____

_____

What active change needs to take place for you to right your walk with the Lord?

_____

_____

What areas of armor are you missing?

_____

_____

How can you get your roar back?

_____

_____

Break the Rules

*I*t seems that when rules and boundaries are placed on our lives outside of the typical norm, we tend to get childish. Common body language responses can often be observed when a rule is set, regardless of age. These can include crossed arms and legs, huffing and puffing, deep sighs, and even curse words. This makes me think of my own kiddos (they don't cuss, thankfully), specifically my eye-rolling, "roaring" son. Yet as adults, aren't we just as guilty? The world is full of "No's," and often it doesn't seem like any of it is fair. But rules are rules, and they are meant to create order and keep us safe, even if they don't seem purposeful all the time.

People who have never had boundaries become very uncomfortable when you put them into play. Sometimes, boundaries may be health related. For example, you can no longer have white grain or artificial sugar. It may be that you can't have a glass of wine every night with dinner or that snacking isn't allowed after a certain hour of the evening. These are body and nutritionally related boundaries, and often people will get over them and recognize the truth in their purpose.

Recently, a new movie surfaced in our house called *Yes Day*. Jennifer Garner, one of my favorite sweet cheeked, dimpled actresses, brought to life the daily comedies of parenthood. As mamas, we have to say "no" a lot. We have a responsibility to make sure they don't get hurt or discombobulated too early and that the world doesn't define their truths before we do. My kids can't wait until we put this day into action. In fact, it's already on the calendar. I'm sure the next book will share all of its researched findings, but for now, I'll sit back and let the movie do the lesson giving... Too many sweets create bellyaches; too much freedom creates confusion; and too many yeses equate to chaos. So even without having our own "Yes Day," my kiddos got a sense of the inevitable outcomes. Regardless, I said yes to the idea and why the heck not? I'm a fun mom.

But what about the boundaries of the heart? What if you can no longer spend time with someone that you used to see every day? What if the boundary means you can't go to a certain place anymore or stay out past a certain hour? These types of boundaries might sound strict. They might even seem absurd and juvenile to the person being affected by the rule. Often that person just doesn't understand the full scenario, and they don't always need to. Or, perhaps they don't have any personal boundaries in place and therefore can't wrap their minds around why you would need them either. Needless to say, boundaries for boundaryless people don't make sense. But, if it's necessary for your well-being, it shouldn't matter who it upsets. The important part is that it sets you up for happiness and success and falls in line with obedience.

The reality for me was that in parenting my own children, my own self-reparenting and my marriage, I had to set boundaries. I needed boundaries that would keep my relationships intact, my health well, and my happiness in check. Again, becoming isn't all glitz and glam. Boundary examples for me include: no alone time with the opposite sex, no extended music listening outside of worship, no movies that entail graphic sexual content, no cursing, and currently, no alcohol. I'm not a prude. I promise. I like to have fun. I do have fun, and my hubby is usually in on the scenario to make it double the fun. I just do so now with practiced self-control.

Boundaries always have exceptions. Sometimes the rules just don't have a meaningful purpose or are being set outside of your belief system. Instead of getting angry, disheartened, or apathetic – why not change it? Be a rule breaker, in the best sense. Take a stand for the purpose and the depth behind it, not because your feelings were hurt. Take a stand because it will create a ripple effect of change. But only do this after digging deeper into the why's, how's, and when's of the issue. Don't blurt out, "that's not fair," and stomp your feet unless you have a solution to share. Listen more than you speak; it teaches patience and keeps you learning. Take a loss as a learning tool; it doesn't make you a loser. It makes you a warrior.

Let me emphasize, however, that boundaries and rules are different. Rules are general guidelines, while boundaries are generally personal. Do commit to memory that when it comes to someone else's boundaries, they aren't rules to be broken. They are requests to be respected. Know the difference.

The latest trend in the fitness world is one that my husband has come to love and teach me about. It's called Gold Medal Bodies (GMB) or what I like to explain as Gymnastics, Mobility & Balance. Obviously, the gymnastics component caught my fancy from the beginning. The mobility component initially had me thinking of vinyasa yoga, which wasn't too far off course. And, as balance beam was always my favorite event, I gave a big check mark pretty quickly to the balance component. But as his workout experience evolved and he came home daily showing me new moves and sharing new ideas of what our body is capable of, I got more intrigued by the movement.

I loved the intention and purpose of the entire genre to not become a "fit-nobot" but instead to develop your body to become a useful, strong, and flexible tool that will assist you throughout your entire life, not just during your younger years of peak performance. This focus on the longevity of your muscles and capabilities so that your body doesn't become frail and immobile as you age, while preserving full range of motion and comfort-ability with strength, is laudable. Imagine waking up every day, even into your 60s, 70s, and 80s feeling prepared and able to do the things you love without risk of hurting yourself or dealing with the aches and pains of a deteriorating body.

The most enticing element of this style of workout is the focus on incorporating fun and play. Some days the chalkboard posted workout isn't about a rep count or a sweat fest but instead is about trying something new, getting a good laugh out of it, and connecting with one another using fundamental components of play. On these days the workout instructions may include: Toss a ball back and forth; Balance this way or that; Hula-hoop like this and climb that. It purposely removes the intensity of push and pull and reverts back to the child-like play of a ball and balance. Everything in fitness (and life) isn't intended to be strict and regimented. Rules and boundaries aren't intended to negatively confine but to protect. And we have the opportunity to say yes to the practice of self-control in the midst of play.

We have the power through our body's performance to set rules and boundaries that make movement possible. The boundaries of our physical body can grow stricter and more confining each birthday, or we can practice fitness in this way, release ourselves from those chains, and break free from the norm.

Don't we want that same performance level in our mental abilities? Don't you want to be mentally fit and to have a sound mind no matter what age? I know I do. I believe we begin this mental process the same way we would begin the physical one – break the rules that society has set as status quo. In this case we are not breaking the personal boundaries of others. It's not personal at all. Respect the person. Question the masses.

People also view religion from this same perspective of rules and boundaries (what's fair and what's not). This can result in highly charged and negative emotional reactions to pre-conceived religious boundaries. Too many people don't have enough insight to move their faith past the man-made rules, the rules of the masses. Maybe you grew up in a certain strict denomination. You may have had to wear a dress, kneel when you prayed, and only sing to the Lord from a hymnbook. I want you to know that I have never been more free to break those rules, and I want you to find the same freedom. This is not freedom to create chaos or to diminish others in their faith. It is instead the freedom to feel empowered and remind others that our purpose isn't to follow man-made rules and experience a streamlined version of life – God has called us to so much more. In fact, the religious were exactly who Jesus recommended we not emulate. We were instructed to not be like the hypocrites who practiced their righteousness in public and prayed so as to be seen by others. Instead we were to do these things privately where our Father in Heaven would see and reward.

This change in perspective has had such a monumental impact on me and has become a shared vision with close friends who are also pastors. Our desire was to spread this perspective, this freedom, within our community by starting our own church. "The Session" was born out of a desire to meet people where they are, to help break down religious rules and boundaries, and to embrace the heart-level connections desired by The Father. We longed for others to get past the Old Testament fear factor and mindset and move into their blessings and callings with a true understanding of God and their relationship with Jesus Christ.

I feel God isn't calling us to compare what's fair and unfair. He isn't even calling us to be rule followers. Yes, His commandments have great weight and great purpose, but they don't shackle us, and they aren't impossible. It depends on how you are living your life.

There are different zones of living. We can live in the comfort zone, the panic zone, or the ideal state of the learning zone. I've moved my faith through all of these zones during my life. I've existed in the relative comfort of "I'm a Christian" and "I'm a rule follower." And I've survived the disaster and devastation of the panic zone where I felt that I couldn't keep it together any longer. It was a time of heartbreak and even the "Is God real?" questions. And now, I'm in the learning zone where I hope to remain Always – Becoming. It's the zone where I get to experience the joy of diving deeper into the "Who am I? Who is He? Why does He love me? How wide does He love me?" questions. I'm ready to teach people how to live in this zone with their own faith and I am empowered to do so because I've experienced all of the zones and felt all of the "that's not fairs" of life as well. I don't need Jesus to be a "yes man" either. His convictions keep me safe, secure, within right standing, and confident.

If you are living your life feeling or believing that "life isn't fair" or there are too many rules and boundaries, you are probably in the panic zone or in a very frail state of comfort. Boundaries are safe borders, safe parameters that keep you under His protection. Start listening and start learning. Start playing and having fun in the gift that is a Christ-centered relationship and understanding of Christianity. And stop battling the concept of losing or getting hurt. Instead, change your perspective on what a loss really is and more importantly on the opportunity that arises after you lose. If it's "not fair," ask yourself, "why?" and figure out what you can do to change it. Do it not just for you but for the ones you love. You won't be sorry. And you'll learn in the end that flexibility takes mobility and movement. Your body has natural boundaries; don't set more for yourself than God intended.

As you become, ask your heart:

What limiting beliefs (lies) are keeping you in bondage?

_____

_____

What rules do you live by that are self-driven and not God driven?

_____

_____

What burdens can you let go of today?

_____

_____

What keeps you in bondage from living free in Christ?

_____

_____

What ways can you experience freedom in Christ?

_____

_____

Pressing In

*G*etting your body to shift its physical form is not an easy, tranquil experience. The challenge is part of the thrill, but you have to be up for it. You have to be prepared mentally and physically to get fit. You have to define your goals and stick to them, day in and day out. You have to fight past the soreness, past the fatigue, past the kitchen calling, past the cravings, past the Netflix bingers, and past the scales and measurements. If it were easy, everyone would do it.

Challenges are what change us. They can make or break us as humans. But there is an additional angle on challenge that I think we should start applying to our health – the pressing process. As we challenge ourselves to obtain and maintain the state of being wholly fit, we press into God in the process.

While I was going through my evolution of mental fitness with my counselors and life coach, I requested for months, through prayer, for God to SHOW ME. I read a book, *The Circle Maker* by Mike Batterson, which stated that I could and should ask God for what I actually want, and that is exactly what I wanted during that season of unknown. I wanted certainty. I wanted reassurance. I wanted a sense of relief that I hadn't quit my previous life and changed my entire path for what felt like emptiness and void. Now my salvation surely isn't nothing, but sometimes on this side of Heaven we can't sense that completion and wholeness. So we are left in doubt, fear, and impatience, at least in the beginning of the pressing process.

Yes, it is true that the future is unknown. If we knew it fully, then why would we need to have faith? Why would we need to trust in God? But eventually, after months of prayer, He showed me. Perhaps you have never been prophesied over or had a God-given vision. But boy, oh boy, I would encourage you to pray for one. Just pray for it! And no, it wasn't given after one prayer request. It took months, but finally it was presented to me, right before my very eyes.

I had been learning through my worship school about the 5-fold ministry. Ephesians 4:11-16 teaches us about the five ways we are equipped within the Kingdom as followers of Jesus. They include, Apostle, Prophet, Pastor, Teacher, and Evangelist. During this time, the gift of prophecy really intrigued me. I was staying up late watching YouTube videos, listening to podcasts, and reading books. And once again during this process of seeking and finding and pressing, I felt perplexed but not in despair.

Within a short time span, God gifted me with several different prophetic experiences. One, which I shared earlier, literally knocked me off my feet. Another was with a stranger who spoke life over areas of destruction that I had yet to ever share with another human, outside of my counseling sessions and my husband. She told me I would speak into young women who had been afflicted by sexual intimacy traumas. She was literally reading my mail. The third experience involved a person who had never met my family. This man laid hands on my husband and me as he prophesied over us and our children. He breathed supernatural affirmation and clarity into the very core of our family, the core that had been jolted and shaken. This occurred not just in the abstract sense but also in the very detailed pieces of each of our spirits. He spoke directly into my son's passion for dancing. He spoke into my daughter's calm spirit. He circled our marriage and the impact we'd make because of the pressing we had experienced. These God encounters will forever be milestones in my faith. They were where I stepped out, where I had more faith than doubt, where I had been hard pressed by God. I needed more from him, and He knew it. But during that time, I stayed planted in Him, in worship, in biblical teachings, and in people who were walking with Him closely.

These experiences, these truths and memories, may feel impossible to you. They may seem like made-up concepts or fairy tales. But I'm documenting them here as proof of what's to come. I hold them close to my heart as trinkets from Heaven, all the while believing that every single experience that the darkness claimed will be reclaimed by the King of Kings, and all things will be used for good. Who knows when it will unfold? Perhaps it's already happening, or maybe it won't come to fruition until my life is fully lived. But the purpose of sharing this with you isn't to give you a table of contents for what my life will look like. The purpose is to challenge you to press into God and recognize that the pressing that happens in the process is not meant to destroy you but instead is meant to bring you strength and life.

2 Corinthians 3: 7-12 - 7 But we have this treasure in jars of clay to show that this all-surpassing power is from God and not from us. 8 We are hard pressed on every side, but not crushed; perplexed, but not in despair; 9 persecuted, but not abandoned; struck down, but not destroyed. 10 We always carry around in our body the death of Jesus, so that the life of Jesus may also be revealed in our body. 11 For we who are alive are always being given over to death for Jesus' sake, so that his life may also be revealed in our mortal body. 12 So then, death is at work in us, but life is at work in you.

Don't press into Him out of doubt; doubt is ever-present as proven time and time again by Jesus's closest companions. One of the disciples was even called Doubting Thomas for a reason. Instead, press into Him out of 100% faith and belief. And if there is a shadow of doubt, but you remain diligent, I believe He will cast out the doubt as He did with me…in an instant…time and time again.

Just as our bodies are capable of the seemingly impossible movements of yogis, gymnasts, and contortionists, our mind is equally as capable. And so is He. After all, He is a miracle worker.

Maybe you've been praying for your miracle for decades and these seemingly quick responses from Heaven feel like a slap in the face to your anxious prayers… I want to reassure you, to God, time does not exist. A million years ago was yesterday and tomorrow is just another page in God's scripted book. He's already written it. It's already been done. He does hear you! The answers to your prayers for a trial you are enduring or a request you have made for your future husband, perfect child, new job, new house, or new financial situation – aren't a matter of how or if. They are a matter of when. God is never early and He is never late. His timing is perfect. He ALWAYS provides. He ALWAYS fulfills. He will not leave you empty handed or broken. Reach out. Reach up. Stand up. Stand out. Prepare yourself for the blessing, and it will come through the process of pressing in.

I'm reminded of Hannah who prayed year after year for a child. She went to the house of the Lord asking, pleading, and weeping in sorrow over her barren womb. She sat in envy and bitterness as the other wives bore children and provoked her into greater despair. Her husband adored her, but even in his kindness she didn't sense the Lord's favor over her prayers. Eventually, she pressed in more deeply than ever before and prayed a prayer that included a promise. She would gift her son back to the Lord if only He would hear her request. Soon after, Samuel was born and named after the Hebrew word "heard by God." In her continued submission and obedience in gifting the child back to the Lord, Hannah had five more children. And her first-born became a prophet of the Lord. He would anoint Saul to be King and later David, who we know is in the lineage of Jesus himself *(Samuel 1 & 2)*. Her blessings became more than she had asked or hoped for.

Use Hannah as your example. Pray like the prayer is answered. Hope like it's already been given. Seek and press into what feels like a challenge in order for God to change your heart because He first changes your mind.

Ever since the various prophetic words were given to me, I've still wondered. I've still had moments of confusion and doubt. I'm not perfect. It wasn't like He wrote out a to-do list or action plan to accomplish any of those things. That part is up to me. We all have free will. My goal is to glorify Him. My goal is to close my eyes and remember the gifts, remember the answered prayers, and remember His presence with the deep knowing that He has never left me, even in the dark. He is constant.

So, when the enemy comes to combat my truth (which is often), I say...not today; I've got work to do to make my Father proud! But, I don't want it to sound easy or effortless. Every day is a challenge. Every day I am faced with reasons I could stop trusting. Every day I see brokenness and hurt around me and sometimes within me. But I now know that I am up for the challenge, and just like Dory from *Finding Nemo*, I just keep swimming.

The challenge in getting fit comes with faith. I get it. Some days it hurts. Some days you are so sore you can't even pick up your kiddos or squat over the toilet. Soreness, like the pains of failure and thoughts of doubt, can be slow to go away. Don't give up. Soreness is good. The initial soreness you experience, just like

Hannah's sore spirit, shows that you put in the effort, you put in the time, you pressed on towards the goal. The delayed onset muscle soreness is an important sign that your intensity level was high enough that you tore your muscles in small amounts. Don't worry; that tearing will lead to positive re-growth of the muscle. I think that's a beautiful representation of the breaking down of our mental state in order to rebuild to the desired state of "fit." The becoming process isn't always pleasing, but it is pressing, and the pressing leads to promise. Have faith that the aches of your soreness will be the fruits of your labor.

As you become, ask your heart:

What pressing in have you been doing with God?

_____

_____

_____

_____

What area have you been ignoring because you feel like it's challenging God?

_____

_____

_____

What if you flip the script and press in despite the pain? Remember, pressing leads to promise.

_____

_____

_____

_____

Fit Tribe

*Y*ou are who you surround yourself with. I remember hearing this as a pre-teen from my parents and teachers. Your friends rub off on you. It's a fact of life. The social realm is a driving force of influence both cognitively and non-cognitively. Unknowingly, we pick up habits, mimic body language, and eventually even goals.

Establishing a group of like-minded individuals who will push you to reach your greatness in all realms will be a make-or-break piece to your success. The recently coined name "fit tribe" wholly captures the intention for success. You want a tribe of people around you who are working towards similar fit, healthy goals for mind, body, soul and spirit.

Accountability is everything. You need people who encourage you, build you up, teach you in moments of confusion, and will be with you when you don't hit the mark. You need people who love you and want what is best for you. If you grant them access to your vision and goals, you can partner with them to help ensure your success; they aren't going to watch you fall without picking you up. They will be your Aarons and Hurs when your arms are tired *(Exodus 17:12).*

After my Young Life school ministry crisis, I struggled for quite a while in the area of loving others and letting others get close to me. At that time I thought that one of my strengths was in establishing friendships, all relationships really, until I realized that one of the deepest relationships I held (with myself) was a fallacy. For a little over a year, I turned away from most people and focused on the inside. I was growing to like myself, to read myself, to know myself, and then from there I was evolving to love myself. It was when I learned how God viewed me – how God loves me – and how God deeply knows and understands me – that I was finally able to embrace loving me, regardless of my shortcomings.

However, when I turned inward, I neglected the outward. I went from having a phone book with an expansive "favorites" list to one with a few reliable people. I know quality over quantity is something you learn with wisdom and life changes; phonebooks inevitably dwindle with age, but I felt a sense of regret that I wasn't other people's "favorite" call. I learned that so much of my identity and concept of love was rooted in what other people thought of me. If I were a "perfect-fun" friend then they would love me, and I would feel loved. But love is so much deeper than how they viewed me or even how they felt towards me. Love starts at a heart level of knowing what love is and loving yourself. God is love.

In comfort I gravitated toward the exterior validation of a fit tribe, focused on health. There are many different groups, just like there are different circles of friends. How you define yourself, what you are looking to accomplish, and your health-value system are some areas of identity that tribes will prescribe to. Perhaps you are in a vegan-runners tribe or a stay-at-home-mom-Whole-30-tribe or a work-from-home-dad-body-building tribe. The list goes on. The tribes are endless. But this concept of like-mindedness started to dwindle for me. It felt surface and I had done too much deep to stay surface level. I didn't want to be in a room with a bunch of people who looked like me and thought like me. After all, becoming was growing, and growing was learning, and therefore I valued the like-heart above the like-mind. Until, of course, I was checked by the Word. I soon discovered the critical importance that God had placed, yet again, on the strength of our mind.

> *Philippians 2:1-3 – Therefore if you have any encouragement in Christ, if any comfort from His love, if any fellowship with the Spirit, if any affection and compassion, then make my joy complete by being like-minded, having the same love, being united in spirit and purpose. Do nothing out of selfish ambition of empty pride, but in humility consider others more important than yourselves...*

Regardless of my mind, at this point my heart was still broken, and if it is true that hurt people hurt people, this time of isolation was critical for my healing and ultimately for the friends I now call family.

Without recognizing and being aware of your own identity, you will never be able to choose the tribe that suits you. But I don't think it's a one and done situation. You may join a tribe for one season, grow into another tribe for a different season, and perhaps even dabble in a few all at once. We each have varying components to our personality, and sometimes our goals are not fully aligned with one group like they may be with another. My suggestion here is to start with what matters most: the health pursuit and alignment desire of the heart.

I think we are all members of tribes without realizing it. Your family is a tribe, although it's not one you get to necessarily pick. Your work friends are a tribe. Your weekend friends are a tribe. I even think there are larger tribes like your generational tribe and your heritage tribe.

I would encourage you to find a connection. Find a place in the conversation, between the lines, where you can relate. Maybe my story isn't up your alley. Maybe my words don't resonate with you. But I believe one of the truest forms of self-awareness comes in the ability to connect with another human being on a heart level. We are meant to be in connection with one another. Our lives don't exist in a vacuum. We co-exist with purpose toward our greater identity as children of God. And while there are cycles and seasons, I truly believe there are times when people will come and go, in and out of our life, with reason and purpose. I think we create vibes that attract different people at different stages of our growth. Our very spirits are sensitive to the spirits of others because God connects us with purpose to serve one another. For example, I wasn't connecting with new moms when I was in my college years, and I'm presently not going out to bars to meet new friends like I was in my early twenties. There's nothing wrong with this ebb and flow of life. But it is important that we recognize its greater purpose rather than just exist.

In this new era of simplicity that I have discovered and evolved into, I am being enriched by a community that has a depth I have never experienced before. This is due to their pursuit of health and a Holy Spirit connection.

Community is, at its truest sense of the definition, when there is communion and true unity. This doesn't have to mean the neighborhood you live in or the city your house is in. I would challenge you to change your perspective on who you are in community with. Ask yourself who is your tribe? It starts with your closest loved ones, those in your home, and expands outward to include those in your extended family, your friends, your church, your work environment, your hobbies, and your hangouts. We are all designed with the desire to be in communion with one another. It's called covenant community – it's God's intention. His purpose is for us to sharpen one another as we become more like Him.

Proverbs 27:17 – As iron sharpens iron, so will one person sharpen another.

Now a huge component of coming into community with others and joining like-hearted and like-minded tribes is the concept of comparison. From the early ages of childhood, we are unknowingly fashioned to compare. We may use comparison as a way to measure our own self-value as we compare our abilities or accomplishments with the abilities or accomplishments of others. Are we faster, smarter, more creative, taller, shorter, or more talented…and the list continues. It's how you win competitions even as an adult. But the comparison game in a tribe, a tribe that is intended to encourage and lift one another up, can be detrimental to success. Community over competition parallels to communion over conflict. We are uniquely designed with great purpose. Similar to the 5-fold ministry gifts that were discussed earlier, your unique gifts have purpose to the body. And just as a body is formed and fashioned using different parts, your role or part in the performance of the body is critical. If you are the foot, you can't be the hand. If you are the hip, you can't be the shoulder *(1 Corinthians 12:27)*.

The Instagram game is so often mislabeled by people who have problems comparing their squares to other people's highlight reels. These are moments in time, captured by a camera. A still shot. If we got to see the live views or the 173 images that were taken before and after getting that perfect, filtered composite, the relatability would be so much higher. We need to not compare. Our purpose isn't to live a life of fake or even pure individuality. Our purpose is to be in one accord – to encourage one another – to spur one another on into our true destinies of purpose as the champions that we are.

> *Hebrews 10:24 –* [24] *And let us consider how we may spur one another on toward love and good deeds,* [25] *not giving up meeting together, as some are in the habit of doing, but encouraging one another—and all the more as you see the Day approaching.*

I have had many seasons where I have felt alone, seasons where I felt as though no one knew me or could understand me. In fact, my feelings were entirely validated when I realized that no one did know me because I didn't know myself. If you aren't honest with yourself, how can you create true relationships? And a relationship based on false premises or surface level concepts has no roots. These kinds of relationships will come and go and leave you in a cyclical pattern of being lonely.

When I began to peel back the onion of my own "who" and get authentic with my own metaphorical stench, the tears began to dry up, and I actually liked the flavor that was mine. So instead of masking my humanity, I started to show people the real me in transparency and vulnerability. I was pleasantly surprised by the response and the immediate connections that were formed. I didn't have to have a hard shell or be the cool kid or the strong mom. I didn't have to be the CEO or the party planner. I got to just rest in the identity of being a daughter.

My new tribe, a raw, real community, was unlike anything I had ever experienced. We cried together, typical response to an onion, I know, but I mean like really cried and comforted each other. I got to a point where sharing my heart with others became such a freeing space of release that I could no longer stomach the mask I had figuratively worn in public for so long.

I started to share the places and pieces of my heart that I had always concealed. And the more my therapists and coach brought these things out into the light of my own awareness, the more honest I became, to the point that a lie, even a little white one, would physically pain me. That may not make sense to everyone... what's a little white lie anyway? Don't they protect feelings? Don't they help ease situations? Don't they provide social coating for strangers and conversations about politics or faith? That may be true for a surface companion who doesn't want to hear the truth, but starting from the ground up with my friendship circle, I didn't want to create that instability ever again. I wanted friendships that lasted the test of time. I wanted to be an Aaron and/or Hur for my friends and knew I'd need that same faithful support in my weaknesses as well.

Before I go any further, and in order to keep you from lighting fires on your way into new relationships, I feel the need to give you a couple of pointers on avoiding common stumbling blocks. Don't go out and air your dirty laundry. People love honesty, not pity parties. Don't be untactful in your words. Be honest, but not at someone else's expense. And I want to shout this one from the rafters – honesty and gossip are not synonymous! I used to be that person, not intentionally mean, that's not in my nature at all, but just talking about others for the sake of conversation. It's destroying. There is nothing beneficial about that process unless of course you are coming up with a solution to someone else's situation. Good news travels fast, they say, and bad news travels faster. I would hate for my honest conversations to be passed along to people who I didn't entrust with the information.

So, recognize the importance of the tribe you choose. They aren't just there as sounding boards; they are there as supporting planks to your purposed path. And their resiliency and steadfast spirits are critical to your sustainability within the friendship.

This brings me to the concept of the inner circle. Your inner circle is a very special kind of tribe, and it should only be so big. I think a safe number is five. I chose that number mainly because of Jim

Rohn's quote, "You are the average of the five people you spend the most time with." Of course your spouse is strategically and importantly included here. And, I must emphasize again that you don't share everything with everyone. There are levels of access to your heart and personhood. Your next level may have 10 – this is a safe place for your children. And eventually your greatest outer circle will be the sphere of influence you may have on others. Those in this circle usually don't have direct access to you.

Jesus, too, had an inner circle of confidants, like His mother Mary and cousin John the Baptist who knew depths to His calling that the others had yet to understand. And then He had layered access to His heart of hearts thereafter with his disciples of 12. These disciples had special access to His thoughts and to His heart. He also had a larger circle of followers. This group included both men and women. And then there were the masses. This group included his critics, and their words weren't what He stood on.

Just as Jesus exposed deep truths only to his close inner circle, you surely don't share things with your siblings or friends that you share with your spouse. And even your children should have a level of protection from every emotion and life situation. But, no matter whom you are interacting with, honesty, as the saying goes, is the best policy. There is no chasing your tail in circles when the only thing that is coming out of your mouth is the truth. Your mind can rest when you have no untruths to plan or work around. Out of your mouth your heart speaks (Luke 6:45). Stay aligned my friends and don't let comparison traps or death traps like gossip skew your heart.

Your tribe is so crucial to your mental health, which is in line with your heart health. I believe when those are aligned your purpose is ignited. I also believe your tribe is intended to help discover and unleash the passions that lay within your purpose. If the people surrounding you aren't pulling out these positives, it's time to reconsider your circle.

You may have heard the saying "You are what you attract." So be sure you take an inventory of yourself before you start pointing fingers at those you consider friends. And begin to recognize their placement and purpose, whether seasonal or forever. As I came into my self-awareness, I became mindful of the "who" in my inner circle and had to make some swift changes in order to stay aligned with God's purpose and calling on my life. I became so passionate about the people I took as company and friends, that it later revealed itself as a part of my calling. Just as Jesus exemplified in his inner circle, it wasn't about their past, their profession, their class, their financial abundance, or physical strength; it was about the heart set of the men who were eager to grow and learn alongside Him.

The masses, too, were attracted to His vibrancy. I believe as we step into our wholeness, bit by bit, our light becomes brighter. And the more we become, the more our influence will grow. With a pure heart set to disciple and introduce others to the light that is within us and that connects us all, we will serve our God in humility and gratefulness as we impact the world around us.

Realizing the true gift that it is, I poured so much of myself into authentic connection during this season. Nothing is better than eye contact and real conversation that leaves you released from negative emotion, while inspiring and replenishing your heart and mind with positivity. I eagerly desire this for others. I want everyone to have a sense of safety and love within their cultivated relationships, where there is a genuine pouring in without expectation of receipt, a spurring in truth and encouragement, and a sharpening and propelling of one another with whole-hearted intent.

Look inward at the heart level before choosing your community by their exterior, just as God instructed Samuel to not to look at the height or stature of a man, but to instead look at his heart *(1 Samuel 16:7).* Find the tribe that motivates you and encourages you in your purpose and passions.

As you become, ask your heart:

Who are you letting into your realm of influence and/
or inner circle?

_____

_____

_____

Do they challenge you in all the right ways?

_____

_____

_____

Are you able to be honest with one another?

_____

_____

_____

Are you encouraging each other towards being the
best version of yourselves?

_____

_____

_____

Flexibility

We had just spent "framily" time with our loved ones (friends who are family = fit tribe) and were traveling the backcountry roads that lead from one city to another. The sun was disappearing behind the trees and illuminating the sky into a magical array of colors. My husband and I often put our kiddos into calm, quiet situations to unpack the beauty of God's gifts. We have even done this with the delicacy and intricacies of our own eyes. We'll make eye contact long enough to not just respond with, "her eyes are blue," but instead to slowly dissect speckles of yellow, nodes of green, black starbursts, and fine grey lines that mold together into a light blue color. Only God.

Anyhow, in this moment we weren't asking anything of them. We were simply listening to a worship song as the hot summer day came to a close and we neared "late o-clock." This is bedtime in our household, a fluctuating time in fact, solely based on the exhaustion level of Mama and Dada. Safe to say, on this day, it would have been before full sunset ensued.

My 5-year-old (at the time) is reflective and fully aware of her surroundings at every given minute while in the car. She's actually better at directional awareness than I am. As we drove that early evening she asked, "What color is God?" I smiled and flipped my driver seat eyes from the road to the rearview mirror to look at her inquisitive, freckled-nose face as she gazed at the horizon. She was truly asking. But, instead of answering or conjuring up a response immediately, I let her simmer within the moment as all of us pondered His reflection in the sunset of Starburst colors (be on the lookout for more starbursts to come).

Since our dating days, my hubby has practiced and preached, "Try to always answer a question with a question." It's an amazing sales tactic, but more than that, it's an incredible opportunity to dive deeper into the psyche of your conversational partner. It also puts them in the hot seat, instead of you, while giving them the often more comfortable state of talking rather than listening. And while I often forget, because (raise hand emoji) talker over here, I quickly recognized that this moment was the perfect opportunity to showcase my listening skills.

"What color do you think He is?" I asked her angel face. "The rainbow. I think He's all colors," she responded. My mind was flashing through the many stories I had heard of people meeting Jesus on their deathbed, the movie scenes where God appears, and even the burning bush encountered by Moses in the Old Testament. From the crystal blue oceans of the world, to the whitest snow blanketed trails of Big Bear Lake in California, and the harvest pumpkin spices of the Shenandoah Valley via hot air balloon, I've been surrounded by Him in every color. So I appreciatively told her, "You're absolutely right."

Our perspectives differ. Our understandings are often simply based on our exposure, which we'll soon unpack. But we have a choice between rigidity and flexibility, a choice, which can lead us to a series of questions:

1. Where did this idea come from?
2. Why is this my understanding or methodology personally and Biblically?
3. Is there a plausible opposing view?

4. How can I adjust or expand my understanding of this concept?
5. What do I believe?

Truly unpacking ideas in our mental, physical, and spiritual beings is no different. One doctor may present one idea; one teacher or trainer may present another. We may perceive The Word based on how we read it today versus the way the Pastor unpacks it on Sunday. Ultimately, it's less about right vs. wrong and more about your openness and flexibility. The more fluidity you have in your journey, even directly correlated to mind and body, the more freedom you will have to discover and embrace what truly matters.

Our family could have stood divided in that moment, arguing over each person's belief or story line of what color He is, but instead, we let it be and rested in the amazing possibility that He is all colors because He is in all things as the creator of all things. How unknowing this little soul was as she spoke wisdom into the worldwide conversations happening around race at that very moment in time. This is not a political book; I am not a political person. But I am human. And I do believe it is through conversations like this one that strongholds can be broken and generational curses can change – for the betterment of the human race. I believe God imparts wisdom deeply into His children, and her innocent question and answer will forever touch my life. I desire to not only see through her child-eyes, but to respond with my husband's interested, present, open mind and heart.

Speaking of his open mind, we're about to take a big turn here. So hold on. When we first moved in together, another before wedlock decision (ugh, God give me the wisdom to preach what I didn't practice for my children one day), he and our all male roommates traveled up to a Redskins game. My mom and I strategically chose that weekend as our moving weekend. We knew we'd have full reign to deep clean and fully redesign their barren bachelor pad. Not only did we refurnish and hang curtains, we also painted the boring white walls in lovely bold hues of Starburst orange, red and yellow. When he returned, he was in shock, and though he'd never hurt a fly or my feelings, years later he shared his distaste for it. He never let on in the moment though. Talk about flexibility… for years his sweet soul rolled with the punches. I insisted on black furniture even though he wanted white. I painted bold while he wanted subtle. We should have taken this as a note to our differences, but we still swore up and down that we were more alike than not. Either way, here we are. And I totally attribute that win to his flexibility. I tend to stand more on the "stubborn as an ox" side of the fence.

Fortunately, as years passed and Jesus began to soften my heart, I realized the things I wanted to be in control of so desperately, like wall color, truly didn't matter at all. The more flexible I became, the more I minimized control and tangible stuff, the more my talking became questions, and the more my life became representative of the sunset rather than the Starburst explosion of our first home.

The fact that I can make the reference I'm about to, may make some cringe. Believe me, it makes me a bit uneasy, too, but it works, and it was literally walked out in my life, step by step. Today's fitness facilities are no different than today's churches.

You try a few out. You establish what you like and what you don't like. You connect to a brand and an atmosphere, perhaps even a people group. You focus on what your personal gain factor will be. And you show up from time to time to put in the work, to hopefully see results, and to live a certain lifestyle connected to a community of other like-minded, like-hearted individuals. We often believe other spaces couldn't possibly suit us or meet us in the same way and that the culture is equally as important to our fit within that space as it is for us to fit-in. If rejected or walking out of flow with their intention, format, or course, we are then on the outskirts of "belonging."

Gyms have styles: CrossFit, HITT, boxing, traditional, women's, barre, Pilates, yoga, spin, etc. Churches, no differently, have denominations, and even within denominations there are variables such as personality and understanding or revelation of the Bible represented. Is one wrong and one right? What if we became more flexible within this variety? This doesn't mean that we are indecisive or wavering in our principles but instead that we are open minded to new ideas or views that may fall outside the generally approved and boxed understanding of beliefs.

In Jesus's day, the Pharisees followed a boxed ideology and rigid laws, and instead of examining and asking questions, their judgment became their blinders. If someone wasn't wearing the right wardrobe or existing in the right hierarchy of class, they were belittled. On the contrary, Jesus walked the streets with everyone and extended an open invitation for questions and answers and for listening and speaking. And yet, still today, churches find their groove in their comfort zone. They are no different than gyms, lacking a depth of modalities and without full exposure or variety. Just as God is every color, wouldn't that then mean that our exposure to every color is critical to our grasping His identity and full beauty?

When we eventually stepped foot in the rooted Pentecostal, newly deemed non-denominational, church with 14 different nationalities represented and this "Holy Spirit" we had never been exposed to, we were shaken to the core. We felt like we had been living a constricted view of what faith, worship, and church community should look like. We were embraced with wide-open arms and treated like family immediately. I could count on one hand how many strangers hugged me at our previous "home" church. A veil had been lifted, and we were shown more colors of Jesus!

Two years later, after witnessing the Holy Spirit move in relationships and in that house and also after embedding vision into our hearts in a new way, we left what was growing to be comfortable to pursue something more out of the box – an actual home church. We met in our very own living room, the same living room where I sat naked and afraid (figuratively speaking) a few years prior, waiting for my storm to pass and decluttering that which had taken my inner self hostage.

In this season of breaking the mold of "church," we experienced fresh awakening as believers all over again. We felt revival in a new way as God took us deeper into the word, into our calling, and into these flourishing relationships. This season changed again when normalcy set in. There were expectations. There were common patterns and practices, and as a leadership team, we felt urged by God to keep moving.

You may hear people mention a plateau that occurs in their health or physical journeys. This is the state in which, despite constant movement, your body becomes so familiar with the moves (food choice, exercise, meal patterns, etc.) that you seem to be at a standstill. This state can then make you feel complacent, even in your positive momentum. A plateau is not a peak. It's a flat line. And even as you move forward, you can feel no energy, upward or downward and no shift in weight, positive or negative. Your goals feel more out of reach than ever before because everything you are doing that used to work, no longer causes change.

I believe the American church has been at a plateau for far too long. It is doing what it feels is necessary, the bare minimum to maintain, and it is not in heavy pursuit of change, even when change is happening all around it. But the Covid-19 pandemic shook the church to shape-shift, to change, for the first time in decades. Gathering looked different. Worship looked different. Attendance and tithing, messages and miracles looked different. The plateaus plummeted and a new question emerged. "How do we show up as the church now?"

If we circle back to the questions previously probed, what would our answers look like through the lens of our church home? Now don't get me wrong. Is it OK to find a groove or a pocket to sit in that really works for you? Absolutely. But our God, even in His steadfast nature, is always on the move. He is not static. Like the ever-running streams and the evolution of ever-changing sunsets, God's movement is organic and intentional. His streams are pathways to life, and His nighttime paintings provide a fresh perspective of His glory and creativity. What if we tried to capture the sunset and planned for it to be the same each day? Nothing about today is the same as yesterday. No matter how routine you get, the people around you are in need of more. Flexibility leads to fruition.

And so we are called to activate out of flexibility, ebbing and flowing with the needs of our mental, physical, and spiritual selves and ultimately leaning into the living Word of God. If something is living, it is breathing and therefore there should always be flexibility for growth and revelation. Even as our home church evolved, what we had planned for it was still limited by our boxed understanding of what "home church" ought to look like. But if WE are the church, shouldn't church take place in our homes night and day? Clearly, no box confines Him. No one gym can do it all. And therefore, the exploration and recognition of all the hues of His presence ultimately reside in our ability to be flexible, flexible to where He shows up, flexible to how we steward what He's given us.

So, do we choose to decide on one understanding, a one size fits all, super-size me, planet way of living, or do we diverge; do we divide? And while we often think that division is bad, aren't we meant to be a peculiar people *(1 Peter 2:9)*, a people that stand out from the crowd, a people called to live fit, not just in body or mind but in our faith? What if the division and calling of our peculiarity led by His will is what leads to our salvation? Are we flexible enough to step out of the boxes of normalcy, complacency, and plateaus in order to pursue the thing He told us to from the beginning?

We're standing before door A and door B. If we choose nothing, if we stand in front of the two doors long enough, we plateau; we get comfortable with standing outside. I don't believe Jesus ever said, "I don't know" or "Maybe." The next time you are confronted in your spirit to say, "I don't know!" why not flip the script, stop talking, and ask the Holy Spirit, "What DO YOU know?"

I think it's the choice we make to be called out and called higher (by way of saying yes to flexibility toward His call), whereby people will ultimately follow and the Church will ultimately thrive. Being flexible doesn't mean you have shaky faith, in fact it shows the fullness of your faith, regardless of situation or circumstance.

At first it seemed as though Covid would get the best of our churches, especially those residing at fixed addresses, but it was in their flexibility and ability to rise to the occasion that the number of church attendees rose higher than any in-person attendance accounted for, where tithing increased, and where homes began to flourish because the spirit resided inside rather than in a boxed location.

Flexibility demonstrates willingness. Jesus healed and performed miracles through willingness *(Mark 1:41)*. He also saw no need to follow the hard doctrines of the times that dealt with the

Sabbath and exemplified in the synagogue that day that flexibility and willingness are more important than religious regulations. A man's hand was restored and a soul was saved through His action. That same action was condemned by the religious leaders (*Mark 3:1-6*). And it was this rigid, unceasing condemnation of His loving, willing actions that led Him to the cross.

It's no surprise that the religious eventually plateau and the spiritual keep ascending. Hypocrisy, blindness, religious law, self-honoring, judgment, and even death have destroyed their blessings, while flexibility through faith is what saved the one lost sheep and fed the 5000.

So there, in the comfort of homes across the globe, where two or more are gathered, He exists. Today, I hope your prayer is over your personal flexibility. May you mentally and soulfully open your mind to His magnitude and miracles. May you physically stretch your body to new limits of strength and endurance. And may you spiritually experience a fresh awakening. While my rainbow wedding and Crayola walls may make it appear otherwise, I don't care about the brand colors or "the vibe" of your gathering and neither will the souls whose lives will be changed. A Starburst awaits, one that my hubby can totally get on board with and my sunset gazing princess has already tasted and seen.

As you become, ask your heart:

When's the last time you were willing to change your mind toward someone else's opinion?

_____

_____

_____

_____

Did you experience church differently during Covid-19?

_____

_____

_____

_____

How have you practiced your own flexibility in your faith?

_____

_____

_____

_____

Excuses

I can often find a reason to bump working out off my priority list. If the kids' schedules are in the way or I have a dinner date with the hubby or friends and need a shower, I often won't have the time to get it all done. Did you notice a couple of excuses woven into just two sentences (time, energy, kids, shower, dinner needs)? Until we make our health a non-negotiable priority, there will always be room for an excuse.

I got tired of making excuses for myself, no matter what area it involved. I want to live my life fully without that constant hindrance. If we are totally honest with ourselves, an excuse is kind of like a little white lie. You are convincing yourself or others that whatever the request or topic, it's not valuable enough. To some this may seem silly, and a little fib seems like no big deal if it's not hurting anyone's feelings. But after my upbringing and my own incessant need to fabricate even the smallest of stories, I have chosen otherwise. A lie is a lie. And though I value Biblical principles, it's not my sole reasoning for it.

You see, when you start with a little white lie, you soon forget it because you don't place significance on it, just like a loose excuse. But eventually, the stories, the fibs, the little lies, become big lies and big stories. I believe I fibbed to myself for a very long time. I made excuses and pardons for my actions and concocted justifications as to why I was the way I was and why I could do the things I did. Lies and excuses can become your belief system and your crutch for simply getting by.

It sounds sad doesn't it? What a way of life. But actually, for a majority of it, I stood in a sea of unawareness. I didn't know, and couldn't determine on my own, the difference between the fallacy and the truth. As a result, I was often a long way away from The Truth. When my counselor sat me down and started dissecting the origins of my thought patterns, actions, and truths, it was the first time in my life that certain memories were accessed, memories based in early childhood sexual abuse trauma that I had hidden from myself and the coping mechanisms I had established to protect myself.

If you knew me even five years ago, you'd say I was happy. You'd say I seemingly had it all together and that my life and marriage were nearly "perfect." Perhaps it was my consistent, upbeat personality and constant smile. When I realized that those two things got positive responses from people, I began to show no other emotion in public. It became a fixed mask, more so out of habit and positive affirmation than anything else, but also because I was stuck in the expectation of others. I just didn't want all of the questions or the comments. "What's wrong?" "Are you ok?" "What's going on?" "You look sad." "You look tired." So, I constantly deferred to a smile.

I do believe consistency in someone's emotional state helps in areas of trust and friendship as a whole. The roller coaster existence of someone who is dramatic or easily offended causes wavering emotional states and conversations that I generally don't like to handle. But in their defense, aren't they being honest with their feelings? I tend to think so, and I have since come to truly value their authenticity.

My smile is often my defense mechanism and also one of my greatest assets. I have found that even in my saddest and most depressed states, where anxiety ran me ragged in my solidarity, I could still muster a smile. I always wanted the other person to feel light-hearted, and I didn't want to make an excuse for what was actually going on. For those reasons, I just pushed through to find happiness in the smallest things, so that I could bring light to others, even in my darkness. It's one of the very reasons my life's empower word has become "Illuminate."

I sat next to a dear friend in a nail salon chair. We were both crying for one reason or another, something neither of us EVER did circa the age of 22 – young, wild, and free – or so we claimed on the exterior. Anyhow, the reason for the tears or the fact that we were crying at all isn't the point of my sharing. She said, "I just don't know how you keep smiling." Almost within the same week, another friend experienced my subtle tears after I had walked a group of women through a personally written meditation before jumping into our meeting. I shared about some life situations, let them know I was grateful for them, and moved on with the rest of the meeting. I could sense her eagle eyes staring me down, but I had a meeting to run. And being that she's one of my best friends, I knew if I looked at her, she might evoke more tears. Everyone left and she said, "I was just watching and wondering how you were still smiling."

Honestly, at that time I could have come up with a million reasons why I shouldn't still be smiling and easily justify 1,000 reasons why I should have been able to eat whatever I wanted. A deep sorrow, caused by prolonged family situations, had ravaged my soul, and if I had climbed into a hole and never come out, the people that knew me well wouldn't have batted an eye. But I refuse to make excuses for remaining in a place of pity. I've wallowed in my own self-pity before. It got me nowhere fun! So I choose to smile. I no longer try to convince myself that anyone needs me to smile; that expectation and belief left me stiff for a while. Instead, I smile because I have so many other amazing reasons to. Gratitude and perspective are the gateway to joy... the real smile that exudes from within.

You can do the same thing; smile. If you can omit the excuses, remind yourself to find happiness, and focus in on the fact that your very existence is a gift to others too. Even if you are in a broken state in other areas of your life, your purpose, position, and sometimes even physical placement are not by mistake and could provide the make or break for someone else. Jesus never chose the whole or the holy; He chose those who were broken, outcast, and lowly... "the least of these."

I understand that excuses can hold much truth as well. As women, we carry so much on our shoulders. (Men, I may be over-generalizing here, but I know many fierce women, and if they don't fit all of these scenarios, they certainly understand most.) We make the task lists, and we also complete them, while our to-dos are usually finished last or not at all. We know where everything is with just a minute of rewind in our brain, but we can't find a thought for ourselves. We are the nurturers and the boo-boo healers, even when we are hurt. We are the needed, even when we are in need. And this doesn't just apply to motherhood; it applies to our lives as wives, as members of our extended family, and sometimes even to our work environment.

When, in the midst of all of that, do we find time for ourselves? How do we make it to the gym without letting these other to-dos get in the way? How do we find a minute to process our own thoughts, nurture our own wounds, or locate a shoulder to cry on? I know from my own experience, I always wanted to be strong. I always wanted to appear like I had it all together. I always wanted to be the best wife and the best mother. I never wanted to be caught in a weak moment. But my husband can surely vouch for the fact that he's seen me at my wits' end, on my knees with nothing left to give of myself. Yet still, I woke up each morning to provide for the babies who couldn't provide for themselves and put them to sleep each night, even if I was in tears during their prayer time.

Ladies, I admire you. I admire the face you put on for your family and friends. I admire the endless smiles you give your kids even when you want to pull your hair out. I admire that you cut calories because you don't have the energy to workout. I admire that you sleep less so that they can sleep more. I admire the time you invest in being the best you in all areas of your life...but are you empty, lost and/or lonely at the end of the day?

I have seen my reflection at the end of all of the giving. I have seen the dark circles under my eyes and the lack of "care" for myself. I have sat alone shaking, thinking I have nothing left. I have been scared of the thoughts in my own head because our mind can be our biggest battlefield. I have questioned my entire existence and the value of it. But my confusion and my mistakes led to miracles because my God had a mission over my life, and I found revelation in my circumstances. One of the pastors who speaks straight to my soul, Steven Furtick, said it this way and I found it perfect for my situation, "I am not stuck; I am stationed."

I have great purpose. I have great value. I have a great mission. And all of these things aren't areas that I HAVE to do – they are areas that I GET to do. The power of perspective over your situation has immeasurable capabilities over your mind.

I pray that wherever you are...maybe elbow deep in diapers everyday and feeling like you do not exist to the outside world, you will understand that you ARE the world to that little child tugging on your shirt, and you will find moments in the coming years where you have a chance to breathe. And yet, when that time comes, you will be wishing them small all over again. Although they don't have to be your entire identity, allow them to be a PART of your identity. Or, maybe you are single and have yet to meet Mr. Right, while all of the women around you are married and having kids. This is the time to invest in yourself, to be the best you, the whole you, so that you are more than capable of loving someone in all of your entirety; he will come.

No matter your situation, know that you are not alone in your emotions. Even the people who appear to have it all together have their moments of weakness. Those weak points for me have been my defining growth points. I could have let them break me. I could have thrown in the towel and sang the "poor me" song, but I didn't. I could have continued on making excuses for my actions. But instead, I took action over them. I dug deeper to discover the WHY behind the excuse.

After what seemed like an immeasurably long period of tears, my well was empty, and the place I found fullness was in my God, He who had never left my side and knew all along that I would find strength in and through my failures. And forget the excuses. They do not add to your growth. Change your mind. Practice gratefulness through a shifted lens of blessing and experience the fresh expression of an internal smile that exudes external reality of that core truth.

As you become, ask your heart:

What's your excuse for not becoming the best version of yourself?

_____

_____

_____

_____

What deflection mechanism have you adopted to protect your true feelings?

_____

_____

_____

_____

Today, can you lay down the excuses and pick up the Truth?

_____

_____

_____

_____

Exposure

ere you introduced to your physical capabilities at a young age? Perhaps you were enrolled in a youth sporting event like me with gymnastics. Perhaps it wasn't until elementary school P.E. (physical education). Regardless, we are all exposed at some point to the body component of our existence and the importance of its function, flexibility, and usage.

When we learn to walk, we become aware of our balance. When we learn to run, we become aware of our speed. When we learn to pick things up, we become aware of our strength. Timing and duration of exposure can give you a leg up in athletics, but what about in other areas of your life? The more often we are exposed to something, the more it becomes ingrained in who we are, how we see the world, and what is deemed normal – good or bad.

Exposure in differing fitness forms is imperative to growth and development. If we only allow our body to become familiar with one genre of exercise, we are inhibiting our muscular ability, especially our flexibility. I do, however, also see the value in commitment to learning a practice wholly. It takes determination, diligence, and commitment, all which are admirable traits. In short, the entirety of our physical practice is what makes us well rounded.

My son is a perfect example of this. By the age of seven, he had been exposed to jujitsu for nearly three years. He comprehends moves and holds, strength and flexibility beyond what I think some adults are even capable of. He has witnessed his body transform physically with little muscles and a 6-pack growing before his eyes. He is agile and a force to be reckoned with and often needs to be reminded of his strength when horsing around with his baby sister. Lord, help me as they get bigger.

Even at his young age, he takes interest in movement beyond one form. This is mainly because his dada is part animal from his flow-based workouts. Regardless, even without Dada's influence, he's been a climber since before he could walk. I remember hearing his body hit the floor during crib escapes at naptime. And now, he's already successfully climbed the most difficult rock scramble in all of Virginia, multiple times, and at a faster pace than most adults. We push him to try new things and experience new opportunities in order to expand his abilities. We could, however, easily limit him to one practice, one demonstration of movement. But just like sitting at the same desk from 9am to 5pm, that would be incredibly restrictive and confining. Our bodies are meant to move and fly; even Lynyrd Skynyrd knew that. (Sorry, not sorry for the Free Bird reference; it seemed so appropriate.)

But truly, confinement can lead to limitation, which leads to close-mindedness, which leads to obsession. The mind plays this game simultaneously. Don't underestimate the power of over-exposure; it can, and likely will, lead to addiction. Somewhere inside of me I'm an addict; I am obsessed. Is it because I was exposed too often, too young? Perhaps it's a root planted from generations past that I am unaware of and always running from. I often wonder if we are all addicted to something. Maybe it's even something healthy like fitness. Maybe it's something seemingly harmless like shopping.

There are numerous kinds of addictions that plague our society today, and they generally fall under two broad categories: Behavioral and Chemical. Sadly, many of us have dealt with loved ones, friends, and acquaintances whose addictions have threatened or destroyed their health, finances, and families. I've watched addiction unfold before my eyes as well, even before I could comprehend what it was.

I was sexually abused before my memory allowed me to recall. During therapy at the age of 29, the original incident unveiled itself as I read a book that dissected my patterns, my choices, my processing, my need, my intrigue, my pitfalls, and my pain points. The vivid memories came rushing back. I could pinpoint where I was, what he was doing, what was asked of me. He covered my mouth with his fingers like the Three Stooges jokingly did to one another. He said, "shhh," and took my hand to do something, something I'm not sure he even comprehended based on his mental and physical state. I was a baby, and my stomach is still in knots as I type this scenario and recall the others that followed. The curiosity and shame seeds were planted. Over the course of my life, it took root and grew in different, unruly ways.

Around the same time frame, I watched someone forced to devour an entire pack of cigarettes at the ripe old age of 16. He had been caught secretly smoking them before he was of legal age. I then witnessed those same cigarettes come back up. The intent was to teach him a lesson and make him never want one again. I also remember sitting at the window and staring at my aunt as she chain-smoked cigarette after cigarette on the back patio in the frigid days of winter. (My mom wouldn't allow it in our home.) I couldn't comprehend at the time why she would put herself through such agony. I was more concerned with her being cold than what the act of smoking was doing. Remember, I'm a beach girl? My sweet angel of a great grandmother also smoked her way into a type of lung cancer that in turn led to the removal of her larynx. This left her with a penny-sized hole in the front of her neck and no voice. She developed quite the beautiful language with her mouth, however, and was still able to communicate with her loved ones and a plethora of backyard animals. I found it mesmerizing as a child.

As a bystander to those situations, I've never touched a cigarette. The 16-year-old is now in his 40s and still smoking, and my great grandmother and aunt are no longer with us. As a child I did go through the local ice cream truck dispensary for the occasional fake cigarette fix. I still didn't see the harm in it until the day I comprehended what real cigarettes were made of. I have briefly considered demonstrating the same atrocious examples to my children in hopes that they never take an interest in smoking either; but likely I'll just recall the stories.

I know that some don't consider cigarettes to be a gateway drug, but I knew many who started there. And because I had witnessed those extreme situations, no cigarettes meant no marijuana for me either. So thankfully, I dodged that one too, even though it did limit my social circles. But I've always been fairly non-judgmental, so I have sat in on a bong rotation, one made out of an apple in fact (oh the hilarity). I've also been in a room where large piles of cocaine were in full view as if it were the typical centerpiece of a college apartment. I tried to pretend that I wasn't fazed by the situation, but I left as quickly as I could. I've also experienced the communal pain of losing a loved one to overuse and almost losing others to intentional overdoses. So, I'm ok with getting called "goody two-shoes," in part because I've been called worse.

Like "slut" for instance... My panties once hung from a light fixture in one guy's apartment. I thought it was funny until I saw them hanging alongside others the next time I was there. I didn't respect my body or myself. I couldn't comprehend that sex was supposed to be for marriage or that I didn't have to perform or that I wasn't solely meant to please in the bedroom. Needless to say, the childhood trauma, blended with my early exposure to pornography, gave way to a hidden addiction to sex. I'll go into that sore, yet healed subject a bit later.

Alcohol has another rooted and repeated story in my life. It's a painful memory lane to walk down. Unfortunately, I've seen so many mirrored examples in friend's lives and in popular sitcoms and movies. Yet, it's still commonplace for people to choose the numbing bottle instead of facing the fears of their rooted emotions. I have to walk this line softly and strategically and without missteps (I'm visualizing the beam again). I say this because this is still a battle I deal with in many areas of life. I say this with the utmost empathy if it is for you as well. I've had to remove the alcohol from my home so it's not visible, even to myself. I've had to have dry spells in hopes of seeing change in others and results for myself. It's not simple. The over exposure and the normalcy of the social practice of drinking creates a tendency for us to turn a blind eye. We even make jokes and laugh to lessen our discomfort with the subject. But like the deflecting smile, the severity of the situation and the brokenness still exist.

Have you ever done that, laughed when something was hard or sad or uncomfortable? I noticed a strong pattern of this in my life as I came into my knowing of self. Even something as seemingly innocent as laughing when someone fell down or when someone called me a bad name had to be dissected. I had to ask myself why I reacted that way? I had to understand why I laughed during awkward or heated conversations. I'd even laugh in the midst of being directly confronted. Man, I thought it was the best argumentative method possible. It made the other person feel completely crazy for their heightened emotion, and I was able to brush it off like it didn't really matter. Even so, I'd simmer on it for weeks to follow until there was resolution. Type 3's don't like to be disliked.

I presume my reasoning is similar to most others. Laughing is a defense mechanism. It protects us from actually having to wrestle with the typical response to a situation such as sadness or anger. It's in fact ok to be sad when someone gets so belligerently drunk that they can't speak or walk or remember what they said the night before. And it's ok if you are angry about the words that they felt the freedom to share with you because they were inebriated.

It's also very wrong of me to laugh when someone is sharing his or her heart, be it in sadness or anger, and especially if I am the reason for that emotion. I remember the first vivid memory of using this tactic to showcase my bravery and control even in pain and hurt. I recall getting socks stuffed in my mouth because I was laughing before I got the belt. It kind of worked though; I didn't get the belt again after that. Regardless, stop laughing to protect yourself, and start exposing your true emotions. Perhaps it will expose the problem and you will find healing instead of deeper sorrow.

Overexposure causes cancer, skin cancer or melanoma, if you want to talk about a literal example. But I mean this in all areas of our mind, body, and soul. I wonder to what extent we have to go in order to have the lesson learned. I surely learned one in each of these situations, even without realizing it at the time. But did the other people involved? Was it the sex or cigarette they craved or just the high? Did the disease of addiction run through their veins and minds so strongly that it drove the actions that masked the deeper emotions? I'm so tired of people creating societal norms out of life destroying addictions, figurative cancers! They are no more normal than actual cancers that wreak havoc on our bodies causing damage and even death.

The term "disease" seems to offend people when something isn't medically diagnosed as a sickness. But if you look up the definition of the word "disease," it is a "particular quality, habit, or disposition regarded as adversely affecting a person or group of people." I've never thought of disease as a habit, have you? Habits are endless, good and bad. And there is no denying that we each have habits, even if it's as seemingly harmless as laughing during an argument. So the question is, do we all have a disease? The duration of the habits and when they become too much, hence addiction, is when they start affecting our own self-functioning and those around us. High-Functioning addicts, no matter their vice, are commonplace in society now.

Why and how are we so good at masking ourselves, even to the point of constantly hiding our hangover? I've had many hangovers in my life formulated from bad habits. Some not even alcohol induced. There are many less publicized hangovers that exist in society today. Let's take a further look:

1. Buyers remorse - shopping hangover
2. Sports Injury or chronic soreness - perhaps athleticism/ fitness hangover
3. Black out - drug or alcohol hangover
4. Full & lethargic or starving - food hangover
5. Shame - perhaps derived from a sexual hangover
6. Financial debt - gambling hangover
7. Exhaustion - busyness hangover
8. Zone out or mental fog - binge gaming or TV hangover
9. Dehydration - alcohol, soda, or coffee hangover
10. Phantom Vibration Syndrome - cell-phone usage hangover
11. Loneliness - social media hangover

Let's go after a lighter example to give a good perspective on how a hangover truly affects the body. I met with a friend who explained a current hangover effect. She's pregnant and had been having these wild dreams of consuming a giant Coca Cola. She grew up with a dietician as a parent, however, and at 29 could count on one hand exactly how many sodas she's had in her entire life. Anyhow, she finally went for it. The night before we had breakfast, she satisfied her craving by enjoying every minute of a massive soda. That evening, she slept restlessly (probably from the amount of caffeine she consumed) and woke up with cottonmouth at about 11pm. And if you know anything about pregnant women, we have to pee a lot. She still didn't have the urge! Her body was dehydrated from the huge cola and not having enough of the one thing she should have been consuming – Water.

Now soda bingeing is not normally considered when discussing a hangover; alcoholism is. And it is a topic I am well versed in because of surrounding influences in my personal life. Long before the popular *Hangover* movie hit screens, hangovers and alcoholism have always been connected. It's been an issue for so long that it's even warned about in the Bible and accompanied by woes and judgments.

> *In Isaiah 5:11 it says: "Woe to those who rise early to run after their drinks, who stay up late at night till they are inflamed with wine."*

That sounds like a heck of a party doesn't it? Perhaps today it would include a DJ or band, a keg or a stocked bar. Regardless, just like the soda example, we are left hungry and parched afterward. The real concern, however, is that we are such an addiction-oriented society, to the extent that it gets excused until it's too rooted and too deep to release and uncover. The exposure is so bright and for so long that we are scorched internally. We accept it. But it's time we condemn it. It is time we change the culture. It is time we take a stand against the hangover. But the only way we can do that is to continually supply ourselves with the Living Water – the only pure substance known to man.

If addiction truly is generational, which it seemingly is in my family, that means it runs in my veins. I've always stood on the outside of it thinking, "no, not me." But as years pass by and you are seemingly unscathed, you may feel like you've escaped the cycle of what alcohol and drugs can do to your body and your life. But one day you get punched in the gut with the realization that it's not always substance abuse that we can become addicted to. Just as I mentioned before, there are multiple ways exposure can lead to addiction.

I've been addicted to working. I've been addicted to unhealthy mindsets. I've been addicted to enmeshed relationships. I've been addicted to body image issues. I've been addicted to food. I've been addicted to perfection seeking. I've been addicted to social media. I've been addicted to working out. I've been addicted to hiding. I've been addicted to lying. I've been addicted to medication. I've been addicted to roles I've played. I've been addicted to not being addicted.

But in those addictions, and every other component of life, there is a "meanwhile." This is a phrase I picked up from the beautiful Lysa Terkeurst at a conference where I pitched this book concept for the first time. And I have kept it close to heart ever since. Within the telling of every story, the concept of meanwhile develops; God is always in the meanwhile. We are doing this, meanwhile, He is doing that. As we go back to the addiction time and time again, He stays constant, moving in and around and through. He has never failed. He has never forgotten. He has never missed. He has never taken it for granted. He has never wasted. He IS always. His "IS-ness" (yes, I just made that up) is always. Who He says He is – He is. What He says he'll do – He does. What He promises comes true. He saves. He provides. He heals. He mends. He redirects. He embraces.

My shortcomings, just like yours, are His greatest opportunities. And He never lets an opportunity pass Him by. He hasn't through each of my obsessive addictions, and He won't with the current one either. So today, I hope you come humbled before Him, reminded that no sin is greater than another, no addiction too impossible to end, and no generational curse too strong. I plan to break the negative chains and shift my focus to Him. I already have. And even when my inadequacies and tendencies to grasp onto things that bring tangible comfort rise up...meanwhile, God. He always prevails.

> *John 4:14 - "but whoever drinks of the water that I will give him shall never thirst; but the water that I will give him will become in him a well of water springing up to eternal life."*
>
> *John 7:38 - "He who believes in Me, as the Scripture said, 'From his innermost being will flow rivers of living water.'"*

He is the cure to your life's hangovers, and what used to be your addictions will likely be the very way in which your overflowing well serves and heals others.

Pastor Steven Furtick, who I mentioned earlier, speaks about standards. He said something that just jumped in my heart for this message and for my own life. "We cannot poison the well and then complain about the water." Let's quench ourselves daily through purification and cleansing. We view our drinking water as a fundamental need for survival, but what if we also had living water running through our veins? If we drink Him in daily through the Word and worship, what difference do you think it would make in our habits and masked addictions?

Alan Jackson says, "Too much of a good thing is a good thing." I believe we can surely formulate positive habits that do not leave us dehydrated in our body, mind, or soul. And I'd like to believe that Alan is talking about Jesus. We can never be too addicted to Him.

Don't allow underexposure or overexposure to derail your perspective. Even seemingly positive arenas like fitness and food can hinder your growth, especially if you've become fixated on body image or dietary components. So instead, root yourself in goodness and wholeness. Stay connected to your right mind and your right body. And then your soul creator will keep any exposure from being too bright or too dim. If we are continually exposed to God, we will build our spiritual muscles, and He will be able to use us, akin to the way our body uses muscle memory. Systematic repetition in Him is how our whole selves become aligned. The more we seek Him, the more He exposes Himself to us, and the more our soul begins to yearn for Him – it's His greatest desire.

As you become, ask your heart:

What have you been over exposed to in your life?

_____

_____

_____

_____

_____

What have you been under exposed to?

_____

_____

_____

_____

How can you partner with the Holy Spirit in your revitalization and the renewing of your right mind, body, and spirit?

_____

_____

_____

_____

_____

206

Maintenance

We've been doing a lot of heavy lifting here y'all (pun intended!). Sometimes you just want to put down the weights and take some time to enjoy the hard work, splurge perhaps on a hearty-meal or sweet treat, take some "time-off" from one season to the next, or enjoy the vacation. It sounds like it's totally worth it. It sounds like you've earned it even. But if you're anything like me, which I imagine you may be considering you're still sitting here reading this book, what you intend to be simply a reward or break, extends into a week or two or a month or two, and before you realize it, an entire season has passed. So my question to you is, what if we questioned the status quo of this light-hearted, seemingly innocent choice and deemed this one "pause" as an actual step backward?

Again, we aren't robots. Do I indulge in a sweet treat? Yes. Do I partake in pizza night? Happily. I even choose to take a rest week from time to time. But guess what responses greet me after those choices? Every. Single. Time. – Apathy. Guilt. Regret. I always experience a sluggish meander back to the starting line or the "I'll wait for Monday" mentality. This pause is never free; it comes with a physical, mental, emotional, and/or spiritual cost. So instead, we must approach every component of our being as if we signed up for the lifetime maintenance package. Or else (dun dun dun.... Don't you hate hearing that sound?) we're going to find ourselves in the shop with a much higher out of pocket expenditure than originally budgeted.

When I started to put health (all areas) as a priority nearly a half decade ago (in the right way…not the magazine airbrush way), I had a tangible transformation that I find fully responsible for the way I treat my body and make my choices today. I'm hoping this is an unlock for you – The pause gives way for a problem. Your subconscious opens the door to filling the void with something else. If your health, your faith, and your well-being were in priority placement, then why would you pause in the first place? Just like the saying goes: If you aren't growing, you're dying. This is no different.

To be clear, resting and pausing are two very different things. So don't let me confuse your spirit or headspace. Active resting is critical to recovery, but the point here is to maintain, remember? Think of it this way, if you put anything in motion, day by day, propelling it forward, it compounds. Therefore, your time of "rest" is actually a time of rejuvenation, not stagnation. This is unlike coming to a halt or pausing, which has negative effects that result from lax decisions or breaks from your health journey.

Our faith is no different than the functionality of the body. We must maintain the forward progression. Our spiritual growth looks different in every season, even day to day depending on the schedule, roadblocks, and job; shoot, even the weather can have its effects on us. But the end goal is the critical outcome desire that keeps us showing up. Freedom and salvation are sweeter than any sweet tooth craving, wouldn't you agree?

If we place a pause on our mental, physical, emotional, or spiritual health, we are telling ourselves, "It's OK to go backward." I don't know about you, but I don't want to live without the knowledge, Truth, joy, and strength that I have now. I want to continue to emerge.

During each decade of our lives we are looking to operate at our highest potential, to reach our peak performance. They say you can run faster in your 30s and hit more ideal BMI targets (not that you should measure your health from that metric solely). But why do you think that is? Are our bodies physically more capable? That doesn't make sense to me with the way my joints feel when I get out of bed now versus the silent functioning of all my parts in my 20s. I think it has much more to do with our maintenance package, the set-up to the performance.

In our 30s we are more in tune with our body. We are less consumed by alcohol and parties. We are more educated. We are discovering new passions and hobbies, slowing down the rat wheel, and getting outside to enjoy the life that's passing us by. We are going to bed earlier. We are taking care of ourselves more. We aren't eating fast food and binge-watching TV. We are more self-aware of our needs and joys. We have more time to thrive because we have fewer "friends," more wholesome intentional relationships, and smaller egos to stroke. We also realize, it's ok to be alone with yourself!

My 30s, thus far, have been the best years of my life. Interestingly enough, this has occurred in conjunction with my continued focus on pouring in, so that I can operate on overflow rather than depletion. Ultimately, as long as we put in the energy necessary to maintain the gift that has been given to us, our peak performance is achievable with each new decade that emerges. It is the knowing that it's not out of striving but out of thriving that we exist in overflow.

However, it would be naïve for me to say that this is everyone's story. Perhaps your previous self was the best version you've known. Perhaps a hardship, health journey, or unexpected plot twist has you in a place where you crave to go backward on a regular basis. This same concept still applies. The only option is progression. The only hope is out. If we are not pressing into God, then life's natural current is carrying us backwards anyway. What if we used the problem as the portal to transform and become even more? Even when Jesus invited His disciples into the boat, He knew there would be a storm. However, God wasn't afraid of the storm. In fact He was expectant and intentional in His methods. He would teach them in the midst. You are no different from those men long ago. You must rest in the place of submission, realizing that it is by His strength that you will be made stronger. Just as the disciples called out in fear to the sleeping Jesus to calm the seas, He will hear you and respond.

I understand it may not be "how you pictured it," but have you ever asked yourself where you got your picture? Was it from a storybook or a Disney movie? Was it your mother's journey? Was it just your wild imagination? I could have stayed in the warped picture of how Playboy defined the purpose of my body. But I made a choice, alongside a lifetime accountability partner, and He showed me what beautiful really looked like. He stripped away my constant need to pause, and He gave me a yearning desire to consistently crave more of His sweetness. And thankfully, today I am reliant on the sustenance only He can provide.

Just like you're never too old to get in shape, you are never too old to sign up for Jesus's insurance and maintenance package. Need a refresh? Come to the well. Need some joy? He's got all the Good News you could ask for. Need a pick me up or a jump-start? Yeah, He's got that too.

Remember, maintaining isn't about putting in "good work" or "good time." It's about true development. I could go to the gym every day of the week. But if I just sit in the locker room on my phone, I'm not actually working my muscles or burning fat. I could go to church on a regular basis, but if I'm not actively listening and engaging, I'm just keeping the seat warm. We are only given one shot here. Our purpose exists within the hard things. It's truly where character is built and God's glory rests. The becoming process of sanctification is fully dependent on the grace and mercy of God within us. Just as David cried out for a clean heart and a renewed spirit, we must recognize the fallen condition of our soul and cry out to our God, the same God who said in Ezekiel 36:26, *I will give you a new heart and put a new spirit in you; I will remove from you your heart of stone and give you a heart of flesh.*

Through it all, though, it's critical to stay in your lane, to know that the people ahead of you aren't there with intent to show off, and that it is not in your best interest to gun your engine and lose your gas before the race is over. We're all driving the same freeway, all trying to get the best gas mileage. Listen to the best directional GPS instructions, aka God Positioning System. And if you are feeling belittled or stuck in comparison, remember all of those ahead of you who are for you and with you and want you to keep going. In fact, they may need you to keep going so that you can help keep them in their lane as well. Everybody's "super car" is purposed to be different. So instead of comparing or challenging another to a race, let's focus on getting everyone to the next pit stop.

We are one body in Christ, one human race, intended to help others function to the fullness of who they were intended to be, all the while maintaining our true purpose and our unique identities. But if you start acting like the tire when you're supposed to be the steering wheel, what do you think happens to the car? We have to work together. We have to stay in our own lanes. And, we have to know the value of ensuring that everyone sticks to their maintenance plan.

I don't know why this book keeps turning into a car show. Maybe it's because my husband drives a hot topic of conversation with all things Elon Musk. But honestly, what if we got SO good at the understanding of our functioning, our purpose, and our ability, that instead of choosing wasteful ingredients to supply our power, we plugged into The Source? What if we sought to get back to ground zero in the garden, choosing to eat from the ground, walking with the Lord in the cool of the day, living without shame or fear or guilt, understanding the deep love He has for us, and fully knowing our utter reliance on Him alone?

I know, I just got finished telling you to move forward in progression, and here I am taking it way back to Genesis and creation. But I never said not to learn from your past in order to propel you forward. In order to know where you're going, you must know where you came from and how you can use that to better your tomorrow and the legacy you leave for those after you. This is actually the exact point of the chapter. Webster's understanding of maintenance is preservation, safeguarding, conserving, and caring for. We spend time maintaining ourselves (mind, body, soul, and spirit) so those that follow in our footsteps will have God-fearing examples of goodness and abundance, regardless of any unexpected pauses.

As you become, ask your heart:

What does your maintenance package look like?

How often are you performing a checks and balance system on your well-being?

How has your current decade been better than the last?

Figure 8

We are all different shapes, different patterns, and different designs. I'm sure you're familiar with the standard body shapes of a woman: pear, apple, triangle, box, and oval. Whoever invented these concepts needed a better creative design. Even sticking with the same category would have been helpful. How do you compare one human's design to a box and the other to a pear? I mean, come on. I don't even know what shape I would be on that scale or what shape I should desire to be.

In addition to this unappealing scale, we've got airbrushed magazine models and health and fitness icons, but honestly, I enjoy viewing the plus-sized, non-manipulated women who showcase the true beauties of their bodies. Some of the people that I enjoy on social media staked their claim to fame by being vulnerable enough to bear it all in their bikini, not for self-seeking affirmation but in truth-telling body image declarations.

Self-image issues are rooted in our awareness of self-worth. But self-awareness is usually an adulthood experience that you don't simply come into with ease. My image issues were hard to ignore when, as a child, 16-20 hours a week were spent in a leotard. I wanted thinner legs, less butt, and more boobs. I wanted to be taller, and then when I was taller, I wanted to be shorter. Although it's not something gymnasts or dancers intend to flaunt, our bodies are on full display. It's the nature of the sport, and there really isn't a way to avoid it. And as we progress through our childhood, we can't help but hit puberty. That's when self-critique and comparison hit hard.

Not only was I dealing with it in my sport and immediate circles of influence, but society, too, began to shift into sexualization as the norm. Commercials, magazines, movies, music...pop culture was no longer just the sex, drugs, and rock n' roll of the 60's; the sexy factor had exploded. It was not unusual to see almost naked, voluptuous women on the billboard or morning MTV music videos.

I was self-conscious and critical. Beauty became extrinsic instead of intrinsic. I remember the shift in my social circles, and unfortunately, I'm watching it happen again with the newest generation as they enter into their young adolescent years. It petrifies me. The opposite sex starts dictating your wardrobe, the way you hold yourself, conversation topics, and even aspirations. They all want to be TikTok and Insta-famous, but for what?

My words may be falling on some deaf ears right now. Perhaps you had your self-awakening before teenage propaganda got a hold of you. If that's you, I'd like to meet you and your parents – and hire you as a nanny, if possible. And if that is you, I'd still encourage you to not skip this chapter, as I hope to give you some insight into the "mean girls" psyche.

I hate to coin myself as such. I tried to be open-minded and open hearted to all types of people and social groups. But my disposable camera negatives show otherwise. We were all the same, and likely all struggling with the same deep demons while fully unaware of what was truly even occurring.

The next staircase I approached was access: constant availability to all the wrong information regarding the blossoming world of puberty, femininity, and masculinity. AOL and recently retired

FIGURE 8

AIM (AOL instant messenger) became a commonplace, evening activity with friends. I couldn't get enough.

"Screen time" wasn't a hot topic at that time. It was uncharted territory. My parents knew how busy I was with positive, healthy, extracurricular activities, so they granted me the time and gift of technology as it became available. It was a mental release, and they knew no better. So parents, take a deep breath before continuing. There are many ways to prevent your little ones from being sucked in, but there are also many ways around any boundaries you may set.

Sexting – messaging with a component of sexual influence in your language. It became my secret addiction. Mind you, texting via the original Nokia phone was limited to a couple characters, and the screen was only an inch bigger than a pager screen, which dealt with only numbers. But don't let me age myself too much – I didn't have a pager.

So instant messenger and chat rooms became a common part of my nightly routine. It wasn't something I was searching for. I didn't hunt the Internet for porn. Actually, pornography was never my vice. However, I do know it consumes 36% of the Internet, and over half of all men and a little under half of all women have admitted to a pornography habit. Most don't even view it as an addiction because they don't recognize the brain warping negativity it causes. The average age of first exposure is before 14 years of age – that's middle school, people! It's an epidemic we should be aware of and not be afraid to talk about. And now, with smart devices in the hands of most of our society, some of it is even out of our control as the sex industry infiltrates conversations on Disney, YouTube, and commercials.

Cybersex was the coined term, and from the first time a high school "love" introduced me to it, I was hooked and wanted more. It was an outlet for an entire other side of my personality. It allowed me to not be my original definition of "perfect" because he viewed this part of me as just that. As a result, it felt even more permissible. It was our secret for a long time, too long. No one knew me in the same capacity. We didn't publicly date for very long. This was probably because I was too self-conscious about actually following through on the actions we spoke about, and well, he wasn't. So while I knew he was pursuing his fantasies in person, I was ok with being his untouchable fantasy. And it didn't matter what boy I was interested in outside of him, even if we were dating, he was still there lingering in the shadows of my phone.

I had opened the door and in walked disgust, guilt, and shame; but unlike my toddler exposures, this felt like my own finger to mouth shushed experience. I knew it was wrong. I knew if it was exposed, I would be mortified. And I knew that my recent, newly discovered Christian faith was not in agreement with this portion of my being. To the outside world, I was walking in perfect light, but bit by bit my shadows were creeping in to disturb the rays of hope.

As access exponentially grew, the addiction did too. It wasn't just nighttime AIM chats, it was daytime texts, nighttime phone conversations, and eventually, inevitably, upon receiving my license, I found myself driving to see him. You can probably unfold the scenario moving forward. We were walked in on "accidentally" during our first time. I was mortified. I had never been seen naked before, and now not just one guy, but two, had me found out. For a long time afterward, it was a one and done experience as my conscious, mortified ego, and Christianity kept me contained. But the guardrails were already removed and the waters had already been contaminated. As a result, my next boyfriend had fewer and fewer boundaries, and little by little the secret was revealed as glorified "cool-guy" points were ranked. I

FIGURE 8

shared earlier that eventually my secret sins were exposed to the school, and the youth group I was serving left me high and dry. At that point I had no reason to listen to my conscience anymore.

College came next, and low and behold the one who dangled the rotten fruit ended up at the same university. I couldn't escape, and I didn't try. He let me be me, or so I thought. I think more than anything my vulnerability was taken advantage of, and I became what he wanted me to be. I found myself going to all the wrong places at all the wrong times with free direct access instead of the sneaking around and the lies. Everyone else was doing it too, so I didn't feel the same weighted guilt.

In the very same breath, I was able to reinvent my public pedestal with new people and a new place, but yet again, he became my secret. And it didn't seem to matter what my figure was or how healthy I tried to be. I was sick all the time. My exterior didn't portray my interior brokenness. My mask had Hollywood written all over it, and I was still the shining star my parents expected and I aspired to be. My light, however, was dimming without me realizing it.

And, I ran. I ran as far from the disappointed angel on my right shoulder (aka my conscience) as I could. My inner circle was participating in the same shenanigans by night and pursuing their "dreams" by day. It's like this season of your life where you are aspiring for the greatness and titles you've been asked about since you were little and yet wasting your soul in the night. Alcohol became the numbing agent to the deep emotions I was experiencing, and I could tell by the passed-out bodies, hang overs, and collective morning walks of shame across campus, it was for many others as well.

No matter your vice, no matter your age, facing the reality of things isn't a cakewalk, and so we instead seek to numb ourselves.

We choose outlets that seem acceptable to society: food, fun (partying), and sometimes even fitness. Letting go of your health generally happens first. You run for the carbs and ice cream or you purge them. I'm a carb loader, though I have wished to be one of those people who lose weight when stressed. But there are battles in that walk, too, that I can't even begin to explore and understand.

I have found that when vulnerability takes over, the most common area of health that we run from is our faith. We can let it go so easily because it's not observable or tangible. We can't see it when we look in the mirror, and so it goes to the wayside without much thought. Feelings become our priority instead of our soul-state of being. We ignore what seems figurative to grasp hold of the absolutes. My body in the mirror was an absolute. This is me in the reflection…or is it?

Yet while you run away, He never leaves your side. You may forget Him. You may ignore Him. You may even doubt and curse Him. Perhaps you never even knew Him to begin with. But the moment you start finding joy in your God-given figure – your inner being – is the moment you discover what mattered all along.

In the midst of all of the college chaos, I was blessed to find him. Not Him Jesus, but the he He made for me. I was introduced to my forever my senior year at school. He made my already fragile knees weak. He loved me before I loved myself. I still can't fathom where the deserving factor comes into play, but I know now the purpose of his early intervention into my life. He walked into my college apartment holding a 6-pack of Modelo. And if you know anything about college parties, the good stuff capped at a Bud Light. The alcohol wasn't what piqued my interest, but the fact that we sat in the kitchen for hours talking, without exorbitant consumption, did.

FIGURE 8

Who was this older guy who didn't seem to have an ulterior motive? He hadn't tried to kiss me. He took me out to lunch or dinner when he was in town. And his texts were kind and inquisitive. I told you his question asking started from day one. He's just gotten sharper at it as we've aged.

He was my hope. He was my light. And though his relationship with the Lord was not much deeper than my own experience, he didn't have my struggles. He helped me uncover my identity, even as I continued to wear portions of my mask. And eventually, his faithfulness led me to my serenity. I say eventually, because we had a bumpy road ahead of us and a lot of mask removing moments of vulnerability to withstand. My insecurities rose to new heights in our relationship.

My fitness, like his, was reprioritized during this time. We both wanted to get back into shape after our crappy college choices in food and beverages. But even though I was adored by him just as I was, I still felt second rate. My insecure leotard body still chased me down. I couldn't do anything about the gymnast thighs or butt, and he even called me "thick," in a loving way of course, but I couldn't shake those magazine models that left me feeling disproportionate and underdeveloped. As a young adult, I joined the "Virginia Beach C" club. If you aren't in the know, it's the standard breast size of the women in our large population. I had always wanted more up top. I thought THIS will be what makes me fully comfortable and confident in my own skin. THIS enhancement will make me whole.

Wrong again. We search in all the wrong places. I was initially shocked and appalled at the transformation. It was one of the first times I recall crying at my own reflection. The doctor even told me that he had never had a patient react like me. Thankfully, I didn't go with his initial suggestion of a DD, or I would have lost it. I still wanted to be athletic looking and fake was not what I was going for. Once I got used to it, however, I fell in love with my new look. I gained confidence in all the wrong ways as I dated my future husband. Thankfully, AIM wasn't popular anymore and that guy and I had finally broken ties, at least in the physical realm. But imprints of sexual intimacy never go away...

I focused on fitness. Now that my body was what I had wished for as a young girl in a leotard, I went "hard in the paint" as my hubby likes to call it. I got my personal training license and started helping others transform their figures too. This is around the same time that I started the boot camp on the beach that I mentioned earlier. So we're bringing this thing full circle. Let's keep going.

At the time, I focused my positivity, energy, and workout regimes into full wellbeing experiences, but looking back, I wish I had the element of faith that I now have, the joy of depositing into people during their health journey. I was a broken girl building exterior bodies not interior souls. And though confidence is a beautiful piece of the puzzle, it's not body-confidence we should be seeking first – that's a byproduct of loving God.

But what happened to me? How did I go from point A to B? It wasn't overnight. There is a nearly 6-year gap between this season of my life and the quarter life crisis. But even with marriage, babies, and businesses, most things stayed fairly neutral. It was a slow transformation of self-awareness coupled with exposing the dark places of my twisted ideology of body shape that ultimately led to the crash and burn I've been sharing about. With a lot of therapy (physical too), church, bible studies, and friends, this change in foundation and formation was a deep adjustment and mending of my broken heart rather than an exterior fix. Simultaneously, though not coincidentally, I was led to other body renovations both on the inside and the out. From the badly needed leg vein-restoration to Lasik surgery, I felt like God was giving me His own version of reconstruction. I still have breast implants, but we've

FIGURE 8

already talked about not getting them replaced when the time comes. My confidence has shifted from the multiple paralleled procedures to my internal cleansing. Bit by bit, I was made new.

I stand in awe of His miracle working ability, His ability to know that these physical ailments were inhibiting me from releasing my full self to His call because they were mental blocks too. I wish now that I had seen the *Heal* documentary before the investments were made on some of these things, but I can't work backwards, and I stand grateful for the comfort and peace I feel in this body today.

As each healing procedure took place, especially with my varicose veins, I was able to get back to the gym with a new and transformed mindset. My "why" was no longer for my selfish reflection or image conscious concerns. It was for my children, for my husband, and for the longevity of my calling. I was walking the walk and talking the talk for the first time in my life when it came to my workout regimen and body positivity.

The very last click for me was the concept of intermittent fasting. Now, I'm not an expert here, and I won't go too deep into declaring a "get ripped quick" diet because I truly don't believe that works. I also don't think your body will respond like my body or her body or the next body. I do, however, share that it works for me. And it's been a lifestyle change just as so many other components I've shared here. My intent in sharing this isn't for you to go out and try it. Instead, I just want you to understand that one day one thing can click and simply be the shift you needed for the last decade, so don't give up on yourself.

I wasn't looking to lose weight. I don't need that. But I do like to feel fit and healthy in my body. I had been putting in a year of Burn Boot Camp workouts and simply wanted to see a greater response to the dedication, especially with the added 5am time slot – I felt like Wonder Woman without the outfit or abs. But, I've never successfully completed a diet in my entire life and only two experiences may have counted as "diets" to some extent. One consisted of chocolate SlimFast shakes that I'd steal from my mom in high school. But they weren't really meal replacements then, just a sweet treat. And the other was when I tried the Special K cereal diet, but my obsession with cereal skewed the results. This diet allowed for one cup of cereal twice a day alongside one healthy balanced meal. Well, one cup was a joke to my popcorn bowl pours. And the diet was further tested each night. Lying in bed, I wouldn't be thinking about ice cream; I'd be thinking about cereal. So I'd have another bowl…oh the struggle is real. And, yes, I realize that I really sound like a skinny girl right now being that my pain point is Special K versus a massive bag of chips or a super-sized McDonald's meal.

Oh, good old Mickey D's. I have to take an intermission from the intermittent fasting story to add a note about this food chain that I never frequent and haven't been to for a solid two decades. I was letting a good friend of ours, who doesn't carry the same physical or nutritional compass that we do as a family, take my kiddo for an afternoon of video games and Star Wars. I know what you're thinking. Stop judging me right now. This was the first time in his 5 years of life we had allowed this, and he was ecstatic about it. So anyway, our friend comes to snag him and giggles about the fact that he's going to take him to McDonald's for dinner. I immediately turned up my nose and said, "Ew," and proceeded to inform him that my child didn't know what that was. I told him the toys at Chick-fil-A were way better anyway, and who wants their food stuffed in a little box? (I couldn't remember the name of the "happy meal" thing.) Anyway, he was repulsed by my lack of patriotism and jokingly told me I was a bad mom. He couldn't wait to tell my son and when he finally got the chance to share the exciting news about their dinner location, my kiddo quickly said,

FIGURE 8

"That's not healthy." I about died laughing, all the while puffing up with mama pride. But I knew, once he sunk his teeth into those salty, greasy fries and he got his first swig of Coca-Cola, he'd be in heaven. Well, not so much…within 18 hours he complained of a tummy ache and said he'd never eat it again. My mama heart was to the moon. I hope that you see that this quick lesson is insight into how we can successfully shift generational perspectives for the revelations and truths of our whole health. This is a stepping-stone I'm glad we've passed.

So, needless to say, I wasn't transitioning from Whoppers to this intermittent fasting thing. Instead, I went from a delicious and hearty, best meal of the day, must have breakfast, to not eating until noon. But just think about it for a minute, the words literally say Break-Fast. Break your fast. I was just choosing to break my fast at noon instead of early morning. And, yes, I've heard all the negative views on this practice, so you wouldn't be telling me anything I don't already know. And don't worry; it's not a hard fast rule, but it has become a daily practice for nearly three years now. I do still love brunching with my besties, however, and some days your girl just needs a good breakfast bowl.

Just to give you a little follow-up fun fact to get your mind spinning a little more, did you know that our American meal cycle was all man made, and the idea of our consuming certain foods for breakfast was in part invented by Mr. Kellogg himself in the 19th century for no other reason than to sell his new product? You got it – sugary cereal – leading us into a new type of addiction – synthetic, processed products. I don't know about you, but man-made anything is up for question in my house, head, and heart. Just chew on that.

So on average, six days a week, I'm on the 18:6 cycle. That's a six-hour window where I allow myself to eat my two well-balanced, organic, paleo meals. And I feel amazing! My energy levels are up, which I believe in part is due to the abundance of water I'm drinking. I also don't have the need for an afternoon nap, though I don't mind taking one when I get the chance. What was once three hours and an addiction to Tylenol PM in college, is now a 20-minute refresher and mental break. And also, equally as exciting, I may be seeing some Wonder Woman abs under there.

Again, this doesn't work for everyone. And don't try it without talking with your doctor or trainers first. The point in my telling you this is that it took me 31 years to find something that I could successfully stick to, made sense to me, I actually liked, and saw results from. My husband doesn't like to say, "I told you so," but he's literally been doing this for years. It just has to be our idea, right ladies? Oh, how stubborn I am. I think that's an enneagram 3 thing too.

At the end of all of this – my figure and physical stature have nothing to do with anything – the reason I'm sharing is to guide you into questioning your habits, your belief systems, and your "ideal figure" desires.

The questions that remain with this topic of figure for today's women, both young and seasoned, are: How do we prevent pop-culture from skewing our body image? What conversations do we need to have in order to harness the inner beauty before eating disorders and sex become an issue? How do we teach the cohesion of mind, body, AND soul beauty and celebrate the variations in our God given-figures?

When I see the number 8, I see a woman's body and the hourglass shape and the curves that God intentionally designed for us in order to bear children and then nurse them. It's a symbol of motherhood and womanhood as well as the sign of infinity. I thought the world owned that symbol. I thought it was a

FIGURE 8

mathematical understanding of the vast array of numbers that we could never comprehend. It was just "BIG."

But recently, while involved in a Bible study, I discovered the covenant God made with Abraham, a covenant made while Abraham slept beside the offering he had just given to the Lord. Covenants, back in Old Testament times, were basically like our common day pinky promise with a bit of blood brothers thrown in through the sacrificing of animals. For understanding purposes, I'll put a bit more perspective on it. When establishing a covenant or promise, animal offerings were cut in two and laid before God. The two participants in the ceremony would then walk in a figure eight formation around and through the two halves of the sacrificed animal as they partnered over the promise with God. In Genesis, God makes a promise of many nations being birthed from Abraham despite his old age.

> *Genesis 7:7 – I will establish my covenant as an everlasting (eternal) covenant between me and you and your descendants after you for the generations to come, to be your God and the God of your descendants after you.*

The key take-away to the grandiose understanding of this number is that God didn't need the promise of man to make this covenant. We, as humans, can break promises. You may recall little pinky promises or pledges that you didn't stick to and maybe even promises you have made to yourself like a fad-diet or workout regimen that you didn't maintain. This isn't to cast blame or have you pick up guilt, but is instead intended to release shame and find freedom in God's promise to His children, His promise to you. God intentionally walked the 8 alone in order to remind us that no matter what fault we may have in our flesh, we are His.

And as His, He vows to protect us, love us, and keep His eternal promise of salvation.

That 8 is now traced on my heart, and I so eagerly want to introduce you to the one who held the pen, the same one who would, could, and will hold it for you. That is the figure that matters, His and His alone. Our figures aren't intended to be criticized, idolized, or memorialized. Instead they are meant to be stewards as vessels to His spirit. The confidence you have in your figure will then stem from Him rather than from a worldly reflection.

FIGURE 8

 ## As you become, ask your heart:

How are you treating your vessel?

_____

_____

_____

What past traumas or imprints have left you
dissatisfied with what you see in the mirror?

_____

_____

_____

Can you partner with God in restoring the body He
has gifted you?

_____

_____

_____

Can you practice loving your figure by affirming your
reflection?

_____

_____

_____

Alignment

By our own strength we are unable to restore and heal from the pain, disease, trauma, and suffering encountered in our lives. The Holy Spirit, however, can. With His miracle working ways and intentionally designed plants and natural medicines, we are more able to establish and maintain health than the doctors, pharmaceutical companies, and infomercials would admit. We are more resilient than the enemy would have us believe. We are continuously blocked and cornered and pushed away from our intended place of purpose – our promised wellness here on earth. But beyond just a balanced diet for our body, we need an aligned mind.

I've known for years now that we are able to crash the chatterbox; that we can stand on top of the naysaying, doubt, and fear that plague our mind; that we can breathe. However, there are more steps in this process of becoming that need to be fulfilled in order for us to fully live free.

We are collectively a mind, a body, and a soul. But without the connection and alignment of wellness, we will always feel a negative pull of instability. Every component of your mental, physical, and spiritual self requires attention and continual correction.

Some days you just want to splurge on anything fried, greasy, and chocolate. I get it. I'm human, remember? But without balance you will quickly find yourself in a place you never intended to be and end up feeling the need for a full-fledged purge. Instead, we want whole-being health. Pay attention to your own equilibrium. If one sector is off, don't panic or mask the emotion with a med or numbing addiction. Instead, adjust your intake vs. outtake, enhance the quality of what you consume (in all areas not just food), start speaking your freedom and health, and start genuinely believing in your wholeness and stability. Our minds can transform our bodies, and our God orchestrates it all. Who are you putting your faith in? Is it your mind, your body, or your God who created both?

I heard a saying that we put more faith in cancer than we do in God. Man, that rocked me to my core. We hear the diagnosis, and we panic and assume there is only one outcome. I believe it's no different than when God sat before His disciples and shared that He would be going to the cross to die. That's surely how the disciples must have felt as well. Panicked. Shocked. Heartbroken. In disbelief.

> *Matthew 16: 21-22 ²¹ From that time on Jesus began to explain to his disciples that he must go to Jerusalem and suffer many things at the hands of the elders, the chief priests and the teachers of the law, and that he must be killed and on the third day be raised to life. ²² Peter took him aside and began to rebuke him. "Never, Lord!" he said. "This shall never happen to you!"*

But three days later they were utterly amazed when He was raised from the dead and brought back to life in the flesh and in the spirit. We have that same resurrection power within us, gifted from God himself. But it's in our acceptance and activation that this becomes true.

Alignment isn't just a consumption discussion. If it were, the chapter would be over, and we'd be moving on to the next step of the becoming process. Alignment is a production conversation and a deletion of the idea of balance. A well-balanced meal or a well-balanced life or a well-balanced beam routine… it's all relative to the person and therefore varied. But like our faith and our alignment, there is nothing relative but instead proven structure and process that bring us into vertical consistency and ultimately a holistic and whole experience with life on this side of Heaven. So the question is less about how balanced are you and more about the pursuit of your alignment.

The Bible tells us that we will reap what we sow. And although it seems on the surface to be a simple agrarian concept, it has tremendous implications for our physical and spiritual existence. We must understand that we are reaping today (disease, poverty, isolation) what we sowed in the past (smoking, frivolous spending, mistreatment of others).

So we must take inventory of our seed. We must learn the importance of timing and orchestrating our energy levels, expectation levels, and hope levels all at the same time. We can't expect to plant all the seeds today and have them grown and ready to be eaten tomorrow. Similarly, we can't be 50 pounds from our goal weight and expect it to be gone when we wake up. There is always a timeframe and energy input associated with sowing and reaping. I don't believe that we would truly appreciate the gift of the harvest or know how to fully steward it if it came too quickly or easily.

The truth behind sowing and reaping is that it gives us the ability to harvest good fruit AND bad. We can't combine various seeds and expect them to thrive in the same soil. We can't plant wickedness and expect abundant righteousness to emerge. But with time, patience, and diligence our efforts will find reward and blessing.

> *Mark 4:26-29 - And He was saying, "The kingdom of God is like a man who casts seed upon the soil; and he goes to bed at night and gets up by day, and the seed sprouts and grows—how, he himself does not know. The soil produces crops by itself; first the blade, then the head, then the mature grain in the head.*

Now listen, I'm a believer in miracles. And I will never limit the God that performs them. But I believe just as much in our required energy input as I do in our reward output. God can harvest anything at any time, but a part of the process, a part of the learning journey, is figuring out the seeding and alignment of each component of our being. This is a process of obedience and faith. Not the fluffy, easy stuff, I know. But what is beautiful in obedience is that the more we commit, the more He gives. Read all of the blessings of obedience below, and I'll bet (on Him) you'll start sowing good seed in your obedience today.

> ***Deuteronomy 28*** *If you fully obey the Lord your God and carefully follow all his commands I give you today, the Lord your God will set you high above all the nations on earth.* ² *All these blessings will come on you and accompany you if you obey the Lord your God:*
>
> ³ *You will be blessed in the city and blessed in the country.*
>
> ⁴ *The fruit of your womb will be blessed, and the crops of your land and the young of your livestock—the calves of your herds and the lambs of your flocks.*
>
> ⁵ *Your basket and your kneading trough will be blessed.*

⁶ You will be blessed when you come in and blessed when you go out.

⁷ The Lord will grant that the enemies who rise up against you will be defeated before you. They will come at you from one direction but flee from you in seven.

⁸ The Lord will send a blessing on your barns and on everything you put *your hand to. The Lord* your God will bless you in the land he is giving you.

⁹ The Lord will establish you as his holy people, as he promised you on oath, if you keep the commands of the *Lord* your *God and walk in obedience to him. ¹⁰ Then all the peoples on earth will see that you are called by the name of the Lord, and they will fear you. ¹¹ The Lord* will grant you abundant prosperity—in the fruit of your womb, the young of your livestock and the crops of your ground—in the land he swore to your ancestors to give you.

¹² The Lord will open the heavens, the storehouse of his bounty, to send rain on you*r land in season and to bless all the work of your hands. You will lend to many nations but will borrow from none. ¹³ The Lord* will make you the head, not the tail. If you pay attention to the commands of the *Lord* your God that I give you this day and care*fully follow them, you will always be at the top, never at the bottom. ¹⁴ Do not turn aside from any of the commands I give you today, to the right or to the left, following other gods and serving them.*

But this can't be done if our alignment is off in mind, body, soul, and spirit. If we are all in our head, we miss what the heart is saying. If we are constantly worrying over our body, we are missing what our mind is trying to overcome. If we are constantly focused on the soul, we will allow ourselves to let go of the body. Spiritual obesity has reigned in religion for far too long. So basically, if you're picking up what I'm putting down – you need to learn to juggle, while also riding a unicycle. Easy, right?

All of this feels like a lot to concern ourselves with, but it's not intended to be a place of worry. It's intended to be a place of rest and life. In fact, Matthew 6:25-34 tells us not to worry over what to wear or what to eat. Instead, we are to pursue the righteousness of God, and all of these things will be given to us. The harvest is becoming, just as we are, in our fixed focus, obedience, and alignment.

Alignment, like harvesting, is more about timing. Fortunately, due to growing up in a military household, time management has always been a strong point for me. I will never forget those 3-minute showers, and yes we were actually timed (partially just for fun). How thankful I am for my tankless hot water heater today. But truly, I believe if you can get your time under control and gain confidence in it, you'll be doing no handed cartwheels on beam in no time as well. Even my children know that "Being on time is being 5 minutes early." To this day I can still hear my student council advisor repeating that at the beginning of every meeting when someone walked in late. It rings so true. And it also gives me a bit of anxiety when I'm late due to something I could not control. Whew, my palms are getting sweaty just thinking about it.

In college I tried to test my time management skills to the max by working as a Resident Advisor for a freshman dorm and accepting a snap bid for a sorority. Even though we weren't allowed to pledge for one and be an RA, I worked the system with a friend and got in. However, when word got out, I was told that I couldn't because there just wasn't enough time to do both. Oh, but I love a good challenge, especially when I know I'm right. Regardless, after several weeks I realized being surrounded by that many women was a bad idea. Later, in therapy, I learned that this was because I wasn't in touch with that side of myself yet, and I was threatened by all of the emotion holed up in one location. I was a guy's girl. And well, there's always a reason for that. And it usually ends on a slippery slope. We'll go into more detail soon.

People often tell me, "You're so busy," and if I listed out my daily schedule for you, you'd probably think the same. However, I feel so aligned in my being and am so aware of my needs at a mind, body, and soul level, that my schedule reflects those things accordingly. It also reflects my intentionality in pursuit of my seed sowing and has proven to produce good fruit, unlike my past, poorly sown, planting processes.

My husband often uses the phrase "break it down to the ridiculous." If you have 24 hours, 7-8 are spent sleeping. But, that's on a good day because mom-life is another story with nighttime potty training, blowing noses, putting on covers that were kicked off, soothing night terrors, and putting dogs out or in or up or something! Thankfully, my husband is amazing and helps (probably more than my ear plugged sleeping self knows). Regardless, I'm proud of myself for having a solid 16 hours of grind. Before my food intake change, I honestly couldn't focus without approximately 10 hours of sleep PLUS a 2-hour nap. That's right. I was a grown adult sleeping like a newborn. And no matter how much coffee or exercise I did, it didn't matter. I would totally crash. If this is an issue for you, go back to the chapters about detox and fuel...it really does matter. Gluten was my culprit.

16 hours, with breaking down to the ridiculous, ends up being 960 minutes or 57,600 seconds in one day. That's 6,700 waking minutes in a week and 403,200 (that's 403 thousand!) seconds. I don't know about you, but that amplifies me. I'm a routine person. I function best with a plan and a to-do list. Without it I feel like I'm wasting what precious time was intended for me that day. That's why you will not often find me on the couch, unless it's a dedicated movie and air-popped popcorn time with my kiddos.

If I know what works and I know how much time I have, it only seems natural in my entrepreneurial spirit to bust out a plan. My morning workout, coffee, prayer, and scheduling session, prior to the rest of the household waking up, sets my day in the right forward momentum. The days I sleep in, even just an hour to skip my workout for more sleep, I'm irritable and cranky because I didn't get that "me" time – which in fact is He time. I also consciously schedule girl time because I need to vent and laugh and learn and dine and rest with them. My creating time for my business doesn't feel like work because it's my passion. I've "worked" before toward a goal, and it was drastically different. I truly believe that if you are in your lane, in your calling, in your mission, God gives you an abundance of energy and focus to accomplish His goal for your life. I plan family time, sports with the kiddos, vacations, and babysitters so my husband and I can have quality time together. I even plan my driving time down to a T. I know who I'm going to call, what podcast, audible book, or clubhouse room I'm listening to, or what prayer request needs to be sent up to the big guy. Y'all, I do all of these things, and I'm usually in bed between 8:30pm and 9pm – Yes, I'm proudly a grandma! My friends' kiddos even refer to me as Grammy Tammy (and I own it). But seriously, it's more about balance than it is about my old soul. Plus, grandpa always said nothing good happens after midnight, and my past life has proven that to be true.

Alignment and productivity go hand in hand. Now for those of you who can't stand a set schedule, you are probably gouging your eyes out right about now. But, if you've never tried it, don't hate just yet. Give it a whirl, and you might just be surprised by the productivity outcome. And if you have tried it but just can't jive with the restriction, there are other ways to create the same momentum with a bit more opportunity for freedom in your day.

Daily goal setting is a great example. Forget the hour-by-hour, minute-by-minute time blocking concept, and just set an accomplishment plan for each day. Of course, you know all of the other intricacies that have to take place such as showering, getting the kids' lunches packed, dinner prep and cooking, bedtime routines, etc. Somewhere in the middle of the must-do's and the honey-do's are the want-to-do's. These are the creating points that bring you to life. It is the time of day where you look at the clock and actually want it to slow down versus speed up. Those are the hours I live for! In fact, I'm doing it right now as I write this book, peering out at the sunrise and the dolphins riding the waves.

Another option is to have a MIT list. I know, we are inundated with acronyms, but this one is good. I'm kind of a freak of nature because I actually like to do all three of these things. I'm sure it is the over achiever personality thing coming out. Regardless, MIT stands for Most Important Task list – I'm speaking to the hearts of the Post-it note people, the ones who usually carry a planner or a notebook with them to jot things down. They always look a little frantic rifling through their purses for their list while trying to capture the thought or the task before it escapes into the vortex of mommy brain.

I tried the planner thing and the notebook thing; it didn't work for me. My running lists are in multiple places. I have the HUB app – which I think is intentionally named for the main place to put everything you do. To me it's my HUBby reminder space. Luckily, he's a list person too, so I'm not quite the crazy micromanaging wife I may appear to be. We include typical running lists of our house projects, home needs, grocery lists, and shopping wants. But we also have our goals, my books-to-read list (which is infinite!), prayer requests for each other, places we want to visit, and even our financial outstanding balances, just to name a few. So truly it is a HUB and so worth the $15 a year.

On the professional side, I use the project management software, Monday.com. This is another shared space where team members and I stay on track with what we have going on in the various funnels. I know when I'm in the "work mode" time-block, which I recently coined my "create mode," I'm on track with my daily schedule and also checking off my goals and MIT's all at one time! I'm doing my little type 3 jig right now. I know raising the roof is dated, but it feels good every once in awhile. No really…try it! You've gotten this far in the book, and I can feel your energy surging towards better balance already…two hands at your shoulders and pump it…Yessss girl!

So at the end of the day, please, don't tell me you don't have time or are too busy. I promise there is time. If you know what happened on last night's episode of *This Is Us* or *The Bachelor*, point proven. If your nails have a new color weekly, point proven. There may be different methods that work for you, but if you aren't growing, you're dying. Let's start today in this arena. Start sowing your seed well with intentionality and alignment.

Focus on the needs vs. the wants and the time you spend "working" vs. the time you spend "creating." If you feel like you don't currently create anything, I'd like to challenge you there too. We all create. We're the most magnificent creation formed – of course a byproduct of being created has to be the gift of creating! Our creator made us in His image, and therefore our natural nature and nurture (no debate needed here) is the cultivation of creativity.

Wow, that was a mouthful. But seriously, if you think about it, even if your "work" doesn't feel very creative, why not shift your mindset on what you are doing? This isn't some "love what you do" passion ploy…though you know I could get on that soapbox. This is about knowing your capabilities and aligning your gifts within your allotted time. The liberty to know that I'm investing in what I'm made to do while spreading that positive self-esteem and message, gives me such release from what used to feel like a burden. Yes, we have to "work," but what if every day you set out to go "create" instead? Even tasks that feel mundane during the sowing and reaping can get you ignited when the first seed sprouts or when you get to feed your family the first meal from what was grown.

I initially made this shift within my own lingo for my children. I didn't want them to have a negative connotation of "work," one that meant their mama was leaving because she was forced into it or is simply trying to make ends meet. No, I go create because it's my passion; it's what I'm good at; it's what I'm called to. I didn't sit down to write this book and invest endless hours away from my family because I had to. I was drawn to it, and I know it's purposed for the big picture. The harvest is coming.

Maybe you're a nurse or a teacher or a firefighter. Maybe you're a lobbyist or a bank teller or an accountant. Maybe you're an assistant or a stay-at-home mom. Any and all of these give you space to create. These roles are so much more than a job or a paycheck. And that goes for any and every position, so don't feel left out or question your current importance in life. I see you, friend. I know your thoughts before you finish them because I've been there.

I was a bartender with a dream after college. I was a personal trainer with a desire to transform so much more than your body. I was a marketing and event director for a dental company with a longing to travel and make people love their smile as much as I did. I was a boutique owner with a wish to make an expectant mom, in all of her pregnancy weight, feel beautiful again. I was a stay-at-home mom with a yearning to find the "me" I had lost and the "me" I wanted to become. Each and every one of those roles was intended and useful for where I am now. I could even go back as far as the roles I played in family dynamics or sports teams or student government or youth groups. If you look back on your life and the roles and jobs you've played or had, they were all purposed; they were all stepping-stones to your more.

We've been marketed the "you are made for more" mantra, and I whole-heartedly chant this in every area of my life, in everything that I do, and in every belief I have for you. Part of your more – actually the key to your more – is a fully aligned, fully present, fully fulfilled sense of spirit and an intentionality in your pursuit of sowing. Our fulfillment, like our harvest, doesn't come from what's around us; it comes from Who is above us and within us.

As you become, ask your heart:

What are you sowing and reaping in your life?

_____

_____

What do you need to uproot and replant?

_____

_____

Are you ready to walk in alignment?

_____

_____

Are you ready to be who you are called to be without limitations of the flesh or blocking banter of the mind?

_____

_____

Are you ready for the Harvest?

_____

_____

Image

Our bodies are designed in the likeness of the strength, durability, flexibility, and fragility that was God manifested in the flesh – Jesus Christ (1Timothy 3:16). So often we neglect its capabilities. We neglect its purpose, just like we so easily discount our life's purpose. Truly, they are one in the same. The way we view our body is the way we tackle our life. The way we fuel our body is the way we ignite our existence.

> *1 Corinthians 6:19-20 marks this truth by saying "Do you not know that your bodies are temples of the Holy Spirit, who is in you, whom you have received from God? You are not your own; you were bought at a price. Therefore, honor your God with your bodies."*

This verse alone compels me to stop, adjust, recommit, and sacrifice myself, knowing the greatest sacrifice has already been given on my behalf.

Let's break this down.

"Our bodies are temples of the Holy Spirit."

The God, our God, of the entire universe constitutes the genetic make-up of our existence. He is within us – His strength – His ability. Imagine an image of that for a moment...your body, a jeweled, precious temple, made perfect in His design. And yet, with that breathtaking image in my mind's eye, I am disappointed by what I see in the mirror... the flaws, the imperfections, and the defects. But, what I critique as ugly or less-than is not mine, I am His creation, and therefore I am criticizing my God by ridiculing myself.

Women are especially susceptible to this hidden sin. I say hidden, because often we don't speak aloud the thoughts and words that cross our mind when we stand in front of a mirror. Our words can be used as weapons – both in truth and in lies. And we discredit our maker when we choose negative words to describe His creation, His temple.

Can you foresee the day when you will see God standing before you, the day when you finally get your first glance of His glory? Will your eyes be drawn to the ugly scars caused by the piercing crown of thorns He wore when He died for you? My daydream is always of perfect skin, no scars, and a divine radiance. But when I meet Him, if His scars are still intact and visible, won't I still fall at His feet in awe of His beauty? Don't you think that's how He sees you?

I know this is deep, jumping from the shape and abilities of our body, to alignment in life, to scheduling, to meeting Jesus face to face when we die. But sometimes, waiting for the punch line isn't worth it. I waited too long for mine, my punch line, that is, the punch line of my life that left me naked in front of the mirror, disgusted by my reflection, and fully unaware that I was looking at God's intended perfect design. Don't worry...we're getting closer to a full understanding of the inner workings of my brain and heart. Even with all of the context thus far, you may feel like something is missing. I still was at this point too.

So that leads to the next part of the verse.

"who is in you, whom you have received from God."

Have you received Him? Is He in you? Are you unsure? This component is life-altering. It is life-giving. It is LIFE. Are you living or are you dead? Are you looking in the mirror at skull and bones? Whether obese or rail thin...the answer could be yes. I don't want to tiptoe around the life-changing point of this section of the verse. I'm going to face it head on because I know now that life is too short to do anything but just that. Face it forward.

For most of my life when I was asked if I was healthy, perhaps by an athletic trainer or doctor, my quick response, without question, was always yes. But what makes up your health? Is it the food you consume? Is it the vitamins you take? Is it the amount of times you go to the gym per week? Is it the checked box of 0, 1-2, or 3-4 alcoholic beverages you consume per week? Is it your BMI or your blood pressure? Is it your weight? Is it your ability to hit a certain athletic milestone of jumping jacks or distance in running?

My answer to all of these questions and so many other sub-surface level questions about health is no. Your health is a heart issue. And while the functionality of your actual pumping heart is imperative, I am speaking of your root heart – your soul. Your health is based on who and what inhabits your soul.

Do you feed yourself, yet you are still starving? Do you workout endlessly, yet still feel weak? Do you take every correct nutritional supplement, yet your sugar levels or blood pressure are still off and you feel incapable of change? Do you read endlessly and know the depths of information regarding your health, yet you still feel empty inside? These questions may be answered in many different ways. You could say no to all of them and still be a non-believer. But I would invite you to read further on the correlation of fitness and faith before you negate His possibility.

Or maybe you are answering no and yet already call yourself a Christian. But you can't figure out why those feelings of inadequacy still exist. I've been there. That's me – rewind to my adolescent years when my reflection first grew dim. I considered myself a Jesus follower. I had been since high school, officially. Although I said my nighttime prayers and went to church occasionally when I was younger, it wasn't until Young Life that I was fully listening to the gospel and applying it when I felt it necessary. By the way, applying anything when you just feel it is necessary doesn't really work. It's like sticking to a goal only halfway – it will never be accomplished if there isn't full commitment. I was a lukewarm Christian, living out of convenience and face value.

So, there I was, a typical high school girl walking down what I thought to be a "good" path, the right path in fact. I read and testified the Bible to my peers. I led worship gatherings and small groups. I spoke in front of hundreds of people sharing with them about my salvation and my "right" walk with God. But slowly, with lack of direction and full honesty, I started leading a life that was far from healthy, regardless of my outer fit-physique. Through my blurred vision, I thought my mirror reflection was good enough. But looking back at pictures of myself, I was not well nourished, despite the big smiles and silly poses.

To be clear, I wasn't having a bunch of one-night stands, but I wasn't the person I was telling my "christian" friends that I was either. I put quotes on Christian because I don't believe many of their actions or responses were very Christ-like. My idea of a Christian has since evolved immensely and includes such beliefs as grace upon grace, present for our sisters and brothers, empathy and acknowledgement, and calling out the good that is within them rather than discrediting or abandoning them in their shame.

These so-called Christians are the church-people and the religious that you may personally know – the ones that never cry, the ones that seemingly have it all together, the ones that talk behind your back or don't truly support you even though they say they do.

I've been that person, in that circle, so I know they exist. And the church that hurt you is in fact made up of broken, hurt, imperfect people. Hurt people hurt people, friend.

> Matthew 7:21-23 - "Not everyone who says to me, 'Lord, Lord,' will enter the kingdom of heaven, but only the one who does the will of my Father who is in heaven. Many will say to me on that day, 'Lord, Lord, did we not prophesy in your name and in your name drive out demons and in your name perform many miracles?' Then I will tell them plainly, 'I never knew you. Away from me, you evildoers!'

That was me. And we are all imperfect. I get it, and I don't try to act otherwise, but I did then. And as you learned from my secret life, I had demons in my closet. We all have shadows. We all have faults. Mine was the struggle of sexual sin. I got sucked into the sexualized world, a world our silence has condoned and allowed to become mainstream. Many years later, and after becoming a mom and a devoted Christian with a deep relationship with Jesus Christ, I now know "too soon" is any time before marriage. But that lesson is often learned the hard way these days, and the resulting wounds steal, kill, and destroy our ability to be fully intimate and fully known by our spouse. Old memories flood our new bedroom. Past experiences taint our purposed, promised love life. We become detached, like hollow souls and bodies, rather than connected and fully present together in God's idea and purpose in sex. *(Pause: Prayer for my children and ALL children)*

As I previously shared, my secret, my sin, became publicly known. The timing was fragile, just like my spirit and heart – right before high school graduation. My core group went missing really quickly. And I had nowhere to go, nowhere to run, and nowhere to cry. I was left alone with only the boys that had led me to that place to begin with. I hid as much as I could. I was ashamed and broken.

I had no way of mending because the "christians" who were my lifeline had vanished, and I lacked a deep enough awareness of God to run to Him. I couldn't tell anyone about it, and because of the deep shame I felt, even my parents were completely unaware. Remember my mask of a smile?

I'm sharing all of this so that you can understand that I have not always been the person I am today. I have not always been healthy. I have moments of binge eating ice cream even still. But that tipping point – that experience of shame, loss, and brokenness – was an important piece of the puzzle that eventually led to my mirror moment years later, the moment where I found myself standing naked and afraid looking at my reflection and wondering how I could be that ugly.

Before I move on, however, I need you to take note of a statement you may have skimmed by. *I* didn't believe that *I* had a deep enough awareness of God, but that doesn't mean He didn't already know my name. In fact, the very people that I felt abandoned me in that season were some of the same people who welcomed me with open arms when I waved the white flag of my salvation. The church that abandoned me before was not the same Church that embraced me. The Church is not the building, and it's not the people. It's the spirit dwelling in the house that embraces the people that embrace you. Oftentimes we point fingers when in reality there are three fingers pointing back at us. So, don't point. Instead try to open your hands, just as Christ did when He broke the bread with the disciples after His resurrection to showcase His humanity *(Luke 24:13-35)*. Be human, be vulnerable, be willing to show your scars, and be loved back instead of running and pointing. I don't accuse or stay trapped beneath what happened to me. God used my weaknesses and my frailties for good. He used that which was meant to harm me to help others. I believe it happened for me so I could write this book for you.

Moving back to the verse that introduced this chapter, it is important for you to understand that He is in you regardless of your acceptance of Him or not. He is the original creator of your DNA – your genealogy has its origins in Noah and Adam and Eve. But… His spirit is not fully in you until you have requested His living waters to flow through you.

Acts 2:38 – "Peter replied, "Repent and be baptized, every one of you, in the name of Jesus Christ for the forgiveness of your sins. And you will receive the gift of the Holy Spirit."

I believe I was a Christian when I first got saved in high school. I don't doubt that God was within me. I don't doubt that my love for Him was real. But I know, through the wisdom acquired by living life, that my re-committed heart is 100 times healthier than the heart I had 15 years earlier. Wisdom is a gift in itself. Sometimes it hurts learning and living through the moments that get you the slogans and one-liners and medals of honor, but it's all worth it. Whether you are 10 years old or 80 years old – the same newness of life envelops your soul when you accept God in your heart. No more running behind a bush, as Adam and Eve did when they realized they were naked (Genesis 3:8). He can still see you, and He knows exactly where you are and what your intentions are. And, He loves you even still.

Today, I know I am saved. His spirit is within me. And the moment you accept that He is in you, your health status changes.

1 Corinthians 6:19-20 – "You are not your own; you were bought at a price. Therefore honor your God with your bodies."

The sacrifice of Jesus is unlike any other storyline in history. The price was surely paid by His death, but it was also paid through His mental and physical suffering leading up to the cross. He was weary and weak, heartbroken and yet still intentional in His purposed plan. In Matthew 26:39, Jesus prays and asks God if the bitter cup can be passed from him. His prayer ends with the understanding that it is not as He wills but as God wills.

He was human. He felt what we feel. Knowing His sacrifice was for my salvation gives me that much more resolve to speak to my body in representation of the beautiful image that it is – The image of a gift – The image of a vessel – The image of a daughter of great worth without need to adorn or construct in a worldly way, but instead in humility and grace and an imperishable beauty of a gentle and quiet spirit *(1 Peter 3:3-4)*.

As you become, ask your heart:

What do you say to yourself in the mirror that would be disproven by your Father?

_____

_____

_____

How does your image on the outside reflect your inside health and heart?

_____

_____

_____

How can you treat yourself differently so that you are a living testimony to the treasure that you are?

_____

_____

_____

Mom-Bod

I surely can't discuss figure, self-image, and design, or even the hourglass 8 without elaborating on the beauty and discomfort of motherhood. But there is too much to be noted in passing, and the girth of the title is impossible to measure in a few sentences.

Our bodies grow humans. It's insane to think about and even more insane to experience. No matter your initial body frame and no matter how many pregnant women you've seen or bellies you've touched, there is no truly accurate depiction of living out the process of baby making (and no, not the pre-conception part. Come on people stay with me here).

At just 20 years old, I chose to dedicate endless hours and research to the phases of maternity, as did 5 other people in my business program. You see, James Madison University has an elite business program with a specialized curriculum for juniors called COB300 (College of Business). If you were a JMU student for any length of time, regardless of your aspiring degree, you knew about this program.

It was tedious both in time and trials. Over the course of a semester you developed an intricate business plan with several other students majoring in different areas of business. After hours of deliberation and study, our team finalized our idea on a business geared toward pre and postnatal women. While most don't experience the ins and outs of motherhood until they have a baby themselves, this began my journey.

Following months of dissection and development of our plan, I had birthed a desire to put my whole heart into this subject. And after participating in a business plan competition with the top 5 plans from the university, I knew we had captured a niche that would not soon be going away. People were popping out babies all the time, and until our government decided to place a ban on it, our trends reported even more growth in the industry.

I graduated without ever writing a resume and began a business with my mother. It was even given the exact name of my school project, Modern Maternity. Before it evolved into the Mom & Me Boutique that it is today, we took many steps to solidify our plan. One of the most useful acquisitions of information was the certification process of becoming a trainer in the pre and postnatal fitness arena. Mind you, this was before I had ever experienced much change in my figure and when babies were just a one-day dream of mine.

As you know, trying to relate to anyone or anything when you haven't walked it out yourself is quite difficult. Empathy hopefully exists in the willingness of relating. But there I was, training these women in my non-pregnant size 6 frame, having never experienced much change in my body besides the freshman 15, while their pant sizes increased to a stretchy band with no belt loops. I probably pushed their physical capabilities more than the women who had already pushed out a baby. In my defense, it was with good intention and total lack of understanding.

Fast forward a few years later when it was my turn for me and my rounded belly to get down on the floor for abs or leg workouts. I would internally curse my own self out with some form of, "What the...was I thinking?" You can comically visualize it, can't you? I watched my shape change and grow. I knew the beauty of what was happening internally, but as the scale kept increasing, I was externally disgusted at times.

I knew what to do and what not to do in the realm of body health and fitness, but my self-image took another hit. In hindsight, I wish I could experience motherhood again in this new confidence and awareness. Maybe someday I will, but it's sad to think I missed out on all the joys that exist in the creation phase. Don't get me wrong; I wasn't this miserable pregnant woman. I actually loved being pregnant and knowing I was carrying life within me. Remember, I wasn't fully aware of my inner damage at this point. It was the reflection I had a hard time with, but I did it, twice. And they are now part of my purpose and inspiration for living life to the full.

Why do I tell you this? Because, I want you to be aware that we all go through times of not being comfortable in our own skin, no matter what the scale or our pant size may reflect. And there are times when what your physical body is experiencing may be tumultuous and unpleasant. It doesn't have to be pregnancy by any means. Men, you obviously won't ever experience this phenomenon, but perhaps a sports or health injury or traumatic accident has you inhibited. We can all relate to distress, somehow, someway.

The prenatal phase was much easier than the postnatal phase in my opinion. At least I had something beautiful inside of me, and I had the expectation and anticipation that there was this remarkable surprise at the end. It's the lack of glamour that accompanies the postpartum period that can make it even more difficult to handle.

Postpartum, I was mentally obese, and by standards of a scale and measuring tape, I was physically obese too. In reality, however, I was being overly hard on myself, considering I just served as an incubator for nine months. Regardless, I wanted the get fit quick fixes. Give me a restrictive tummy band. Give me tight jeans that will hopefully shrink my uterus when I wear them. Give me a trainer, a slim shake, and some veggies, even though my body was craving carbs and ocean sized glasses of water as I nursed these tiny babies into their own health.

I was one of the lucky ones and was able to get into a bikini the same year I gave birth. I insisted I be one of them. I put to work all of my studies of fitness. All of this may have played a part in my postpartum depression; even though they say the natural physical endorphins help release the dopamine levels to see you through it. The pressure I was putting on myself was too big. And the crazy thing is, my husband reminded me daily of my beauty and worth, but it fell on the deaf ears of an unhealthy mind and heart. I wanted to be that "perfect 10" mom. MILF (mother I'd like to ****. You can fill in the blank.) they call it. How horrible and vulgar is that? Regardless if you are joking around with your mom-friends or your husband is commenting on your new voluptuous, milk-enhanced shape, it's outrageous. The ILF of the acronym makes me cringe, as does my state of mind concerning my prenatal and postnatal figure.

If you are reading this and have yet to conceive a child, never will, or never can, I want you to know that this is likely a fraction of psyche from your mother. And if that is you, and you are angry with me for taking such a viewpoint on the splendor and gift that is childbearing, I apologize, and I hear you. After experiencing my season of self-awakening, which led me to the awe that I now fully embrace in this precious ability and true gift, I find it quite offensive myself.

As mothers we are/were literal vessels for life. And God has granted us this supernatural power to design. Motherhood, whether through adoption, fostering, in-vitro, or good ole regular baby making, is one of the purest, largest blessings on this side of Heaven. I view your pregnant and postpartum body as the temple that it is. You are lovely, striking, and magnificent.

Being a mom shapes you. Ugh, even in the most unappealing pancake ways, if you catch my drift. Breastfeeding is one of the most incredible experiences of intimacy I've ever had. My aftermath experience was a bit different because of the aforementioned C-cup, but I feel for my sisters who have to pick up their nipples to fit inside their bra. I will say, even getting past all the vanity that occurred with my implants, this was one thing I was thankful for. And if you are that mama struggling with the deflated, post-party boobies, I would certainly not judge you if you want to get them fixed. Girl, you deserve it after that selfless, life changing experience.

Maybe a better way to say it is, motherhood molds you. Physically, obviously. Mentally, undoubtedly (#mombrain is a thing). And Spiritually, surely. Don't let your own negative self-image harm what was intended to bring joy. Seek help. Seek light. It is nothing to be ashamed of. You have everything to gain when you realize the beauty of all the sacrifices.

I experienced postpartum, even without the boobage situation. It was dreadful and lonely and confusing and scary. Three weeks after my summer baby was born, I was lying in the pool while he rocked peacefully in the shade. I remember floating and my mom coming out to check on us. She asked how I was, and I just knew I couldn't formulate words for all of the bubbling emotions within me. As I sat with my mouth below water, treading slowly to stay afloat with the least amount of physical exertion (I was exhausted), I sank below the water to stop the tears from overflowing and the looming question she would ask.

How could I not be overwhelmingly joyful about this sweet, perfect human I had just given birth to. He had the most ideal instant latch. He was sleeping wonderfully. He was drop dead adorable with his fo-hawked long brown hair. The meal train was still happening. My husband was home and incredibly helpful. And I was already wearing a bikini. "What is wrong with me?"

I didn't have a week worth of live-in help from anyone. I didn't have any fellow mommy friends to really connect with since I was among the first to have a child in our circle. I couldn't go to all of the hangouts and summer concert festivities like I had previously. I wasn't the weekend party planner for the whole gang anymore. I wasn't going to the beach for hours on end like I used to. I felt stranded. I felt helpless. I lacked conversation. I lacked connection. I felt like I lacked purpose as well.

Yet, here I was giving life to a human! Here I was doing exactly what I was designed to do with my femininity. Here I was with the answered prayer of a baby I struggled to conceive. But yet, I couldn't get a grip on the desolate feeling within me. I never told the doctor. I didn't talk to my friends about something they probably wouldn't understand. I never asked for help from anyone. I did a lot of crying on my mom's shoulder. Super dad came to the rescue. And eventually I suppressed it enough to feel normal.

And then, I got pregnant, intentionally, with my second child when my first was only 8 months old. Brilliant, right? Not so much. I had been determined to self-generate a picture perfect idea of what my family should look like. My overly obsessive timing strategy to have siblings close to one another, like my brother and me, ended up adding to the emotional turmoil within me.

Now don't get me wrong. If I wasn't intended to have my baby girl, it wouldn't have happened. And she turned out to be just the angel I needed all along. She's my calm and my peace. She's my sweetest smart cookie. And in hindsight I wouldn't change anything about her or the timing of our children.

Even so, I wasn't my best me while I was pregnant. Nursing and raising an infant while maintaining a business and working on launching and designing another was stressful. And trying to manage a marriage that intimately I couldn't show up for (I felt disgusting all over again) just added to my negative outlook. I was the epitome of a hot mess express. Which, if you know me well, you know I don't love that terminology or claim it at all. So, that should tell you the severity of the situation.

All of that added pressure, without a release, can result in an explosion. The release I chose wasn't positive. And it ended up leaving me without any confidence or self-worth at all. Don't let yourself get to that place. Don't try to be superwoman; she's a fictitious character for a reason. Asking for help isn't going to make you look bad, and at the end of the day, if someone cares, they are likely dealing with their own self-confidence issues and understand your pain.

Well, there is no better time to transition to the next topic than right after we dissect the mom-bod. Let's talk about the enemy tactic that has proven to be a mass trial, a tactic that knows no generational (mom or not) boundary – let's talk "skinny." And don't worry. I want to crush your anxiety or simply your expectations around this concept, so don't skim past what can serve you.

Skinny has been trending for far too long. I'm so thrilled to see that models, actors, and marketing companies alike are going after the average woman now versus the magazine airbrushed version of a girl. Even Barbie got some edits. Unfortunately, this transition has not been established quickly.

The diet industry is a skyrocketing $70 billion dollar enterprise and one that utilizes "skinny" as a source of obscene profits at the expense of our health and our children's health. It is now a constant in our daily lives that is advertised through products like Skinny Pop, Skinny Margaritas, Skinny Cow Cheese, etc. If our society had a heart or even used its eyes and ears, it would realize the powerful impact that these marketing ploys are having on women, men, and children alike.

Skinny is not ideal. It's impractical and unhealthy. And the tactics used by the diet industry are complicit in the pain felt by 11 million people struggling with body image disorders like anorexia and bulimia. Now, admitting truth, we can't blame only current culture. Corsets and diets were trending even in the early 1900's and thin, with the Virginia Beach C, has been a desire far longer than old photographs prove.

So how do you combat the skinny mindset when it represents all you've ever been shown as "pretty"? You don't forego the outer image, but instead return to the awareness of the gut. The competing brands speaking to gut health are transforming people for the better, and it's not about belly fat but instead about inner wellness. The success stories based around physical gut health are inspiring to watch, but alongside body transformations, He's calling us to something more.

You must cleanse yourself from the pills, the scales, the diets, the processed foods, and the imagery of beauty that's constantly shoved in our faces. Start to witness the strength and purpose of the inner you as day by day you work towards healthy, even perhaps lean, reciting the words that give you the power to get outside of the cultural mindset of what size jeans you wear. It's not about that.

And I know what you're thinking. This advice may seem disingenuous coming from a girl that seemingly has the body type of one of those fit models, but that has not come with ease or without selfish, vain desires to obtain the skinny snapshot. I've never battled an eating disorder, but when you fight any mental battle of self-image, it's still debilitating on a soul and body level.

Even with the awareness of health that was established in my life from childhood, my mind was weak. And when your mind is weak, you cave to transformation and the expectations of others. I would look in the mirror and pick myself apart. My thighs touched. My butt wasn't the right perky. My arms were beginning to take on flab. My abs weren't visible like they once were. My stretch marks and wrinkles aged me. And even with implants, I thought my boobs were small post nursing. My hair was too thin. My nose was too big. I critiqued every area, even the ones complemented by my very adoring husband. And wasn't his the only opinion that mattered in every one of those areas? I was obsessed with comparison and failing to see myself as anything besides inadequate.

We live at the beach. Skinny is expected come summertime. I think everyone is familiar with the New Year's resolution gym membership spike. Newbies take over the floor space and the machines. But it inevitably dies down...until about May when Memorial Day BBQ's are upon us. How people convince themselves that three weeks' effort will get them in last year's bathing suit is beyond me. But in reality, it's less about them and more about the perception of others.

After kids was the most difficult time for me. My body had just accomplished the most miraculous development and transformation, and while I was wowed by the ability, I was disgusted with the outcome. Even though two weeks postpartum I was able to get in a bathing suit and enjoy a pool party with friends (who complimented my figure), they didn't know the mental struggle. I was one of the first in my group of friends to have kids, so it became a negative self-evaluation battle with no support group in sight.

What will they think? What will they say? But ladies AND gentleman, THEY don't matter. You matter – Your health – Your heart. The mirror can be our worst nightmare or our biggest motivator. Don't look at the curves and the crevices. Don't look at the warts and wrinkles. Look into the eyes – peer into the soul. Our wondrous bodies and brains are the most complex machines on the earth. Some of our abilities aren't even scientifically identifiable, and yet we still criticize. How self-absorbed we are as a society.

Our job isn't about critiquing; it's about upholding, stewarding, cultivating, and nourishing so that we may live a life of activation and calling for His greater purpose. We do need to purge, but not in a harmful, literal way. When we can purge the junk, we can access the part of ourselves that was always there and always beautiful.

Thin yourself of the junk. Thin yourself of the ridicule and negative imagery. Thin yourself of the cultural expectations. Thin yourself of the stresses and the burdens. Thin yourself of the unhealthy consumption. Thin yourself from societal pressures. Thin yourself from the expectations of others. Thin yourself of debilitating "churchy" mindsets. Thin yourself of the titles and the materialism. Thin yourself of it all and healthy, lean and long, fit and fueled, will be your natural state of being.

I still order from the "Skinny" menu. But it's not because I'm concerned about what will become of the consumption, it's about the compilation of ingredients. Our nation is finally bringing to the forefront the truths of our food, what's in it and how certain industries have monetized on the decline of our health. Please consider watching documentaries like *What the Health, The Magic Pill,* or *Hungry for Change.* Don't turn a blind eye to this insidious plan.

I don't often attack the skinny argument because it can be offensive to many who are fighting thyroid issues or chronic illnesses that don't give them options in the realm of weight gain. My hope in sharing this message isn't about your pant size or scale number but instead about the cleanliness of your nutrition and the outcome of your physical, mental, and emotional health based on your intake. Being wholly FIT is the new skinny – and dare I make a silly pun, HOLY FIT beats it all.

So if you still choose to stick with the skinny mindset, at least attack it from the slang definition of the phrase. The skinny = "The straight story" or more precisely, the inside story, the real truth. The real truth is that The Truth has already decided who you are. He says you are beautiful because you are made in His image. The inside story, your heart's story, not your body's image, is where the health journey begins and ends. Our bodies are simply vessels to help us complete our God given purposes here on Earth. Unfortunately, I believe that many won't fulfill their complete mission, not because they aren't mentally or spiritually equipped, but because they haven't put in the hard work to be physically well. I don't want that to be you.

When you look in the mirror, look beyond the physical existence of your image and grasp hold of the spirit of your being and the entire compilation of your light. You see, you are literally a light, comprised of Him and exuding Him. Science proves that we emit light that is 1000 times lower than the sensitivity of the human eye. But just as the book and movie, *The Shack,* so beautifully depict, we glow. And that is beautiful... No matter your size.

My challenge to you in combating your skinny mindset is to get the True skinny on who you are, whose you are, and how He sees you. And treat yourself in accordance with the delicacy and beauty to which you were formed and continue to live. This includes your physical fitness regimen, your eating choices, your sleep patterns, your audible and visual consumption, and every other component of daily existence.

If you need a reminder, paste this on your mirror. When you brush your teeth, when you put on your makeup, when you brush your hair, remind yourself – multiple times a day.

Song of Solomon 4:7 - You are altogether beautiful, my love; there is no flaw in you.

Thinking deeper on this concept, I looked into the eyes of my children, and I rewound the last four and five years of their lives. In the same reflection, I imagined myself as an infant and a toddler and a waddler and a kiddo and a teenager and a young adult and a pregnant lady and a now, still emerging and growing, woman. The changes wrought by the world are evident, even on my babies, even as much as we try to shelter and preserve them from anything besides goodness and love. Day by day they are infiltrated with thoughts that they are not perfect or beautiful because they aren't this or that.

My sweet son has longer hair than me. We did cut the baby fohawk eventually, but there came a point that he asked to grow it. I somehow became one of those hippy moms who let my kid wear his hair in a man bun or waving down his back and swooped in front of his eye. But I've watched his confidence sore because he loves his hair so much. And when Thor and Aqua Man are rocking the same hairstyle on regular, it got even better for this kid. But I've also held him in my arms when other little boys teased him on the playground because he looked like a girl or when the server at the restaurant told us our girls were so pretty. He can't comprehend it. I mean the boy is rocking a hoodie and camo while my girl is in sparkly everything with a bow. I don't know if I can chalk it up to a lack of attention on behalf of the adults or not, but you can bet my mama bear instincts had to be hand-cuffed to my chair in order not to go after the elementary bullies. My son is perfect. His hair is amazing. And he loves it. Why would I make him cut something that currently makes him proud just because the common boy-cut is still an expectation of our society? No, I don't want him to be traumatized or have confidence issues later, but if you ever get the chance to meet my son, you will instantly see that confidence (just like with his dada) is not an issue.

If we were born in the image of God and therefore automatically knowing and confident of our birthright as princes and princesses of the King, how then can we preserve that knowledge? How as a mother can I cultivate that identity for my children? How can I reclaim my own? God tells us and shows us and leads us into and through the trials that combat our concept of self-image. He has more power and sovereignty than the enemy has or will ever have. Yet it is evident that the bad guy has infiltrated our lives and negatively impacted our mental health, physical health, and surely our spiritual health.

John 16:33 - I have said these things to you, that in me you may have peace. In the world you will have tribulation. But take heart; I have overcome the world."

Let no man, let no enemy, let no demon, let no word, let no song, let no sign, let no theme, let no show, let no movie, let no book, let no marketing, let no sound, let no leader, let no pulpit, let no family, let no friend, let no politician, let no creature, let nothing and no one stand in between you and your deserved, designed, and delivered confidence. You are all together beautiful!

Tell yourself right now – You are beautiful. You are a princess. You are loved. You are gifted. You are purposed. You are creative. You are talented. You are strong. You are intelligent. You are a miracle. You are more than you've ever been told you are by anyone here on earth! Your Father in Heaven sees you, mama and friend. He knows you. He made you. And He believes in you.

Own your identity and confidence today and every day through the image and knowing of Christ Jesus. And remind your babies who they are too! Understand that the you that is so beautiful can stand in confidence, not by your mirror, not by your works, but by His gift.

The self-love and self-care movement trickling into society today is another way to create false idols within us. In fact, it was guaranteed this would happen *(2 Timothy 3:1-5)*. We are instructed to steer very clear of those who claim they are self-made or man-made. Even with great trainers, teachers, and counselors, our existence and always becoming alignment is owed to the price He paid on our behalf – Selflessly.

Stand against the very idea that "I did this" instead of "He did this." Without Christ we are nothing and surely not the full mother our kiddos deserve. But through this journey of becoming, through this alignment zone of being all you are created to be, your humility will be the bright light that proves to the world that as we die to self, we are raised to life. And no external validation, mom-bod, or skinny teeny bikini, can gain us treasures here on earth that are worth living for. But instead, the treasures worth living for are those we store up in Heaven. The Bible tells us that where our treasure is, there too will be our hearts. As you build and sow, He establishes you further. As a result, not only do you reap the healthy harvest of His promises, but those who are connected to you do so as well. Our children will be blessed in the bounty of our sowing good seed and living freely from the confines of the mom-bod and the "skinny" mindset that once held us hostage.

Confidence isn't arrogance; it's proof that He exists all the more.

As you become, ask your heart:

Are you criticizing the very frame that provided the brilliant gift of motherhood?

How do your children hear you speak of your body?

How can you reframe your mom-bod mentality to express gratitude and glory to our intentional maker?

Replenish

I know we already spoke about fueling our bodies and the importance of putting in the right gasoline. But here, instead of fuel, we will focus on the value of replenishment. And since we just got off the topic of skinny, I don't want your brain allowing you to run to the pantry to falsely fuel up.

When you're working out, it's important to repair, maintain, and grow the muscles that you have just broken down. Protein is the essential element to do this. Although there are many food triangle options to put in your body, it's actually the protein that helps build the muscle mass. And though carbohydrates are what we often crave to fill us, they turn to glucose, which if eaten in large quantities can be stored as fat.

I believe that working our bodies from weakness to strength and unhealthy to fit is valuable far beyond the mirror reflection. It is also beneficial for those in our realm of influence. I watch my husband impact people daily through conversations about health, food intake, and fitness. He is a motivator and a value-add to people, even strangers. They see his frame and they immediately need to know what he does that they don't do. He has even challenged seemingly fit individuals who thought they had reached their peak performance. GMB will always leave you in the learning zone of fitness, just like the Bible will for your faith.

Replenishment of the body, from a standpoint of growth and wholeness, comes from the sustenance consumed. Unfortunately, society has even devalued our food. With documentaries like *What the Health* and *The Magic Pill,* people are finally realizing how deceptive and false the labels on "healthy" foods are. The sugar and grain industries have capitalized long enough, whether the conspiracy claims surrounding the labels are true or not... remember politics and I are more like oil and water than peanut butter and jelly.

Regardless, people are finally getting back to the roots of the issue. Literally. Whole foods – organic foods – raw foods – are becoming all the rage. It was somewhat perplexing to me that people were shocked by the health factors and benefits of eating natural. The original design of any earthly gift is always purest at its most natural form. We can learn the same exact lesson from the food sources for our bodies as we can with our mental, emotional, and spiritual sources.

Values, living at the root of someone's heart and soul, make them who they are. Or at least that is supposed to be true. But nowadays people have the ability to wrap themselves in a pretty box and bow without disclosing the true ingredients. Don't be fooled by the packaging and labels whether they are on people or products. The beauty of the gift can sometimes disguise the truth of the inner self, the inner contents, leaving them missing the mark on authenticity.

True understanding of decluttering, also known as landscape design, must take place not just in your kitchen but also in the closets of your head, home, and heart. By design, this idea is meant to create healthy boundaries for you and your family. It started with our home space (recall our decluttering project). It then rolled over into our kitchen pantry, especially as our kiddos got older and "snack foods" became incessant diverters of health.

I mean organic goldfish, really? We cleared the shelves of products that had no expiration date and ingredients we couldn't even pronounce.

Our kiddos know that if they want a snack, the fridge is open at all hours of the day. What's inside has expiration, came from the earth, and provides full nutritional goodness to their tiny growing bodies. The pantry, however, is a "must ask" location to enter. Snacks may include rice cakes or vegetable noodles that need to be cooked. Although these choices may not sound as appetizing as double stuffed Oreos or animal crackers, I know there won't be any sugar crashes or mood swings. And isn't it my job to protect them from head to toe? If we could see their gut with our own eyes and the inner workings of their bodily systems that have to digest and control their well-being, I believe we'd be making more educated choices in their foods. And if we believe that God has given us all we need, then we might also believe that Mr. Kellogg likely had ulterior motives to his cereal antics.

It doesn't stop there. I've told you previously that I let go of a lot of things. Landscape design is the concept that applies to each of those cut ties – relationships, limiting beliefs, old habits, etc. I'm sure the word prude has circled your mind once or twice as you've read about my transformation and the beliefs I now hold. Alongside that descriptor are some other, perhaps more vulgar, names based on my past activities and perspectives. But I've learned, as exemplified biblically and through incredible friends, to turn the other cheek, especially when I know the name-calling comes from a place of not knowing or understanding (remember what your hand looks like when you point).

These ideas of void nutrition, lack of knowledge, and landscape design can be matched to one's prayer life too. If you are praying for health and yet spending your day smoking, how can you expect God to do his handy work? If you are praying to lose weight yet stuffing your face with donuts and fine white grains, you likely aren't going to get a result.

I don't mean this from the perspective of "How can God?" because God is a miracle worker – He's proven a great many times that He can shift one's entire being with the touch of a hand, through one spoken word, without a moment's notice (study His miracles in the New Testament for proof). Although human effort is not needed for God to work His miracles, He is not a vending machine. Instead, He is a loving, caring father who wants to do what is best for us. That requires that we invest in what is good for us as well. Otherwise, His answer to our prayers will be bestowed upon people with no knowledge or understanding of how to maintain the gift that is given. Again, may I remind you that becoming is an action. And even while He pursues us as His children, we must reflect the likeness of the prodigal son, who made the long journey to come home, step by step. He removed himself from a destructive and self-made landscape and chose to return to his Father's loving arms and to the humble, healthy beginnings of his Father's house (*Luke 15:11-32*).

One of my favorite pastoral analogies that has stuck with me in my own becoming process is that Sundays are meant to set the table for the week, but it is up to us to prepare the meal, day by day. I used to fill my week with many appetizers, but I believe after further introspection, I was missing the meat of the meal. I was missing the protein all together. And I am not a vegetarian – so I was hungry! And that hunger, even with a full pantry and fridge, left me starving. So I designed a new meal plan. Just as I suggest you do.

The Bible is the meat. We have to devour the protein to build the muscle. If you are vegan or vegetarian or pescatarian or any other hearty meat eliminating person, don't take me too literally here. I respect your food choices…choose your analogy respectively.

Plus, if you are really doing your due diligence in meal prep, you know protein can be found in many food items other than meat alone.

Living out the value of loving the Bible, of teaching the Bible, of living in it and having faith in it, requires us first to read it, all of it. We must stop allowing other people's insights or a few short Bible verses or pithy billboards on the drive to work to be our only form of meal prep. These things, though meant for good, can leave us feeling condemned or confused and often provide no spiritual sustenance. I pray a lot. It gets me through my day. And while prayer was an imperative part of my journey to becoming the Christian I am today, it will not be the only piece to the puzzle that eventually transforms me into the fit daughter I still desire to be and am always becoming.

To know is to study and to understand in intimate ways. Just like in a new relationship, I don't get to say, "I know him/her," without first spending time with them and learning about them. I have to sit and experience and ask questions and witness. I want to know Him, and I want Him to speak to me through scripture just as I have heard Him do so often with spiritual leaders. I'm sure that you would appreciate and devour these revelations too. Knowing Him is a gift. Pursuing Him is a choice. And becoming more like Him is an imitation process *(Ephesians 5:2)*. Just as my children imitate my belief about McDonalds or my choice in food or music or language, they could not recall these teachings without being close to me – intimate in nature.

I am confident that by living out the practice of reading the Bible on a consistent basis, replenishing our spirits with His truths, and designing our lives with a righteous, healthy landscape, we will enjoy the relationship building process and experience oneness with the Lord – but most importantly we will have cultivated a more devoted and steadfast faith in Him. I believe if we can engrain this in our daily routines, it will filter and flow into all areas of our life, just as God's living water overflows abundantly into all things.

The journey of replenishment starts from a place of pouring out the old, clearing the cabinets, and starting with a clean slate. But replenishment can only begin fully after acceptance and repentance have occurred. We talked previously about the importance of submission – the letting go despite the fear or perhaps the letting go because of the fear. We, too, must let go, just as Noah let go of the home he once knew and what others around him thought about his crazy antics. He accepted his call, repented of his past failures, and activated in pursuit of God's own heart and will. As a result he witnessed the flood, which washed away destructive cities, filth and brokenness, poor seed and rotten fruit and made way for the promise of the rainbow and the replenishment of the earth. Noah's submission, acceptance, and repentance brought forth a fresh vibrancy, new life, fresh seed, and a healthy harvest.

Becoming fully renewed and replenished happens in the steps following acceptance and repentance. My weaknesses, my past, had brought me to a place of bare cabinets with no way to prepare a meal or set the table. This is why, as I shared earlier, church became a home rather than a Sunday practice. I needed fuel. I needed food. And soon, I began to know Him. I began to understand how to replenish my own pantry and how landscape design leads to health instead of heartburn.

I had many conversations in my brokenness and hunger asking God to show me all the places where I was weak, why I was weak, and how He could help me gain strength in my weaknesses. I was no longer afraid that I would be left void, empty, or malnourished from the food of the world. I was given the bread of life. And you too have this same promise, this same rainbow.

Before this phase of replenishment, when hunger was only stomach deep, I used to chew on a favorite verse I had memorized when I was younger.

> *Philippians 4:6-7: "Do not be anxious over anything, but in everything, by prayer and petition, with thanksgiving, present your request to God. And the peace of God, which transcends all understanding, will guard your hearts and yours minds in Christ Jesus."*

After my replenishment began, my mind, body, soul, and spirit were awakened to the endless banquet table of fulfillment and nourishment. I like to imagine the movie *Hook* with Robin Williams, when Pan and the lost boys delighted over the table of imaginary, delicious, rainbow delights. And I know now, that verse wasn't ever really my favorite (though I am fond of it), it was just the only one I knew. Sad really, when I think about it, because The Lord has given us The Word, He is The Word, and yet I diminished its power by neglecting it and allowing others to dictate my landscape and fuel my hearty appetite with junk.

Are you ready to try the next step in the equation of full wholeness, the critical piece of replenishment which allows the starved soul, the vacant or distracted mind, and the broken hearts and tarnished bodies to exist in overflow? For we were never meant to live on bread alone, but instead by every word that comes from the mouth of God *(Matthew 4:4).*

As you become, ask your heart:

What does your current landscape design look like?

_____

_____

_____

What are your pantries full of?

_____

_____

_____

What can you remove and pour out in order to be replenished with His nourishment?

_____

_____

_____

What do you need to accept in order to replenish?

_____

_____

What do you need to repent in order to replenish?

_____

_____

Stress

*Y*ou may have already gathered from the information thus far that I lived most of my life in a place of constant stress. From the shame that hid under my masked smile, the perfectionism race that never won a medal, to the body that I was constantly trying to self-design – I was internally raging. Externally, I didn't look like I had put my finger in the electrical outlet, and I wasn't pulling out my hair or even curled up in a ball with a migraine. I simply found ways to "manage it." Well, that's what I previously thought. Now I know I was using coping strategies to suppress it.

Managing your stress is very different from, and much healthier than, suppressing it. Fitness, in fact, is a great way to manage stress because of the release of endorphins and the quality time spent on you or with workout buddies. Or it can be successfully managed by way of a vacation or a personal health day. "Sick days" no longer exist in my contracts because I'm not often (knock on the invisible wood of my glass desk) sick. With such concentration on my health – mentally, physically, and spiritually – my sick days have morphed into personal health days. I wish I had known about these years ago; I realize now that I have needed them ever since high school. It's a time I utilize to do exactly what we're talking about – manage my stress. You should try it. And don't you even dare think of packing it with doctor appointments or errands – that entirely defeats the purpose, even if it does suit the concept of "personal health" on a physical level. Make margin to release, sister!

I've been dropping some pretty heavy truth bombs on you throughout this read, both in personal testimony and transformational tools. And I hope I haven't totally destroyed my reputation, though again, loss of titles coincides with loss of need for affirmation, and mental and spiritual growth means you have the freedom to move past small things that used to feel so massive. I also hope I haven't left you completely hopeless in humanity or your own ability to find freedom. In fact, I've prayed for quite the opposite. I believe and know that if we walk in the truth of our testimony, we can fully release others from their bondage, not by our own might or strategy but by His name and His ways (*Psalm 119:45-47*).

I'm giving you a few tangibles in order to help you handle the constant stress of most situations. Even as we breakdown the typical pattern of a workout regimen, mind, body, soul, and spirit with this book (I hope by now you've picked up on that from the chapter titles), there can be strain engrained in those steps. I mean, let's be honest; we have been stretching a lot thus far, and even my previous gymnast self feels the pains of stretching. So, unless you're Stretch Armstrong, it's ok to need to take a breather.

Remember the splits story from earlier? Eventually, I did get the splits. It was just in my own timing. Similar to the season that I was learning my backhand spring and I kept, without fail, bending my arms. Not only was my coach concerned for my spine, he also just wanted me to get over it already and do it. So he tried to force me into it. He said if I bent my arms, I'd have to run around the entire circumference of the gym with a massive orange construction cone on my head, chanting, "I'm a Cornball"; my maiden name was Cornwell, and he clearly thought he was funnier than he was. But just like the splits, I eventually got it, again in my own timing, just like most things in life.

You can't force time. But stress can surely force you into things that make time stand still and make pains seem to linger forever. You do realize, however, that you have a choice in this matter – A choice to block stress rather than receive it – A choice to relieve stress rather than ignore it. I'm assuming you're nodding your head right now. That means you also know that you can make changes to your schedule, your eating and fitness patterns, your thought cycles, your spiritual practices, etc., in order to fix these things before they combust.

I thought I knew this. I even thought I tried but probably not as hard as I should have. And the more these things compounded to add pressure, the more stress began to emerge in other areas of my mind, body, and soul.

When I met my husband, I knew he was something unique and rare. We became best friends long before we became lovers, but I fell in love with him instantly, and he knew it. In fact, I drunkenly told him how I felt a few times before we had a more meaningful conversation in person. I was in college, so remember this was my pre-knowing Jesus days (and remember grace). Despite how trashy it sounds in retrospect, he loved me back. And, like the control freak I was, I even orchestrated telling him first since he wasn't moving at my typical quick pace. I sent him on a scavenger hunt around our apartment to tell him firsthand. I was never as confident as I was at that moment. He loved me back.

I knew it by his acts of service, gifts, and immense quality time. He spoiled me rotten with every possible love language, and this was long before we read Gary Chapman's book, *The 5 Love Languages*. But even with all of that love, he still perplexed the hell out of me. He was the first guy I had ever been with since high school that wouldn't kiss me on the first date or the second or the thirtieth. I was frustrated. Sexually frustrated. And confused. Even my aunts were asking, "Is he gay?"

Before I move on, I really pray that my son or daughter doesn't fall in love with someone that needs their physical love before their precious, and hopefully correctly prioritized, emotional love.

Our first kiss was 11 months after we met and three months after we started officially seeing each other literally every day. The same night was our first...you know...encounter. Yah, he took things slow, but then I wrecked the smooth-sailing ship as soon as he provided access via a Colbie Caillat song in my new car. At the time it was comical to all of our friends. In hindsight, always 20-20, it was not my proudest feminine moment. Sorry, Dad.

From there, it was cheap wine and movie nights on the regular. Even his roommates found it humorous coming home to the same Usher soundtrack over and over. It was a running joke. Again, my mama heart is exploding with anger and disappointment thinking about these things. But honestly, until I had children, it never seemed that unacceptable or unfortunate. We were young and in love. Isn't that what we were supposed to be doing? Everyone else was.

We did in fact consider ourselves to be Christians at the time. We even went to church fairly regularly and lived out a seemingly Christian lifestyle, if you don't count the sex and living together before marriage thing. And I can't forget that I also took a promise ring oath with my dad when I was 15. I was going to save myself for my husband, but you already know the ending to that story. I loved God just as much then as I did in high school, even when I felt betrayed by "His people." I believed God loved me and created me and wanted good things for me. And I knew Gary was one of those good things. But I rejected a deeper sense of knowing. I rejected true commitment.

But, just like I didn't keep the commitment in high school to the small group of women I shared only one side of my heart with or to my dad who bought me the ring I asked for, I wasn't keeping it at that point in my life either. Promises were broken. And because we weren't married, within my own mind, I was able to defend my decisions and make excuses. It was just a text... It was just words that weren't followed through with action... But it was ALL action, no matter which way I spun it. I suppressed the situations. I lied or ignored it time after time after time. I couldn't understand why I chose to respond in this unseemly way to a friend or colleague, or why I reached out to them at all when I clearly wasn't missing human connection. I couldn't comprehend the true damage being done by the inner turmoil I was causing myself or the stress that needed to be released from my body. I didn't want it, but I also didn't press to get rid of it. I simply would vow to myself – never again.

Although some of the contents of this book may call for reader age restrictions, this is real life, and heaven knows our youth have access to far too many things beyond their years. So, if you're a young or unmarried girl reading this – love yourself enough to respect yourself, your parents, your future husband, your future son or daughter, and most importantly your creator – choose to wait!

Hebrews 13:4 - Let marriage be held in honor among all, and let the marriage bed be undefiled, for God will judge the sexually immoral and adulterous.

Sex before marriage, in all of its various forms, is immoral. I have the pleasure of knowing many amazing women who learned this lesson before it was too late, unlike me. Their marriages are evidently better for it. And their souls must be too! I also know women who discovered the same truths too late, or at least so they thought, but have since forged amazing new relationships based on this fundamentally important and scripturally sound concept. Think about it, even if you aren't a Christian, this still makes a ton of sense. You circumvent jealousy, comparison, confusion, and mistrust. So, start today. Renew yourself from the inside out. It is possible through repentance and restoration. Intimacy is In-To-Me-You-See. It requires that we be willing to let someone get close enough to see our hidden places, our weaknesses, and our secrets. But the immorality of my sins caused a massive barricade between my Great love (Jesus), my husband, and even my mirror moments with just me.

Unfortunately, even after marriage, I felt constricted and confined by decades of suppressed stress and the secrecy of a life lived in flight mode. I had no idea that trauma could imprint at such depths within the human body, even as deep as our organs. Without truth, without acknowledgement, without direct action over the stress, our relationship and marriage was continually being built on a lie. This was never in a million years who I expected to become or how I expected my fairytale, which began with that fateful wedding day story, to unravel. But there I was, living the exterior dream, dealing with the internal nightmare. And no one knew.

I found myself married with two beautiful babies. And though I was deeply in love with my husband, I was in constant hiding. My self-imposed shackles held me back from being able to be with him fully or ever feeling fully loved because I didn't love myself. The pressures of life, careers, and family continued to compound, and eventually, what I had built on a faulty foundation collapsed. I put myself in harm's way, even knowing the emotions and mental struggles that these actions were causing. I was in unsafe situations with people who didn't value the promises and commitments I had made. And I wasn't being led by the Spirit because I had yet to fully hand my sin and need for control over to Him. I was using alcohol to mask the pressure. Whether with my words, through my actions, or even within my mind, I was not living in integrity or pursuing what I now know as my fundamental, purposed, first ministry – my family.

But just as I preached earlier, I make no excuses. I take full ownership of my actions knowing that I am a grown adult, and like you, one who is completely human and totally flawed. Yet, amidst my brokenness – my husband held me – cheek to cheek. You heard that right…HE held ME! How did I deserve this? How could he be so strong? How in the world was he still finding the love within himself to hold my hand and look me in the eye? How could he care enough to hold me at night as I questioned my existence and sat in full body shakes of fear and shame? I was lost within an identity that I rejected. I had no understanding of who I was and surely didn't understand how he could see deeper, beyond my broken heart and my broken choices.

Even years later when I ask myself, "How could he still hold me?" I know fully that God is the only answer. But how do I know, you ask? Fast-forward weeks later past the couch experience I shared earlier, where I entered in utter shame and left with sunshine surrounding me. Fast-forward past the seemingly endless and expensive therapy sessions. Fast-forward past all the loss that left me whole. Fast-forward past the dozens of books, conferences, church services, questions and answer sessions, painful storytelling, memory revealing, and unfolding lies. Fast-forward past my inner healing and self-identity exploration and decluttering ownership journey. Fast-forward to first steps of vulnerability and righteous communication. Fast-forward to reestablishing my physical well-being and mental strength. Fast-forward to the moments I could look at myself in the mirror with a pleased and humble heart. Fast-forward to the moments of spiritual peace and clarity on my calling. Fast-forward to newly established relationships and businesses. Fast-forward to our baptism on the west coast by the same woman who married us, our very own fairy God-mama who knew the depths of our story and loved us through it. Fast-forward to the emotional times of exploring sex within the beautiful confines of marriage. Fast-forward to truly comprehending intimacy and love. Fast-forward to the moment that I realized that it could only be God that gave him such incredible strength to stand by me in that incredibly impossible time – To that moment where I discovered my sweet, kind, strong husband…was also human…

I was the woman he loved through her darkest hour. I was the mother of his children who he saw transform from a mess of weeds to a bountiful, beautiful garden. I was the woman who put every ounce of energy into her recovery, while simultaneously dealing with so many external factors and relational sorrows with family members. I was the woman who showed up day after day in apology, by way of words, but even more so in actions. I was the woman who unpacked childhood trauma, released heavy burdens of shame, and had emerged as healed and whole. And I was that woman who now lay crumbled before him, just as he was years before at her feet, over the same exact enemy tactic – to destroy our marriage by way of sexual sin. We forget sometimes that even superheroes take off their capes. And in that moment, under intense stress unlike any I had ever experienced before, I had a choice.

Crazy dramatic plot line twists, huh? Believe me, it took me some time to swallow it as well. But I had only one example to go by in order to breathe again. I had a very real choice to act out of flesh and flee from pain and hurt and confusion or to be more like Jesus. So I rose up from my brokenness and found my footing amidst all the pain, stress, and confusion – and I held him – cheek to cheek – just like he did for me. And I stayed there with him as he went on his own journey to wholeness.

We can't possibly be prepared for the mess that life can become or the turbulence that we will face. It's promised in fact, even as Christians, that there will be trials and tribulations. Even with my history of bumpy roads and learning the hard way, I wasn't prepared for that curve ball. But we chose the same path of healing. We chose the same stance of standing upright to the challenge. And this time, instead of coating myself with incessant amounts of icy-hot to dull the back pain, we got ourselves a new bed – both literally and physically.

Stress response is usually fight or flight. It's a physiological reaction when we are faced with turmoil or threats. Fighters, as you can expect, usually throw the first punch or vocalize with harmful, deflective words. Flight, however, is the exact opposite. We run away from the turmoil or threat in order to silence everything and remove ourselves as far from the situation as possible. Out of sight, out of mind, right? Not true.

We are adaptable and therefore teachable. Fight or flight responses, though embedded chemically, can be averted if we take preventative measures to keep stressful situations from escalating to the point of no return. Jesus himself chose both of these responses during different circumstances. In John 6:15, Jesus withdrew to the hills to avoid the approaching crowd that wanted to make him king by force, but he also chose to fight in Matthew 21:12-13 by overturning the tables of those who were using his father's temple to buy and sell. This may bring you fist throwers some peace, but it doesn't necessarily give you the right of way to proceed. Remember, we're also instructed to turn the other cheek. I've previously mentioned several unhealthy choices such as alcohol, shopping, or excessive exercise – these would be suppression tools versus healthy options – fist throwing likely makes that list too.

Thankfully, my life shifted from suppressing stress to releasing stress. I assure you, not only will your body thank you, but your mind and heart will too. Freedom exists in stress release, in turning over the heavy burden to God himself. On the surface this can look like positive affirmations of who God says you are or getting out into nature and becoming grounded with the Truth and what really matters. I've heard it described as a "forest bath" where you reconnect with your senses and get your bare feet on the ground, sand, or grass in order to remind you of your place on the earth.

One place I can assuredly go to take a forest bath is my oasis of a garden. You know the saying, "the grass isn't always greener on the other side"? Yah, well that one took on an entirely new meaning when I started understanding the process of healthy stress release and gardening, both in my actual yard and our personal "yard" as a married couple. A number of truths were revealed to me through this process of "yard care." I learned that the yard can only be weeded when you get knee deep in the weeds, the grass is always greener where you water it, and you can stand in ego at the gates of the garden, thinking you can maintain it alone, or you can have help from the one true Gardner who cultivated the ecosystem on which you are standing. Ego vs. eco, you choose.

If you want to start positive change within yourself, it's no different. The same vibrancy exists within you that exists in the abundant flowers you nurture. But like the shifting seasons, it doesn't happen overnight, and it takes constant love and attention. I've since become an indoor plant person as well (less maintenance obvi), not to circumvent the effort, but instead to enjoy the life-giving oxygen that is released from these natural, God gifted sources. Seek stress relief wisely before you get to the full fight or flight nervous system response. I've been able to address things more quickly, catching the weed as it breaks the surface of the soil, rather than waiting until an entire area has been choked. Regardless, garden or ocean, find your calm so the storms don't feel so overwhelming.

Working out is another way to combat stress. As we exercise we release positive endorphins, which are basically neurotransmitters to the brain that make you "feel good." It's why you never regret working out, even when you're sore. You always feel better afterward because it's basically meditation in motion, not only relieving stress, but symptoms of anxiety, depression, and burnout as well. Working out problems is quite a bit different, but if we put the same emphasis into our emotional, mental, and spiritual health, we would surely feel the benefits there too.

I stand today, toes in the same sand I got married in nine years ago, in sheer amazement of a God who gives hope, who restores brokenness, who reclaims covenants, and ignites embers that the enemy consistently tried to put out. And if you know the science behind a fire, then you know smoke isn't a signal that the fire has gone out. It may simply be a signal for help, which we clearly needed, and God responded by sending a gentle breeze to ignite the still hot embers of our love for one another.

We are purposed to live an abundant life, but just as the diamonds are formed under pressure, stress is inevitable and sometimes even useful. The hard stuff, the stressful stuff, is where our weaknesses are exposed and the glory of God is revealed. When Paul and Silas were placed in a stressful situation, imprisoned in fact, instead of relying on their own strength or might, they turned to prayer and worship *(Acts 16:16-40)*. God became their rescuer through their actions, as He did in so many biblical stories. Your prison doors, like theirs, will open, and your shackles will be removed through your choice of action. Instead of relying on your own might to fix or mend or break free, present your situation to God and worship Him, even still, for His goodness reigns no matter in what literal or figurative jail cell you may find yourself. And the best part is, within the miracle moment when the bondage and death cloths are removed, others get to be in witness to His greatness. This book is my prison door opening to showcase His greatness.

But be prepared. Even on their mission, Paul and Silas had an unexpected situation unravel. Just as I sat in anguish and disbelief with my husband's confession of a sin that I thought was mine alone, the curve balls of life can come plowing through the batter's box, expected or not, and hit you dead center in the middle of your forehead. I can assure you, God is greater and He's in the meanwhile. There is nothing in any area of our entirety that is too broken, too dirty, or too burnt-out for Him. Our weaknesses are in fact His opportunity to showcase the fullness of His grace and His perfect power *(2 Corinthians 12:9).*

But you have to let go of some pretty difficult things in order to experience full wholeness, joy, and health. We have to stop trying to unshackle ourselves because that effort is what creates further stress. If we stay stagnant, blinded, and even content, He can still move. He's all mighty. BUT you will be impeding all that He has in store for your tomorrow. Stop holding on to things you were never intended to hold. Only when your clenched fists become open can He take hold of your hand and move you into the place of freedom.

This was a chapter I never intended to write when I set out on this journey. It's raw and fragile and insanely hard to put into words. But in the end, I believe it may be the chapter that touches you so deeply that you will make this the starting point, the signal point of your nearly quenched fire. God already sees you. He already knows your stresses; he's ready to hold you cheek to cheek. But you have to be bold enough to wave your white flag and allow my truth to ignite the fire within your soul. Only then will you be able to live out your own truth by abiding in The Truth. Grace, mercy, and peace are yours for the taking, and they'll follow you all the days of your life, through Him alone and in truth and love *(2 John 1:3).*

As you become, ask your heart:

Where are you overloaded with stressors?

How are you acting out to combat them?

Are you a fight or flight responder?

What roots need tilling before they grow weeds?

What are positive ways to start releasing stress today?

Salutation

$\mathcal{S}$tanding at the ocean's shoreline. Sand in all the wrong places. Over a decade later. I danced. Freely. Music was resonating with my thought patterns as waves audibly soothed my soul. I stood, not concerned about my waistline or on-lookers' opinions, not needing constant interaction or affirmation from others. I was simply relishing in being alone alongside my creator and the created. No cloud in sight. Washed white. My happy place. My heaven on earth.

I went to bed the night before slightly guilty that I was choosing to sleep instead of participate in the women's worship gathering that I regularly attended. But Grace resonated with the new mercies given to me the very next morning. I was well rested and my soul was eager to gather and meet with Him in my own personal timing and receipt. I tuned into the soundtrack that I had missed, knowing that I would hear multitudes of women singing their personal and communal praises – Competition out the window – Comparison set aside –Togetherness and community at its finest. And He did not disappoint. The playlist was cultivated to speak to me in that very moment, in solitude.

Moments after shoreline burpees, push-ups naturally inclined by tidal lines, and squats to the beat of the worship music (yes, Christians have groove too), I released the workout plan. I became present with my body, my mind, and my spirit. I was moving with the words and the emotions of my soul. I could have concerned myself with the passersby on their morning walk. I could have sat resting. But I was propelled into movement. Dancing like the tiny dancer from my childhood classes – the tiny dancer without limitations to the performance – the tiny dancer without rules from the instructor. My arms and heart were open to the gift of the moment as I stared out over the vast ocean, feeling perfectly safe, fully seen, and incredibly known, even in recognition of the magnitude of the world existing around me.

The fins, I believe perfectly timed by God himself, greeted me, and then came the waterspout blow. The question, "Do dolphins do that?" spun through my head in amazement. I turned off the music and pulled out my camera to relish in the moment and to share the beauty of how God said hello to me that morning. I couldn't wait to show my kiddos the early season sighting. Seconds later a humpback whale shot out of the water yards in front of me and back-dove playfully into the waves. I screamed and jumped. My fluid dance moves turned into childlike exuberance with more passion in my spring than any gymnastics 9.0+ ever provided. I cried and yelled to the heavens, "SHOW OFF FOR ME JESUS!"

I'll never forget that moment. Within it, God assured me that my going to bed early, exhausted from a full day, in the quiet of my home, prayerfully falling asleep, was just what I needed mentally, physically, and spiritually. By listening to my body and mind, giving myself grace instead of guilt, I made way for Him to surprise me. I made way for me to show up eager for more of Him, expectant in my solidarity that He would speak to me. I made way for me to see that I hadn't missed "the party" with the 100 women the night before. It was a valuable reminder of the importance of choosing me and putting my needs before others' expectations and desires. It was a reminder that God speaks to us all in our own special, purposed ways. He knew that "God wink" from Heaven was my own version of Hot and Holy. Yes, that's the name of the local women's gathering – on fire for the Lord and pursuing His holiness through our daily actions, mindsets, and heart placements – with a sense of humor included. (Don't get all religiously judgy on me now!)

I wept. Not just for the gift of nature or the grandiose heavenly gesture, but for the years of trial and tribulations followed by the years of dedication and obedience that led me to this very moment. I wept tears of joy. Child-like wonder peaked in my spirit yet again. He knew me. And He affirmed me.

As you proceed through the evolution of your becoming routine, I promise, because He promises, that He will never not show up when you pursue Him with eagerness and willingness, when you seek Him even beyond the crashing waves that can pull you into the depths of the unknown. Life situations, mental battles, other people, roadblocks, physical ailments, external forces, and spiritual battles will try to overcome your strength and resiliency. You'll be pushed off course, right where the enemy wants you, in the rip tide of his conniving schemes. Right outside of your safety zone. Right outside of your confidence. Right outside of your intended blessing. Right outside of your purposed realm of influence. Back into your struggle. Back into your comfort zone. Back into complacency. Back into glass half empty. Back into hurt and exhaustion. Back into restlessness and fear. Back into the negative self-mirror. Back into the circling mindsets. Back into your childhood loneliness. Back into your shackles.

Don't lose hope. Press on again, not by doing, not by exercising, but in your significant being, aligned and willing to start anew where Grace abounds.

Learn to take a knee. Learn to listen. Learn to back down if the subject matter isn't life threatening. Learn to admit that you were wrong. Learn to take a day off and get a massage so the knots don't become true injuries. Don't let society pigeonhole you into believing that winning is everything. It's not. I've had more success and joy in the triumph following my failures than I ever did controlling a win. And even if you have a repeat cycle of success, pay close attention to the recovery process after each win. Without the proper cool down, you are at risk for future failure, further injury, and fatigue. It's a mental game just as much as it is a physical one. The cool down is imperative, win or lose.

The three W's are my cool down. As with the other pieces of this journey, I hope you adopt this too. It's freely yours. And since no one was there to give me a blueprint in dealing with my own L, I hope to get you to the W faster, not in the typical sense of the scoreboard wins and losses but instead with a new set of W's: Word, Worship, and Warfare.

The Word is used to feed and refuel through His promises and prayer. It reminds us of who He is and reassures us in who He says we are. Stay rooted in good seed and His righteous wisdom.

Next, allow Worship to infiltrate your environment. Praise penetrates and leaves our hearts in a state of gratitude for the awesome wonders we have witnessed with our own eyes *(Deuteronomy 10:21)*. For without Him, I wouldn't have made it here to this whale watching, dancing moment.

And lastly, is Warfare. It is the putting on of that daily armor, aligning your personal landscape design to His will and your roadmap to His call. For each step, just like each day and each minute, matters significantly in the ripple you are creating for the greater Kingdom purpose. Be willing to exist outside of yourself. Turn the "I" lifestyle we see emulated by the world into the "He" showcase.

Often, we desire to accelerate the recovery and cool down process. I know I did. Each time I learned something new I'd praise myself. But it was never about me to begin with. It was all for His glory. He did it. He choreographed each new dance step in my becoming routine, and through my obedience the rewards were gifted – fresh revelations and deeper understandings. I had aha moment after aha moment, unearthing the roots to expose my truths, which were in fact lies. And ultimately I discovered His Truth in the tilling. He reestablished my self-worth and identity. He nurtured and re-parented the little girl who was lost and scared, and I humbly watched the butterfly emerge from its long confining and limiting cocoon.

For the first time in my life, I tangibly feel Him and His presence. I can comprehend His love and I am loving myself and others in His likeness. I feel free. And while all of those are massive milestones, my life is not over; the battle is not won. I've been fair warned that the enemy is still coming after me (and you), and if I let my limbs go limp now or my guard falls, I risk losing all of the muscles I've trained for and gained thus far. What a shame if the colorful butterfly never fluttered and took flight. What a miss if I didn't stand freely to watch the whale breach.

Becoming is never over until we sit at the right hand of Jesus in Heaven. Here on earth we must keep saying yes to the opportunity of being stretched out of our comfort zones. We must be stretched beyond what we can physically comprehend or handle, leaning into our weaknesses and being exposed to further conviction in order to experience His beautiful, loving Truths. We won't always get it right in our imperfection. Even as a proclaimed Christian, my billboard is imperfectly perfect, always becoming. Sin is inevitable, but the process of redemption is always ours for the taking. His steadfast love and mercies are new every day. And the promise of His rainbow keeps me yearning to learn about every color of His creation.

> *Lamentations 3:22-23 - "The steadfast love of the Lord never ceases; his mercies never come to an end; they are new every morning, great is your faithfulness."*

He is love and He is salvation. Stretch your arms to the skies my friend. Boldly and in public, unashamedly bask in His glorious light. Let no man take you captive. Let no weakness hold you hostage. Let no judgment hold you back from your freedom dance and whale breaching moment. Hydrate yourself in the beauties of His blessings.

As you journey through the intimate workings of your mind, body and soul experience, you may find yourself stuck in different phases. Detoxing and finding your tribe don't happen overnight. But be courageous my friend; press on past the pain and excuses and fear of exposure. And as you simplify, as you let the stress subside, and as you routinely speak life over yourself in the mirror, you will discover true meaning through your vertically, spiritually aligned being. Don't give up.

The battle is not over, but it has been won, and He is the victor over every situation. So don't stop dancing now, sis. Don't let the hard, hurtful, hearsay, hell of the world send you back to your grave; you've already been resurrected. Stay in the earned and carefully cultivated space of physical, mental, emotional, and spiritual strength. You have worked too hard for this remission. Remission, which means cancellation of debt (aka sin) and forgiveness, is the entire reason Jesus walked the earth and the very reason the next step in your becoming journey matters greatly in His plan. Remission is the exact space for you to remember your mission!

Don't let anyone, anything, any wave, or any thought take that from you.
Don't let any storm distract you from His rainbow of promises.
Let go of stigma, impressions, and expectations while allowing Him to train you up from childhood all over again.
Let go of the end game and find peace in the journey while setting healthy goals to accomplish His will in your life.
Let go of the titles and claim His name over yours.
Let go of the reward in order to stake claim in the manna being showered daily.
Let go of the constant effort that exhausts you and be fueled by His energy.
Let go of the baggage that weighed you down or tripped you up and pick up His promise.
Let go of craving more in the flesh and be nourished in the soul by the abundance of His gifts.
Let go of the fear and grasp hold of The Light that keeps you out of the dark.
Let go of the lies that say you are not made for more because in fact your very birth proves otherwise.
Let go of the relationships that have held you captive.
Let go of the scales of comparison that have you stuck in the mirror and lying to yourself; you are beautiful.
Let go of the words that caused you to press pause on your life; you are called.
Let go of the past that shackles you and stand in admiration of The Freedom.
Let go of the stuff and even the people that held you back from His will and calling.
Let go of the weight that has kept you from the heights and journey you need to walk to serve others.
Let go of the expectations others have placed on you and stand within the identity of who you are in His eyes.
Let go of your expectations over others, exemplifying the same grace that has been given to you.
Let go of your past failures and cling tight to the harvest you are cultivating with His good seed.
Let go of societal pressures to be perfect and lean into your always becoming, worthy sonship.

God has you purposed – you are not your past, your pain, or your problems. You are His precious, intentionally designed child, and you have a calling to answer to. He is stronger and more glorified in your weakness. The mission piece of your puzzle is connected to the puzzle pieces waiting to be put into place as you stand in your rightful position – perhaps on the shoreline of the sea, weeping as strangers witness your personal miracle moment. Your rightful position, where you will joyfully experience intimacy through His palpable, sweet, love. Your rightful position, where His love will replenish you from the inside out. Your rightful position, where He will provide you the deep-rooted strength to be truly fit in faith and gracefully surrendered and always becoming…

Write a review for the book for a chance to win FREE access to the course. New winner picked regularly!

The purpose of this course is to catapult your calling! To expand & design your God-dream! To help you establish your business premise on the one true solid foundation, The Rock, by which your purpose and passions will take flight. By staking claim on your purposed identity as a Kingdom Entrepreneur, we will develop the mindsets, methods and models to bring to life the vision He has planned for you before you were knit in your mother's womb.

The Fit in Faith movement was birthed through my own trial and error discovery of mind, body and soul alignment. I learned first hand that being fit isn't about our physique at all, its about the wholeness of our heart and the root of our joy. This is an opportunity to join me alongside other big dreamers, innovative movers and lifestyle shakers, as we explore and share our messy comeback stories to wholeness. The mind - body - and soul connection catapults us to living our lives fully alive and fully well! If you're one step away from achieving your idea of something 'more', tune in for practical, fun, and healthy ways to ignite yourself into 'evermore'.

SUBSCRIBE & LEAVE A REVIEW FOR A SHOUTOUT ON AIR!

Thank You

Thank You For Reading My Book!

I really appreciate all of your feedback, and I love hearing what you have to say.

I need your input to make the next version of this book and my future books even better.

Please leave me a helpful review on Amazon letting me know your thoughts, transformations and truths.

Love and light,
Tamra Andress

CPSIA information can be obtained
at www.ICGtesting.com
Printed in the USA
BVHW061112070122
625565BV00005B/12